LIFE STREAMS

QUEST BOOKS
are published by
The Theosophical Society in America,
Wheaton, Illinois 60189-0270,
a branch of a world organization
dedicated to the promotion of brotherhood and
the encouragement of the study of religion,
philosophy, and science, to the end that man may
better understand himself and his place in
the universe. The Society stands for complete
freedom of individual search and belief.
In the Classics Series well-known
theosophical works are made
available in popular editions.

Cover art by *Jane A. Evans*

LIFE STREAMS

Journeys into Meditation and Music

Hal A. Lingerman

*This publication made possible with
the assistance of the Kern Foundation*

The Theosophical Publishing House
Wheaton, Ill. U.S.A.
Madras, India/London, England

The Theosophical Publishing House
306 West Geneva Road
Wheaton, IL 60187
A publication of the Theosophical Publishing House, a department of the Theosophical Society in America.

Library of Congress Cataloging in Publication Data

Lingerman, Hal A., 1943-
  Life streams.
  "A Quest original"—T.p. verso.
  Bibliography: p.
  1. Meditations. 2. Music—Miscellanea. 3. Devotional calendars. I. Title.
BL627.L565   1988   299'.934   87-40522
ISBN 0-8356-0629-5 (pbk.)

Printed in the United States of America

Contents

Foreword

Life Streams offers a variety of approaches that you can use practically for effective spiritual centering and relief from stress. By spending just ten to twenty minutes daily in focused reflection, you can learn to clear your energy flow and enrich the quality of your life. Daily themes for meditation, short readings and imagery, combined with suggestions of particular pieces of music, are offered to help quicken your imagination, insight and creative response. They open doors into the Silence.

These simple daily practices can help you integrate your deeper Self with your personality and temperament. Your highest ideals for spiritual progress must find anchors in your personality; spiritual ideals must connect with ways that you express your life response through your temperament.

Your personality, which consists of your mind, emotions and body, serves as a clearing-house for your energy output. You release energy whenever you use your body, emotions, mind, or your deeper intuitive faculties. How you release energy depends on how deeply you are contacting the spectrum of your personality with its wide range of different frequencies, intensities and shadings. There are many latent tonalities and melodies waiting to be played on the keyboard of the human personality—subtleties of physical movement and activity, varieties and intensities of feelings and emotions, and many layers of thought and perception. There are also energies to be released from the Self, a deeper consciousness that undergirds the personality.

Your temperament consists of your habitual behaviors, the ways you respond repeatedly to life situations. Temperament is the cumulative expression of your feelings, in all the different shadings and movements of your personality tones. Your emotions change continuously and undulate with successive waves of life; your temperament describes the feeling tones that regularly arise in you and are released as energy.

The ancient Greeks tried to categorize the human temperament into four basic ingredients or "humors": choleric, sanguine, melancholic and phlegmatic. According to this approach, temperament is determined by the relative combinations and proportions of these humors in one's total make-up.

Pythagoras, a Master-teacher among the ancient Greeks, built upon this idea. He demonstrated how a person can hear different notes of the musical scale and see the various colors of the spectrum. In a similar way, Pythagoras suggested "behavior tones" of the human temperament. He believed there is a correspondence between the varieties of human behavior and different cosmic energy vibrations, which he indicated by numbers. He represented the basic themes and issues of life as expressed through the human temperament, in his descriptions of larger, "numerical essences." For example, certain patterns of emotional response, such as "sympathy," might express aspects of a certain vibration, called "2" or "twoness," while a different flavor of emotion, such as "romance," might better describe an aspect of a different energy rhythm, called "3" or "threeness." In this way Pythagoras suggested an inner mathematics that describes the basic energy flow of the individual psyche.

Pythagoras described nine primary currents of energy vibration, to which he arbitrarily assigned the numbers 1 through 9. These currents contain vast potentials for human response— physical, emotional, mental and intuitive.

The rhythms and needs of each person are always changing. Likewise, the tones of each day are different. In the spirit of Pythagoras' insights, I have arranged daily themes for meditation according to nine primary "tones" and their many variations. My choices are not random or haphazard—each day has an appropriate theme and energy vibration, as shown in the following table:

Number	Days of Month	Themes
1	- 1, 10, 19, 28:	Focus upon the quickening of the mind—new areas of insight, discovery, research in pioneering territory (mental focus).
2	- 2, 11, 20, 29:	Center upon the emotional needs for closeness, partnership, linking and emotional supportiveness and intimacy; one-on-one relationships and details (emotional focus).
3	- 3, 12, 21, 30:	Consider the creative imagination, imagery, the arts, and self-expression that describes the beautiful and the romance of life (emotional focus).
4	- 4, 13, 22, 31:	Concentrate upon planning, form, productivity, regularity and dependability; do the task well (physical focus).
5	- 5, 14, 23:	Enjoy variety, change, physical sensation, travel, contact, and move the body to release energy (physical focus).
6	- 6, 15, 24:	Serve the community, group and family needs. Socialize (emotional focus).
7	- 7, 16, 25:	Enter the silence and the deeper fields of knowledge, research and meaning. Find out who you are in your divine essence and in your character (intuitive-thinking focus).
8	- 8, 17, 26:	Take charge and manage what needs to be done. Find the decisions that must be made; use power and money wisely and benevolently. Use willpower and be successful (mental-will focus).
9	- 9, 18, 27:	Live for brotherhood, global unity and harmony, as all lives work

> together in the one Life. Practice
> forgiveness and compassion. Syn-
> thesis can lead to transcendence
> (intuitive-feeling focus).

In the same spirit that I have chosen the themes for each day, I have also included many appropriate passages from the writings of great spiritual teachers from all cultures and faiths, and from composers whose musical compositions enhance the daily meditational theme. Each of these is followed by a brief guided imagery in keeping with the theme for the day. You may wish to free associate with each theme or to keep a journal.

At least two musical selections (sometimes more if they are especially appropriate) are suggested for each day. Usually one is classical and designed to penetrate powerfully into areas in the psyche of the listener. The other is usually more contemporary and frequently New Age. New Age music is an emerging genre of sound that often makes fewer demands upon the listener. In New Age music the dynamic contrasts are usually much less intense than in classical music. It contains several other distinguishing characteristics:

1) Unusual instruments: Celtic harp, oud, pan flute, ocarina, koto, sitar, bells and gongs, vibraphone, acoustical piano, windchimes, synthesizers and others.

2) Nature sounds sometimes integrated into the soundscape: ocean, birds, thunder, streams, rivers, tropical forests, rain, wind, waterfalls, animals' calls, by themselves or with instruments.

3) Cross-cultural influences: different ethnic traditions, and mixtures of spiritual and musical styles, such as Persian, Balinese, Celtic, African, Polynesian, Native American, Japanese, Chinese, South American.

4) An emphasis upon spontaneity and improvisation; at times definite melodies may be less noticeable or less developed. Often, New Age composers borrow from classical masterpieces. Among these are Steven Halpern, Raphael, Daniel Kobialka.

5) Sometimes music that is undirected and just floats in the

atmosphere, like a pleasing fragrance. This may help to release stress, quicken the imagination, or lead the listener into a deeper, meditative state. Such New Age music reminds us that we are voyagers through space. We rest in the Infinite.

6) An ambience that can enhance relaxation. The serenity and openness of some of the music can help to alter brain waves, lower blood pressure, etc. It may induce healing.

7) A frequent emphasis on an Aquarian Age vision of increased brotherhood and global unity, an emerging era of expanded relationships and planetary well-being.

8) Frequently small ensembles with interesting combinations of sound and timbre, such as Celtic harp, birds, and ocean waves.

I have found that it is helpful to use a variety of music and have done my best to suggest selections with many flavors. Some strong classical music is therapeutic and breaks up blockage and resistances in the psyche. Great classics can also provide a bridge to higher consciousness. In New Age music, which is just evolving, I have chosen selections that can best relieve stress and heighten one's consciousness. I have not included others that seem to me more shapeless and spineless, repetitive, sugary, even ugly, chaotic and disruptive to one's inner harmony. I have drawn on works that have proved helpful to many persons I have worked with during the past fifteen years in counseling, teaching and workshops. These pieces have been carefully selected from thousands of recordings experienced in classes, workshops and individually. Sometimes the selections coincide with composers' birthdays.

Finally, I have tried to describe each selection of music in ways that make it more accessible to the listener. I have also included artists and labels, so that the recording (record, tape or compact disc) can be located. A Schwann Catalogue will enable you to look up any recording that interests you. You may find many recordings in libraries, on radio programs, or in stores.

I welcome your additional suggestions of music and recordings that have especially helped you. You can write me c/o The Theosophical Publishing House, P.O. Box 270, Wheaton, IL 60189.

January 1	# Aspire

Focus There is no dream that is too great for any human being, no aspiration too high, no ideal too wonderful.

What we are capable of conceiving in our souls, is also capable of being manifested in the outward world.

More than that, what we truly conceive within our souls and work for cannot help appearing in our lives.
Derek Neville

Meditation With the new year, new possibilities ahead are opening to you now.

You can feel the dream taking shape; watch it emerging before your eyes.

New possibilities are already unfolding; you can move into the opening; your dream can be fulfilled.

Musical Keynotes Jeremiah Clarke, *Trumpet Voluntary, Prince of Denmark* (Biggs, Ormandy—Columbia). This dynamic music heralds an expansive energy. It arouses creative response. Whether performed on organ or trumpets, clairvoyants mention that the music emanates gold and purple. Many listeners have found this music to be catalytic and electrifying in its energies.

1

Magical Strings, *On the Burren* (Zensong—
Wilkinson, 651 W. 7th Ave., Escondido, CA
92025). Beautiful melodies and the sounds of harps,
whistles, pianos, harmonium and hammered
dulcimer enliven you and impart a sense of
direction.

January 2   ## Closeness

Focus   Love, one for another, between us, shows itself in
               bursts of song; . . . great thoughts are symphonies;
               and as we answer love to love, and thought to
               thought, all the air about us is filled with tones and
               supertones, with harmonies, songs, chants and
               great chorales. . . .   Geoffrey Hodson

Meditation   Great powers surround you, emanating vibrations
               of music and beauty.

               Breathe naturally and open up to these flowing
               harmonies.

               Let your mind rise into sunbursts of song.

Musical   Max Bruch, Violin Concerto No. 1 in G (Lin,
Keynotes   Slatkin—Columbia). This concerto, for violin and
               orchestra, offers a closeness and an intimacy that
               bring openings. The music allows the heart to
               reach and explore in a zone of reassurance.

               Carolyn Margrete, *The Emerald Season* (Sunburst
               Music). This music, for solo piano, is calming, in-
               timate, and kindles hope. It was recorded at Mount
               Tamalpais, California, in the radiance of nature,
               and it brings the power of renewal. Note especially
               "Heart's Seasons" and "Woodland Peace."

January 3   *Praise*

Focus   Let the bright Seraphim in burning row,
               Their loud uplifted angel-trumpets blow;
               Let the Cherubic host, in tuneful choirs
               Touch their immortal harps with golden wires.
               Let their celestial concerts all unite,
               Ever to sound His praise in endless morn of Light.
                                         George Frideric Handel

Meditation   With praise your heart center opens.

               Relax now, in a beautiful place; pick a scene—
               water, mountain, sands or grassy meadow.

               You can feel the expanse—the clear view around
               you.

               Release praise into openness, breathing praises and
               glory and singing them.

               Great beings are singing with you. Glory answers.

Musical   George Frideric Handel, *Let the Bright Seraphim*
Keynotes   from *Samson* (Te Kanawa—Philips). In this praise-
               filled piece, soloist and orchestra help to awaken
               feelings of joy and celebration.

               Gheorghe Zamfir, *Classical Zamfir* (Mercury).
               Haunting sounds of the pan flute, accompanied by
               orchestra, permeate this music of praise and
               joyfulness.

January 4   *Ripening Purpose*

Focus   Wherefore I put you in remembrance to stir up the
               gift of God which is in you....

> For God has...given us...power to love and be
> of sound mind.   II Timothy 1:6,7

Meditation   For this you were born this lifetime.

The purpose and plan unfold before you.

You can take a step today to being more productive and useful as your skills unfold.

The pieces of your life begin to fit together; your greater purpose is emerging.

Musical   Josef Suk, *Ripening* (Neumann—Supraphon). "A
Keynotes   work based on the highest source—love....Purified, it proceeds through Nature, to become a victorious song of life." All stages of human feeling and purpose are described through this beautiful music.

Yanni, *Keys to the Imagination* (Published by Private Music, Inc.). The music is daring and dynamic and can empower the listener with new vitality. It is music of action which can stimulate purpose. The energy is mainly yang and moves outward. Synthesizers and brilliant sounding strings produce a powerful yet clear sound.

January 5   ***Love in Action***

Focus   Let us be open to God so that He can use us. Let us put love into our actions, beginning in the family, in the neighborhood, in the street.

God gives what is needed. Work is our way of expressing our love for God. Our love must pour on someone. People are a means of expressing our love of God.   Mother Teresa

Meditation   Imagine the abundance of opportunities that flow into your life daily.

You can welcome whatever the new day brings.

The banquet of life is prepared for you; feast upon the great variety of opportunities that await you. Taste the menu of this new day!

Musical Keynotes   Felix Mendelssohn, Symphony No. 4, *Italian* (Maag—MCA; Davis—Philips). This orchestral music offers a freshness and effervescence which sparkle with delight. Beautiful melodies release colors and new vitality.

Bruce BecVar, *Take It to Heart* (Shining Star). The music is fresh and kaleidoscopic, offering many varieties of rhythm, melody and timbre. The mingling of guitars and synthesizers produces a welcoming sensation and awakens the sense of new opportunities. Note especially *Song for Jenna* and *Hymn for a New Age*.

January 6   *Epiphany*

Focus   Passion of an instant
Births of all eternity;
Space illuminates
Depth's darkness
Infinity breathes
The worlds of universe—
Ringing sounds
Envelop silence.
                 Aleksandr Scriabin

Meditation   Epiphany brings new manifestations of light and wonder.

Beyond yourself, glory enters you in a moment of love, a dream revealed, a gift of insight, a closer friendship.

Epiphany, the touch of glory, can enter your life today, filling your silence.

Musical
Keynotes

Giacomo Puccini, *Gloria Mass* (Corboz—Erato). This radiant and joyful music, for choir and orchestra, fills the atmosphere with its own glow of Epiphany and splendor. The music is especially nurturing.

Ottorino Respighi, *Epiphany* from *Roman Festivals* (Muti-Angel). The strong rhythms of trumpets fill the music with a vigorous, celebrational atmosphere. The work ends in a blaze of energy and power—very yang music.

January 7   **Humility**

Focus

I try in my music to give an impression of fervor, and especially of humility, which to me is the most beautiful aspect of prayer.

Francis Poulenc

Meditation

In quiet moments the heart is humble.

In simplicity the soil waits receptively for the coming rain, and the richness of the harvest emerges.

Unpretentious, without drawing attention to itself, the life unfolds a plenitude of beauty and radiates its own fulfillment.

In quiet humility you will be empowered.

Musical
Keynotes

César Franck, *Panis Angelicus* (Pavarotti—London); Wolfgang Amadeus Mozart, *Ave Verum*

Corpus (Te Kanawa—Philips). These two sacred pieces, for chorus and orchestra, can lead the listener into the silent reaches of eternity. They are both transparent and open the heart and soul. Beautiful melodies carry the power, and celestial forces echo the light of the heavens.

Richard Musk, *Illumination* (Golden Nimbus). The music moves the listener inward. *Windchimes in Turquoise* is especially haunting and timeless, combining the mantric sounds of ocean waves and windchimes. The music connects the listener with feelings of the cosmic Presence and humility felt as a traveler through the eternal.

January 8	## *Stewardship*
Focus	I am a citizen of the world.... I feel that music should be humanitarian in its approach and message; it should be universal in scope. Jaromir Weinberger
Meditation	Good stewardship means taking care of whatever has been entrusted to our keeping. It also means using the power of your riches and position to help the greater needs of humanity. Stewardship and service are the reach of love.
Musical Keynotes	Beethoven, Violin Concerto in D (Mutter, Karajan—DGG). This masterpiece, composed for violin and orchestra, brings power and focus. The middle movement is more quiet and searching. Beautiful melodies and strong rhythms help to center the listener. Janalea Hoffman, *Music for Mellow Minds* (Mellow Minds, Box 6431, Shawnee Mission, KS

66206). The sounds of solo piano are especially
helpful for focusing and organizing the day.

January 9	## *Humanity*

Focus

To be the center of a living multitude, the heart
of their hearts, the brain from which thoughts, as
waves, pass through them—this is the best and
purest joy which a human creature can know.

Edward Dowden

Meditation

You can find yourself by losing yourself.

Today it can be helpful to focus upon the needs
of others, to use your abilities to inspire and uplift
suffering.

You can make some contribution that in some way
is constructive to humanity.

*Musical
Keynotes*

John Knowles Paine, Mass in D, *Gloria*
(Schuller—New World Records). The music is expansive, awakening feelings of an individual in the
midst of larger humanity.

Constance Demby, *Novus Magnificat: Through
the Stargate* (Hearts of Space, San Francisco). Por-
tions of this piece are quite open and far-reaching.
A new vision of humanity and constructive synthesis comes through the combination of choral and
electronic sounds.

January 10	## *Rock and Silent Stars*

Focus

Lean on the silent rock until you feel its divinity
make your veins cold; look at the silent stars, let
your eyes climb the great ladder out of yourself and

man. Things are so beautiful your love will follow
your eyes. Things are the GOD, you will love God,
and not in vain, for what we love, we grow to,
we share its nature.

                                        Robinson Jeffers

Meditation   You can feel the power radiating throughout
                nature.

                Imagine yourself in a powerful scene—ocean,
                mountain, desert or wind.

                Breathing naturally, you can feel the energy of God
                pouring through you, cleansing, purifying and em-
                powering you.

                Courage now arises with the cleansing. You can
                move into whatever awaits you.

Musical   Beethoven, Piano Concerto No. 5, *Emperor*, First
Keynotes   Movement (Arrau, Davis—Philips). The music
                carries an energy which is bold and majestic; the
                piano expresses daring and forward momentum,
                and is supported by the strong underpinning of the
                orchestra. It is dynamic yet pliable.

                Paul Sutin, *Serendipity* (Real to Reel, 1001 J.
                Bridgeway, Suite 440, Sausalito, CA 94965). This
                is strong and joyful music for keyboard, acoustic
                guitar, flowing water, birds and light percussion.
                The energy is open, kinetic and strengthening.

January 11   **Cooperation**

Focus   When the heart is ready, the Light enters it.
                                        Flower A. Newhouse

Meditation   When you act in the spirit of cooperation, the
                power of the results is squared. Stronger energy
                emerges out of a shared vision.

Look at how you are blending and cooperating
with those around you. Can you find new ways
of harmonizing and communicating more closely
with others?

Musical   George Frideric Handel, *Largo* from the oratorio
Keynotes   *Xerxes* (Ormandy—Columbia). The music for
               strings is filled with a sense of devotion and
               reassurance. The tone is intimate and awakens
               cooperation and sharing.

               Christian Sinding, Suite for Violin and Orchestra
               (Perlman, Previn—Angel). The music is lyrical,
               stimulating the sense of warmth and cooperation.

               The New Troubadours, *Winds of Birth*
               (Findhorn—Scotland). Songs and music proclaim
               a sense of partnership and working together in the
               spirit of friendship.

January 12   **Laughter and Mirth**

Focus   I believe in a passionately strong feeling for the
               poetry of life—for the beautiful, the mysterious,
               the romantic, the ecstatic—the loveliness of
               Nature, the lovability of people, everything that
               excites us, everything that starts our imagination
               working, LAUGHTER, gaiety, strength, heroism,
               love, tenderness, every time we see—however
               dimly—the godlike that is in everyone—and want
               to kneel in reverence.

                                            Leopold Stokowski

Meditation   Laughter relieves the heavy moments; it breaks up
               too much seriousness and self-importance.

               Laughter and tears are always related in feelings
               that are mysteriously beautiful.

Musical
Keynotes

F. J. Haydn, Leopold Mozart, *Toy Symphony* (Marriner—Angel). Good spirits abound here. A sense of playfulness and jaunty rhythms emanate from the music. The sounds free up rigidity, and there is a child-like quality which is fun-filled and magical.

Evenson, *High Joy* (Soundings of the Planet). A blend of sounds, produced by autoharp, violin, flute, piano, voice and nature, brings joy and good spirits. The music is very freeing.

January 13   **Obligation**

Focus

Heaven is under our feet as well as over our heads. We live in a world in which there is a demand for ice-creams, but not for truth. There is one obligation, and that is the obligation to obey the highest dictate.   Henry David Thoreau

Meditation

What is most important to you?

How true are you to what you value highly?

Consider your standards: how can you deepen your ties with what is most meaningful?

Being true to your obligations, you live each day more authentically.

Musical
Keynotes

Richard Addinsell, *Warsaw Concerto* (Adni, Alwyn—Angel). This music, for piano and orchestra, is strong and filled with a sense of dedication. Beautiful melodies connect the heart with determination for action.

Tom Barabas, *You're the End of the Rainbow* (Invincible). Strong and flowing piano tones help the listener to turn inward and assess life's deepest values.

January 14   **Action**

Focus   In action lies wisdom and confidence. A person
                who acts can attain the higher wisdom and know
                that life is conflict and victory.
                                            Albert Schweitzer

Meditation   Opportunities often pass us by if we wait too long.

                Between inertia and impulsiveness there is action
                which is swift and sure.

                Consider the need for action in your life: is there
                something you need to do now—a phone call, a
                task, a letter, a change of direction?

                Now is your chance to act!

Musical   Beethoven, Symphony No. 7, Fourth Movement
Keynotes   (Karajan—DGG). The energy of the music is very
                activating. The orchestra plays rhythms and
                melodies that are filled with changing shapes and
                colors which are good for breaking up rigidity and
                inertia.

                Kitaro, *Return to Orion* (arranged by Richard
                Goldsmith—Sound Design). The vibrations are
                strong and powerful. An epic quality comes
                through the orchestra, which empowers the
                listener with new vitality.

January 15   **Approval**

Focus   For they loved the praise of men more than the
                praise of God.   John 12:43

Meditation   There is the devotion of a loving heart, and there
                is a concern to please others.

A loving heart loves because it is transmitting the love of God for all creation.

If you can inwardly approve of your own life, living each day in the spirit of the highest that you know, others' approval will not be necessary.

Musical   Ralph Vaughan-Williams, *Dives and Lazarus*
Keynotes   (Boult—Angel). The music moves quietly and lovingly; there is a sense of devotion and caring. A quiet reassurance shines through. A quality emerges which is beyond personal responses or desires. The orchestral colors nurture the listener.

Kim Robertson and Singh Kaur, *Crimson*, Volume 1 (Invincible Records). This is gorgeous music of exaltation and liberation. A single, feminine vocalist spins out melodies of devotion, and accompanying her are open and fluid sounds of harp and synthesizers. Note especially *Guru Ram Das*.

January 16   **God First**

Focus   Be in love with God Light more than you are with yourself, your appetites or your material interests.

Love God more than self or any other person or pleasure.   Anonymous

Meditation   Loving God first opens doors of clarity and attunement with all persons.

Feeling the transpersonal love of God enables us to come closer to the hearts of others.

You can feel today a closer sense of divine love—unchangeable and always full.

In this love you can expand your capacity to touch others' lives with deeper sensitivity.

Musical *Keynotes*	Camille Saint-Saëns, Symphony No. 3, *Organ Symphony*, Second Movement (Litaize, Martinon—Angel-Seraphim). The noble serenity of the great organ is accompanied by strings and full orchestra. God's grandeur unfolds as human aspiration quietly reaches toward celestial regions. A shining archetype of some great edifice radiates the heavenly glory later in the symphony. Daniel Kobialka, *Path of Joy* (Li-Sem Enterprises). A contemporary rendition of J. S. Bach's *Jesu, Joy of Man's Desiring* provides a meditation on the love of God. The heart chakra opens to the devotional tones of violin and strings.

January 17   # Self-Management

Focus

Rules for Self-Command

— Become acquainted with the Supreme Being.
— Refrain from censure and detraction.
— Avoid deceit, envy, fraud, flattery, hatred, malice, lying and ingratitude.
— Develop fortitude under affliction.
— Have tenderness for the weak.
— Show reverent respect for the ancient.
— Show kindness to neighbors.
— Be good-natured and hospitable to strangers.
— Develop service in the cause of mankind.
— Realize the capacity of an individual to become effective.
— Form a good plan and make it your business to execute it.
— Prayer achieves a sympathetic resonance with a more majestic force than man can control or comprehend.

Benjamin Franklin

Meditation   Effective management over oneself is essential to wise management of others.

Taking charge, setting limits and establishing policies can be done in ways that empower others.

You can find ways to use the power entrusted to you to release others' confidence and strength.

Genuine self-management leads to benevolent rule over others.

Musical
Keynotes   Ralph Vaughan-Williams, *Serenade to Music* (Boult—EMI). The music for orchestra (and optional chorus) suggests the beauty and order of life. The melodies rise to a crescendo of power, then subside into peace.

Zamfir, *To Thee, O God* (Mercury). This is a hymn to the Infinite, alternating a haunting, gentle lyricism with the mighty power of the pipe organ. It is both gentle and strong, a good tool for self-management that blends mind and heart.

January 18   **The New Song**

Focus   See what the new song has!
From stones, men,
From beasts it has made men.
Those otherwise dead, those without a share in life
     that is really life
At the mere sound of this song
Have come back to life....
Moreover He has structured the whole universe
     musically
And the discord of elements He has brought
     together in an ordered symphony
So that the whole Cosmos is for Him in
     harmony....
This word of God, looking beyond lyre and harp,
     mindless instruments,
By His Holy Spirit tunes the Cosmos
Especially this little cosmos, man, mind and body;

And He sings to God with this many-voiced
    instrument—
He accompanies His song with the instrument of
    man:
For thou art to me a harp, a flute and a temple,
A harp by the unity of parts in one whole
A flute by the living breath
A temple by thy reason:
A harp that rings in harmony
A flute that breathes melody,
A temple that is the Lord's house.

                                Clement of Alexandria

Meditation   Amid struggles and testings, your new song is
                emerging.

                Dissonance finds a new harmony; there is a larger
                harmony that resolves chaos.

                In your own way you are creating a new song.
                Your song may help someone else to find his or her
                voice for the first time.

Musical   Wolfgang Amadeus Mozart, Concerto for Flute
Keynotes   and Harp (Böhm—DGG). Interaction of flute,
                harp and orchestra produces musical melodies that
                are always new and alive. You can hear a new song
                in this music.

                Alex Jones and Heidemarie Garbe, *Pranava* (Alex
                Jones Tapes). The music for flute and harp is
                quieting and peaceful. Especially lovely is the
                meditative piece *Sunshine of His Love*.

January 19   **New Unfoldment**

Focus   When we die and go to Heaven, our Maker is not
                going to ask, "Why didn't you discover the cure

for such and such?" or "Why didn't you become the Messiah?" The only question we will be asked in that precious moment is "Why didn't you become you?"   Elie Wiesel

Meditation   Becoming your highest expression of You is a life-long process.

Most important is to continue learning. Learning is larger than knowing.

Continuous unfoldment becomes more enjoyable than striving or competing.

Discovering the larger resources in yourself and finding productive use for your abilities make every moment creative and new.

Today, realize some new learning.

Musical   Sir Edward Elgar, *Enigma Variations* (Jochum—
Keynotes   DGG). This music is a kaleidoscope of different moods and tunes. The energy is always changing, and rhythms activate and quiet the listener at different times. *Nimrod* is especially stilling.

Kim Robertson and Singh Kaur, *Crimson II* (Invincible Records). The music, for female voice, harp and synthesizers, is continuously mantric. The tone is devotional and worshipful. Especially appealing is *Mool Mantra*.

January 20   **Blending**

Focus   From two's, three's and four's, etc., we build towards a world of several million souls who can be blended together in time in the vast communion of life; thus Christ is completing Himself.
                    Teilhard de Chardin

Meditation   Different players and notes blend together to produce the sonorities in a great symphony.

Any meeting you have with others invites you to
orchestrate and bond meaningfully.

Take time today to reflect upon how you are blending. With whom are you making music instead of
noise? In the spirit of Saint Sebastian, how can you
be a carrier of peace in the midst of conflicts?

Musical   Wolfgang Mozart, Sinfonia Concertante in E-flat,
Keynotes   K. 364 (Böhm—DGG). Lovely themes and
cooperative blending characterize the music. Good
spirits and a mutuality emerge from the many
voices of individual players and orchestra.

Guillaume Lekeu, Violin Sonata in G (Grumiaux
and Varsi—Philips). This is an especially warm
and lyrical blend of sounds. The music carries a
strength and a quietness that are especially good
for attunement.

Georgia Kelly, *The Sound of Spirit* (Heru Records,
Box 954, Topanga, CA 90290). *Morning Song* (solo
harp) and *Bird in Flight* (harp, violin and viola)
mingle to produce a beautiful, quiet meditation.
The music illustrates a true blending of the players.

January 21   *Joyfulness*

Focus   Joy is the echo of God's song, sounding through
your soul.   Anonymous

Meditation   In the midst of all circumstances, you can prac-
tice joyfulness.

You can feel delight and gladness for the divine
goodness that fills your life.

No matter what is happening in your life, joy can be there; look for the good that can emerge from every problem, failure and disappointment.

Your joyfulness is the bridge that carries you across the threshold to new energy and empowerment.

Musical   Maurice Ravel, *The Fairy Garden*, from *Mother*
Keynotes   *Goose* (Martinon—RCA). This music is magical and full of enchantment. The finale is filled with high sprirts and excitement.

Ernest Chausson, *Selections from King Arthur* (Erato). Chausson's masterpiece contains many sections of music which is joyful and filled with the sense of the quest for the Holy Grail.

Radhika Miller, *Lotus Love Call* (Art of Relaxation). Especially beautiful is *Dawn*, a song of joyfulness, brimming with birds and streams and the open transparency of the flute.

January 22   **Realization**

Focus   *Your Life Purpose*
1. To become more conscious of your inner life and immortality.
2. To realize more fully the Great Plan of Life under which you grow.
3. To come into a larger harmonious fellowship with the Angelic and other Higher Kingdoms of being.

Flower A. Newhouse

Meditation Today consider your most important ideals for this lifetime. How are you grounding and living these ideals daily?

As a practical idealist, you can find ways to tether your greatest dreams.

Like a balloon, you can soar high over the horizon,
but remember to touch down on the earth.

Musical   Charles Tournemire, Selections from *The Mystical*
Keynotes   *Organ* (Delvallée—Musical Heritage Society). This
                 music for solo organ is a soaring vision of divine
                 Presence. It is inward-looking and carries its own
                 serenity.

                 Paul Halley, *Nightwatch* (Gramavision). This
                 music for solo pipe organ is contemporary and ma-
                 jestic. The mighty pipe organ of the Cathedral of
                 Saint John the Divine, in New York City, rings out
                 in mystery and power. Especially moving is the
                 great ambience of the cathedral acoustics.

January 23   *The Immortal Hour*

Focus   What ache of longing lay behind the song. He seeks
                 to know the joy that is more great than joy the
                 beauty of the old green earth can give. He has
                 known dreams, and because bitter dreams have
                 sweeter been than honey, he has sought the open
                 road that lies 'mid shadowy things. A king of men
                 has wooed the Immortal Hour.
                             Fiona Macleod, Rutland Boughton

Meditation   The immortal hour of your life is that time when
                 you seek the finest—which is in this moment, yet
                 just beyond it.

                 Today you can be filled with the thrill of this very
                 moment, and you can feel the Immortal Hour—
                 the greater experience which awaits you.

Musical   Rutland Boughton, *The Immortal Hour*
Keynotes   (Melville—Hyperion). This opera, based upon the
                 poetry of the Celtic poet Fiona Macleod (William

Sharp), brings its own magical qualities and enchantment. Especially beautiful are the unseen
voices of the choruses.

> "How beautiful they are, the lordly ones,
>   Who dwell in the hills, the hollow hills."

Sylvia Woods, *The Harp of Brandiswhiere*
(Tonmeister). Again, this music for Celtic harp and
cymbalum, trumpet, penny whistle, etc., brings
its own sense of faerie enchantment. The energy
of the music is more outward, but stimulates the
imagination.

January 24	## *Magnanimity*
Focus	Magnanimity means greatness of spirit—a spirit not common to the natural heart. The natural heart is self-seeking, not self-effacing. To be magnanimous, then, means to be greater than one's natural self, to rise on occasions to unaccustomed generosity in deference to someone else's need or claim. Magnanimity may make large demands upon cherished plans that involve one's whole future. H. M. Tippett
Meditation	You are magnanimous when you can rise above meanness and pettiness. Aspects of magnanimity are generosity and noble-mindedness. Today you can feel the bigness in you that can stand free of littleness.
Musical Keynotes	Beethoven, Symphony No. 6, *The Brook*, Second Movement (Klemperer or Jochum—EMI). In this music for full orchestra, the mood is tranquil and warm. The murmur of the brook is heard in the

second violins and violas in the beginning. Calls of the nightingale, cuckoo and quail are imitated at the end of the movement.

Brian Hands Concert Orchestra, *Melody of the Birds* (Viking—New Zealand). New Zealand birds of the forest, such as bellbird, yellowhead and tui, mix with orchestral sounds to create a friendly, nurturing landscape.

January 25	## *Reverence*
Focus	Life is feeling, experience, suffering....

Wherever you see life—that is yourself....

Reverence is the sense of the unfathomable mystery of existence—different in its outward appearance and yet inwardly of the same character as our own, terribly similar, awesomely related.

In reverence the strangeness between us and other creatures is removed. Reverence for the infinity of life means removal of the alienation and restoration of empathy, compassion and sympathy.

Reverence means our duty to share and maintain life.   Albert Schweitzer

Meditation To be reverent means to live in continuous adoration of life. It is to feel the awe and wonder of every living form in all its manifestations.

You can reflect today with reverence; you can feel the struggle of every life to survive and grow. Each life form brings its own particular meaning.

Honor the sacredness of every life.

Musical   Antonin Dvorak, *Largo*, from Symphony No. 9,
Keynotes   *From the New World* (Kertesz—London

Treasury). There is a marvelous sense of adoration and quiet appreciation in this music. It glows with peace and power. A contemporary setting of this selection, *Goin' Home*, makes a beautiful meditation. (Daniel Kobialka—Li-Sem)

Abraham Kaplan, *K'Dusha Symphony, Sanctification* (Congregation B'Nai Amoona, 324 S. Mason Rd., St. Louis, MO 63141). This noble orchestral and choral work lifts the listener into a prayerful consciousness.

January 26	## *Courage*
Focus	The highest form of courage is being happy under testing. Esther Sullivan
Meditation	Challenges in life build spiritual muscle. You can be happy for your testings and use them to grow. You can accept everything with joyfulness. Being happy under testings brings new strength and courage for overcoming.
Musical Keynotes	J. S. Bach, Brandenburg Concerto No. 4 (Casals—Columbia). The music is joyful and strong, bringing its own empowering resilient qualities. Richard Wagner, Overture to *Die Meistersinger* (Païta—Lodia). This strong and uplifting music rises to a great final crescendo. Vangelis, *Chariots of Fire*, Soundtrack (Polydor) This piece is very powerful in places, dynamic and motivational, with some mighty melodies and currents of strengthening orchestral color.

January 27   **Charity**

Focus   His love for his brothers, his cooperative and af-
               firmative nature, his charity, his deep joy
               whenever he could serve one of his brethren with
               his special talents, these were his great qualities.
                                          Brother Hensler
                                   from Mozart's Memorial Service

Meditation   You express charity when you are able to love
               others for themselves.

               Like the Good Samaritan, you are loving and
               charitable when you love those who may never
               acknowledge or reciprocate your giving.

               Your expression of charity opens the doors of seren-
               dipity and unexpected blessings.

Musical   Mozart, *Laudate Dominum* from *Solemn Vespers*
Keynotes   (Te Kanawa—Philips); Symphony No. 40, Second
               Movement (Britten—London). Both these pieces
               and others by Mozart radiate a deep and
               penetrating goodness. The music helps the heart
               open to the larger horizons that are magnetized by
               charity.

               Mike Rowland, *The Fairy Ring* (Sona Gaia). The
               sounds of piano and strings are gentle and embrac-
               ing. The music awakens givingness and helps
               release hurts of the past.

January 28   **Catalyst**

Focus   When all goes well with me. . ., the thoughts come
               streaming upon me most fluently; if I am not
               disturbed, my soul is fixed, and the thing grows
               greater, broader and clearer, and I have it all in

my head; I see it like a beautiful picture..., the whole at once.

Composing is like a beautiful and vivid dream, but hearing it is best of all.

Wolfgang Amadeus Mozart

Meditation   A catalyst in your life stimulates and accelerates your response so that you can notice quickenings in your life.

Consider today whatever or whomever stimulates you—in your feelings, thinking and action.

Find the catalysts that help you to grow and progress: persons, books, places, music, activities.

Musical Keynotes   Jan Sibelius, *Karelia Suite* (Järvi—Bis). This is music of nature in its many moods. The orchestra ebbs and flows, and beautiful melodies abound. It has good energy, especially in the overture.

Light Rain, *Sundown Silhouette* from *Arabesque* (Hearts of Space, San Francisco, CA). From the musical traditions of the Middle East, these exotic sounds bring stimulating rhythms and beautiful melodies.

January 29   *Sensitivity*

Focus   Music is an outburst of the soul.

Frederick Delius

Meditation   Focus upon the many nuances and shadings of feeling.

Your feelings allow you to express sensitivity: you can laugh, cry, exult, sympathize, sing, love, in countless shadings of tone and color.

Reflect today upon the many ways to express sensitivity: what persons, things or events call forth your greatest sensitivity?

What are your favorite ways to show your feelings to others?

Musical   Frederick Delius, *Florida Suite* (Beecham—EMI).
Keynotes   This orchestral piece is beautiful nature music, suggesting the fragrances of orange groves and the river flowing into the rising sun. It is especially good for evoking feelings and memories.

Celebration, *Journey of the Heart* (Celebration, 4118 Adams Ave., San Diego, CA 92116). Nondirectional, pleasant sounds, wisps of melody; harps, guitar, flute and voices create an open, ambient soundscape good for relaxation and guided imagery.

January 30   **Imagination**

Focus   Through vibration comes motion;
               Through motion comes color;
               Through color comes tone.

                                        Pythagoras

Meditation   Imagination has been described as "ways in which the soul beholds things that are absent." You have the ability to feel and imagine what is suggested but not yet experienced.

Your imagination can bring through archetypes that already exist in the higher worlds of thought.

Today, visually, sonically and kinesthetically, your imagination can magnetize new seeds of discovery that surround your consciousness.

| Musical Keynotes | Charles Loeffler, *The Death of Tintagiles* (Nelson—New World Records). This music is exotic and magical, taking the listener into landscapes of enchantment. The viola d'amore plays its haunting, melancholy moods accompanied by full orchestra. |

Maloah Stillwater, *Shores of Paradise* (Heavensong Music). Gentle sounds of zither, ocean surf, guitar and birds suggest distant, tropical horizons. This music not only stimulates the imagination, but is helpful for stress reduction. It is open and spatial, not good for grounding or focusing.

| *January 31* | ## *Full Productivity* |

| Focus | Let these eyes, illuminated by Thy Glory, be filled to the brim.   Franz Schubert |

| Meditation | Today's theme emphasizes abundance of life. |

You can find what is most important and necessary in your life.

Your desire for fullness creates space to be filled creatively.

You can make room for what you really want to do. Allow the doors to open!

| Musical Keynotes | Franz Schubert, Mass No. 6 in E-flat (St. Johns, Guest—Argo). Beautiful choral singing and orchestral color release energies of abundance and power. |

Dyveke Spino, *Morning Dance* (Dyveke Spino Productions). The combination of piano, flute and voice make this a vitalizing musical experience. Note especially the glorious openings and expansive melodies of *Meadow Vista*.

The Yearning

Focus

Ah, sweet mystery of life,
    at last I've found Thee,
Ah, I know at last the secret
    of it all;
All the longing, seeking, striving,
    waiting, yearning,
The burning hopes, the joy
    and idle tears that fall;
For 'tis love and love alone
    the world is seeking
And 'tis love and love alone
    that can repay.
'Tis the answer, 'tis the end
    and all of living
For it is love alone
    that rules fore'er.

                Victor Herbert

Meditation

What is your deepest yearning in life?

Consider the deepest, happiest experience you can remember. Can you again contact the feelings of that moment?

What is it or who is it that brings out your deepest yearning? How are you expressing this feeling?

How do you want to open your heart?

Musical Keynotes

Victor Herbert, *Ah, Sweet Mystery of Life* (Sills, Kostelanetz—Angel). This song, for soloist and orchestra, is very heart-expanding. The notes rise into a final, freeing crescendo, and openings occur.

Paul Horn, *Inside the Taj Mahal* (Teldec). The ambience of the Taj Mahal in India provides a stunning quality that lifts the flute tones upward toward the heavens. (Omit the vocals on alternate bands.) The sonorities ascend like a spiral, weaving their way toward celestial reaches, much like a mass by Palestrina in earlier periods. However, this music is not helpful for grounded activity. It centers energy in the higher chakras.

February 2	## *Attunement*

Focus

There can hardly be a greater pleasure than to hear beautiful music.

Felix Mendelssohn

Meditation

You have the ability to attune yourself with beautiful vibrations.

Higher reaches of divinity are within your hearing and sensing.

Finding accord with lives around you helps you to reach greater attunement.

Today look for new ways to realize better attunement and harmony with all of life.

Musical Keynotes

Mischa Elman, *Elman Plays Fritz Kreisler Favorites* (Vanguard). These melodies are especially good for realizing finer attunement. Kreisler pretended that they were composed by others, but after his passing, it became clear that they were his own creations.

Annie Locke, *The Living Earth* (Search for Serenity). Gentle and mysterious sounds take you inside the peace of a crystal cave. This restful music is especially good for imaging.

February 3   ## *Visualization*

Focus

There must be something to occupy the heart and elevate it far above failures, strife and isolated things.   Felix Mendelssohn

Meditation

One way to change a situation is to *replace your focus.*

You can focus upon a problem or a solution.

Replace the problem with some visualization of a more beautiful alternative.

When you are in a stressful situation or environment, visualize a favorite spot that is peaceful and renewing. Feel that you are there, experiencing the scene.

Change your focus in a way that harmonizes with the larger plan and possibilities for your life.

Musical Keynotes

Felix Mendelssohn, *Calm Sea and Prosperous Voyage* (Muti-Angel); Claude Debussy, *Claire de Lune* and *Prelude to the Afternoon of a Faun* (Ormandy—Columbia). These impressionistic pieces, for full orchestra, offer a spacious quality that allows you to fill in the scene. Both selections have the power to take you into a landscape of your own choosing. You can use the music to change your focus and move into openness.

John Barry, *Somewhere in Time*, Soundtrack (MCA). This music for orchestra is dream-like and mysterious. Beautiful melodies weave together to express a sense of longing and loving. The music stimulates the imagination and is the opposite of focus and grounded activities.

February 4   **Memory**

Focus   For myself, music performs a special action in
                 arousing my memory....More than once music
                 has enabled me to retrieve from its hiding place,
                 quite suddenly, some reluctant and elusive
                 memory.   Mario Pilo

Meditation   Beautiful music can stimulate your consciousness.

                 Certain melodies can open up forgotten memories,
                 faces, smells or scenes. Today, you can use the
                 musical selections to free associate.

                 You can let the sounds awaken memories: perhaps
                 a place, a taste or color, a person, now coming into
                 view.

                 Let the music guide you across your stream of
                 memory.

Musical   Ralph Vaughan-Williams, *Lark Ascending* (Bean,
Keynotes   Boult—Angel). The music, for violin and or-
                 chestra, ebbs and flows, allowing you to take a
                 journey of your own choosing. A strong sense of
                 the open air helps you take wing.

                 Annie Locke, *Portraits* (Search for Serenity). The
                 music of a synthesizer will take you into mysterious
                 and open spaces. It is gentle and not demanding,
                 like a crystal, emanating many colors. Its trans-
                 parency will enable you to fill in your own spaces.

February 5   **Releasing Blocks**

Focus   Through its influence upon the unconscious, music
                 can have a specific healing effect. It can help in
                 eliminating repressions and resistances, and it can
                 bring into the field of waking consciousness many
                 drives, emotions and complexes which were creat-
                 ing difficulties in the unconscious.
                                            Roberto Assagioli

Meditation   Deep sadness or anger can rob you of your vitality.
                This is a day to release your tensions and angers,
                your pockets of blocked energy.

                Let yourself go into strong velocities of sound. Let
                the energy field of the music vibrate through you,
                as you breathe out all blockage and interferences.

                After you release into the music, write down any
                memories or scenes that may have emerged for you
                to let go.

Musical   Johann Sebastian Bach, Toccata and Fugue in D,
Keynotes   orchestrated by Leopold Stokowski (Seraphim).
                The music for large orchestra is vast and cosmic.
                Great power and capacity of sound allow you to
                release any anger or sadness into the music. In-
                finities of space contain and transmute tension or
                sorrow.

                inti-illimani, *Palimpsesto* (Redwood Records).
                Strong and rhythmical sounds of South America
                provide joyful, exuberant release. A strong festive
                quality emerges, allowing catharsis and out-
                pouring.

February 6   ## Devotion and Friendship

Focus   You know that however much time passes without
                your hearing from me, there is not a day that does
                not in some way or other bring me nearer to you
                or remind me of your friendship.
                                            Felix Mendelssohn

Meditation   Use today to review your friendships.

                Who nurtures you, and how good a friend are you
                to others?

Your love and affection flow out to others like fragrant roses. Generosity and kindness from you magnetize old and new relationships.

Today you can be a friend to someone, and you can be a good receiver of love from others.

Musical *Keynotes*   Sergei Rachmaninoff, *18th Variation, Rhapsody on a Theme of Paganini* (Rubinstein, Reiner—RCA); Frederic Chopin, *Piano Concerto No. 1, Second Movement* (Gilels, Ormandy—Columbia). Both selections contain vibrations of love and kindness. Your heart can expand into the music, awakening devotion and feelings of friendship.

Daniel Kobialka, *Softness of a Moment* (LiSem Enterprises). Beautiful settings of music by Rameau and J. S. Bach, played on violin, viola, mandolin, flute, English horn, oboe and synthesizer, can open your heart to affection. The music flows peacefully.

February 7   # Spirituality

Focus   To be spiritual is a matter of looking into the hearts of others, sharing their joys and anguishes, and feeling that you can strengthen the weak and purify the muddy and ugly places of the world.
C. Jinarajadasa

Meditation   Genuine spirituality is never aloof or superior in its expression.

Your spirituality toward others can feel the joy of bending low—in a spirit of service and helpfulness.

You can transmute interferences by others into overcomings and progress. Welcome demands and inconveniences that are not expected.

Musical   Anton Bruckner, Symphony No. 8, Third Move-
Keynotes   ment (Haitink—Philips). This music, for full or-
               chestra, is mystical and illuminating. Gradually,
               the journey in the night seems to climb to a great
               height; on the mountain peak you can feel the ra-
               diance of resplendent light and power. Then the
               music recedes into peacefulness.

               Gustav Mahler, Symphony No. 4, Third Move-
               ment (Szell—Columbia). The music of the full or-
               chestra presents a scene in nature—quiet, searching
               and intimate. Gradually, the music builds up to
               a mighty crescendo, then descends quietly. The
               music is powerful and meditative.

February 8   ## Will Power

Focus   There is a kind of music which arouses the will and
               incites to action. Such music has stimulated in-
               numerable individuals to noble deeds, and heroic
               self-sacrifice for an ideal.

                                              Roberto Assagioli

Meditation   This is a day to consider willpower.

               If there are times when you hesitate or feel stuck
               in fear, music can help you break free and move
               forward.

               Look at any area of life that may be causing you
               to avoid necessary action: then let the music enter
               into you, bringing you power, gladness and
               courage.

               Move ahead and do what must be done.

Musical   Ludwig van Beethoven, Symphony No. 5 in C-
Keynotes   minor (Klemperer—Angel). This music, for full or-
               chestra, is one of the most powerful works ever

composed. It affirms life and strength, and helps you overcome inertia and passivity.

Ray Lynch, *Your Feeling Shoulders* from *Deep Breakfast* (Ray Lynch Productions). The music, for piano, guitar and synthesizers, is deep and soulful. The melodies can carry you on the ocean of power and arouse feelings of strength and cosmic immensity.

February 9	*Compassion*

Focus

Compassion will involve you in suffering. When you callously ignore the suffering of others, you lose the capacity to share their happiness, too. And however little joy we may see in this world, the sharing of it, together with the good we ourselves create, produces the only happiness which makes life tolerable.   Albert Schweitzer

Meditation

"Love until it hurts!" So speaks Mother Teresa.

Feeling with another involves you with the widest range of bittersweet experiences that life offers.

Reflect today upon your desire and ability to reach out to others' needs, to feel their joys and sorrows intermingling with your own.

Expanding your capacity for compassion each day, you will gradually grow into the Christ spirit, which knows and feels the hearts of all mankind.

Musical Keynotes

Alban Berg, Violin Concerto (Suk, Ancerl—Quintessence). This beautiful work, his last composition in any form, shows Berg to be a melodist in the midst of a twelve-tone style. It is dedicated to "the memory of an angel," in particular the daughter of Alma Mahler. The music, for violin and orchestra, suggests the passing of the young girl and then the eternal rest of her soul in the next dimension. It is deeply felt, compassionate music.

To Thy Loving Heart, Yoga Center Chants (Helix Center, El Toro, CA). These are devotional choral chants, inspired by the life of Sri Ramakrishna. The music evokes love and compassion.

February 10   **Giving of Oneself**

Focus   At early dawn when sleep is
Sweet with dreaming, dreaming,
The accordion sang out again
At the parting hour.

Life is thus a moment only,
Only a dissolving
Of ourselves in other selves
As a hearty gift.

Life is but a wedding gift
Bursting from the light,
Like a song, a dream, a pigeon
Winging in the blue.
                              Boris Pasternak

Meditation   Your life becomes more precious as you sense the days passing more quickly.

At times, perhaps, in the capsule of a moment, the gift of your lifetime reaches stillpoint and total clarity.

Today, you can see your life flowing into the lives of others.

In the giving of yourself, you find your life bursting from light.

Musical Keynotes	Felix Mendelssohn, *Te Deum* (Bernius—Carus; Verlag—Stuttgart); *On Wings of Song* (Lough—EMI). This is devotional music, for solo voice, choir and orchestra.
	Christopher Parkening, *Simple Gifts* (Word). Particularly lovely here are the meditative pieces for solo guitar, *Simple Gifts* and *Glorious Things of Thee Are Spoken.* The music has a simple joy and songfulness.

February 11	## Encouragement
Focus	O my Beautiful, come into my heart. What is the song without the singer? And what is the singer without thee? O my Beautiful, come into my heart, And set its music free. <div align="right">Indian Fishermen's Song from Clara Codd *Trust Yourself to Life*</div>
Meditation	Consider today how you can encourage others.
	Whenever you can enhearten another, joy and encouragement come to you.
	You can find new words, deeper feelings, impressions freely offered, in a spirit of helpfulness.
	By encouraging someone, you can remove discouragement.
Musical Keynotes	J. S. Bach, *Jesu, Joy of Man's Desiring* (Stokowski—Vanguard; Flagstad—London); *Sheep May Safely Graze* (Stokowski—Vanguard). This is perhaps the most encouraging of all music. Bach's text is as follows:

> Jesu, joy of man's desiring,
> Holy wisdom, love most bright:
> Drawn by Thee, our souls aspiring
> Soar to uncreated Light....
> Hark what peaceful music rings,
> Where the flock in Thee confiding
> Drink of joy in deathless springs....
> Thou dost ever lead Thine own
> In the love of joys unknown.
>
> Robert Bridges

Paramahansa Yogananda, *The Divine Gypsy* (Self-Realization Fellowship). In the Hindu tradition, these lovely, quieting pieces come from Yogananda's *Cosmic Chants.* Especially beautiful and reassuring are *They Have Heard Thy Name* and *O God Beautiful.*

February 12   ## *Longing*

Focus   The creative impulse...is a longing for TRUTH. Always it is a lonesome hunger that gnaws within the human heart, forcing us to search for understandable expression.

Roy Harris

Meditation   There is always the divine moreness—the great immensity which enlarges us and feeds us.

Express your longings and thirst for greater horizons of understanding and expression.

Energy increases as you feel the great longing for the Infinite that stretches you and opens you into the further reaches of eternity.

Musical Keynotes   Aaron Copland, *Fanfare for the Common Man* (Ormandy—Columbia); *A Lincoln Portrait* (Carl Sandburg, Kostelanetz—Columbia). Both pieces, for full orchestra, express a longing for freedom and a nobility. Their strong melodies and rhythms energize and stimulate ideals. This is music of empowerment.

Roy Harris, Symphony No. 6, *Gettysburg* (Clark—Andante). This wonderful symphony portrays the times of Lincoln and the Civil War. A strong sense of truth and integrity comes through.

Steven Boone, *Lazaris Remembers Lemuria* (Concept Synergy). David Frank's arrangement of these memories stirs longings and dreamscapes. The music is open and spatial, good for the expansion of feelings and imagination.

February 13	## *Building Values*
Focus	Music became for me a sort of vessel in which to gather permanent values of life upon which I could depend and on which I could build my whole world around me. Roy Harris
Meditation	All around you actions reveal values. What are your values? Which are most important to you?
	Today, let your values rise in your consciousness: list the most important ones.
	Look at the way you are demonstrating these values in the choices and behaviors you are making. (You may wish to read S. Simon's fine work, *Values Clarification*).
Musical Keynotes	Giovanni Pergolesi, *Glory to God in the Highest* (Mormon Tabernacle Choir—Columbia). This music is strong and solid, good for engendering purpose and dependability.
	Abraham Kaplan, *Halleluya* and *I Will Lift Up Mine Eyes* from *Glorious* (North American Liturgy Resources). This stirring music is good for strengthening values.

February 14   ## Love (Saint Valentine's Day)

Focus   I love thee freely, as men strive for Right,
                  I love thee purely as they turn from Praise.
                                          Johannes Brahms

Meditation   Feel your heart outpouring.

                  Begin by feeling love for the gift of your life.

                  Consider those who love you and have given love
                  to you.

                  See yourself as a loving person, giving of yourself
                  and your means to others.

                  Enjoy the deep feelings of loving and being loved
                  for who you are and who you are becoming.

Musical   Gustav Mahler, *Adagietto*, from Symphony No. 5
Keynotes   (Kubelik—DGG; Walter—Odyssey). This heart-
                  rending music for strings carries a spectrum of feel-
                  ings, and describes the deepest ranges of love, with
                  its joys and sorrows.

                  Sergei Rachmaninoff, *Adagio*, from Symphony
                  No. 2 (Previn—Angel or Telarc). This is a medita-
                  tion on love, for full orchestra. It is like the waves
                  of a great ocean, gradually rolling in and then
                  receding into the infinite Silence.

February 15   ## Rhythms

Focus   The psychological life of the individual as well as
                  that of his body has its various and complex
                  rhythms: the rhythms of elation and depression;
                  alternations of sorrow and joy, of fervor and
                  lassitude, of strength and weakness, of extrover-
                  sion and introversion. All these conditions are ex-

tremely sensitive to the influence of the rhythm of
music.   Roberto Assagioli

Meditation   Be aware of the alternating rhythms of your life.

In everything there is a measure of motion.

Rhythms express the polarity of life. You swing
toward one tendency and then toward the other.

You can establish a rhythm to your days. If you
go too far in one direction, you can cultivate the
opposite rhythm so that balance is achieved.

Musical   Michael Praetorius, *Dances from Terpsichore*
Keynotes   (Munrow—Angel). These lively dances carry the
Renaissance spirit and are filled with rhythmical
vitality. The music has a marvelous energizing
quality.

Henry Wolff, Nancy Hennings, *Tibetan Bells* (An-
tilles). A marvelous variety of tone and timbre
sounds forth in varying rhythms that are
stimulating and invigorating. The music vibrates
in ways that can help release blocked energy.

February 16   **Truth**

Focus   An upright person has the hardest stand to make,
knowing that the public are more attracted by outward show than by TRUTH.
                          Felix Mendelssohn

Meditation   There is glamor, and there is truth. Today reflect
upon the simplicity of being true.

When it is easier to say what others want to hear,
you can easily choose to be true.

Not speaking the truth means jamming your energy
system.

Speaking and acting in the light of truth brings
inner peace. When you are true to yourself and the
highest that you know, you will sleep well and find
harmony in yourself.

Musical   Johannes Brahms, Piano Concerto No. 2, Third
Keynotes   Movement (Gilels, Jochum—DGG). The music for
                   full orchestra is highlighted by the solo voices of
                   the cello and piano. It is direct and deeply
                   heartfelt.

                   Norman Miller, *Enoch* (Norman Miller, Box A,
                   Malibu, CA 90265). This strong and triumphant
                   music, for chorus and orchestra, brings in a heroic
                   quality.

February 17   **Aria**

Focus   The human voice and music can combine to
                   transform...persons into poets, great lovers and
                   visionaries...."It is the best of all trades to make
                   songs, and the second best, to sing them."
                                   Alan P. Tory and Hilaire Belloc

Meditation   Aria suggests an air, a melody or a tune. A melody
                   is accompanied by a single voice that brings deep
                   feeling, such as joy, nostalgia or longing.

                   Think today of the single voices that bring music
                   to your life.

                   Can you now hear a single song, word, laugh or
                   cry?

                   You can let this sound and this tone vibrate through
                   you, bringing deeper meaning and beauty into
                   your life.

Musical Keynotes	Arcangelo Corelli, Concerti Grossi (Vox). This music has great warmth and a friendly focus. It is direct and also very lyrical and melodic.

Wolfgang Amadeus Mozart, *Exultate, Jubilate* (Te Kanawa—Philips). This music is joyful and jubilant. The soprano "takes off" and lifts the listener with the high notes of exaltation. The piece is especially good for lifting your spirits.

February 18   **The Joy of Work**

Focus

A person must work. Only then can one see God.... The water cannot be seen without pushing aside the green scum that covers it; that is to say, one cannot develop love of God or obtain the vision of Him without work. Work means meditation, worship and the like....Work with longing for God in your heart. If you have longing, you will receive God's grace.

Ramakrishna

Meditation

Mother Teresa has said, "Your work is only an expression of the love you have for God."

Reflect today about your work and tasks.

The more you can truly love your work, the more God's power strengthens you.

You can let your labor be your love.

Doing the task well, you help to add beauty and joy to the world.

Musical Keynotes

Syrinx-Vivaldi, *Il Cardellino*, Flute Concerto, Opus 10, No. 3 (Erato). The music is joyful and filled with rhythms that energize and delight a

listener. The tunes are easy to hum and help work
to go smoothly.

Whistle While You Work from *Snow White and
the Seven Dwarfs* (Mormon Tabernacle Choir—
Columbia). Peppy tunes from the world of Walt
Disney are especially energizing and motivate a
person for work.

Also suitable are the beautiful chants inspired by
the life of Sri Ramakrishna, as played in the tape
To Thy Loving Heart (see February 9).

February 19	# Discovery
Focus	And it was Olav Trygvason, Suddenly he did behold High rising o'er him temples lofty, White walls and domes of gold. Seized with a mighty longing, He strives to reach the land now dawning. Like the Viking we are praying, Homage to the Highest paying, Spirits tremble, hearts are bounding, Joyfully His praises sounding. That thy faith may strong be builded, Pure as ice by sunlight gilded, Rise from Nature's best endeavor, Seek thy God, seek Him forever. Seek thy God, Seek thy God! <div align="right">Björnsterne Björnson</div>
Meditation	Seek thy God on the oceans of discovery! Visualize yourself flowing along the waves of newness.

Your day is always new and filled with opportunity.

Keep the thrill of continuous learning and discovery.

Musical Keynotes   Edvard Grieg, *Olav Trygvason* (Dreier—Unicorn Records). This powerful music recalls the great oceanic journeys and discoveries of the Vikings. Strong melodies and orchestral/choral colors awaken a spirit of adventure.

Luigi Boccherini, Guitar Quintets (P. Romero—Philips). These are lively, quickening pieces. The energy is always new and dynamic, yet the music is also warm and melodic.

Joanna Brouk, *Invocation*, from *Sounds of the Sea* (Hummingbird Prod.). Open air music, suggesting the timeless sweep of ocean waves creating a womb-like, watery lullaby. You can relax into the music, letting it take you on a voyage of discovery. The synthesizers and flute sounds are spacious and reassuring.

February 20   **Choice**

Focus   There are always two choices, two paths to take. One is easy. And its only reward is that it is easy. The other is difficult. Few challenge it. But the rewards are truly great.

Chariots of Fire

Meditation   Someone has said, "When there are two choices, take the one that is more difficult."

Consider today the choices in your life.

Think of the possible consequences of your choice—both short term and long range.

You can make the choice that is most appropriate to your life path and the highest that you have been seeking. You will not be disappointed.

You can choose what is most harmonious with who you really are.

Musical Keynotes

Music of Jubilee, *J. S. Bach Favorites for Organ and Orchestra* (Biggs, Rozsnyai—Columbia). This music is heroic and strong, as well as nurturing. It brings out willpower and the ability to make constructive decisions.

Judith Pintar, *Changes Like the Moon* (Sona Gaia). This music, played on the Celtic harp, offers a fine variety of moods and melodies. I especially like the beauty and clarity of *In the Garden* and *Longing for the Sea*.

February 21

Celebration

Focus

Be not lax
in celebrating,
Be not lazy
in the festive service of God.

Be ablaze with enthusiasm.
It is in praise and service
that the surprise of God is consummated.
Hildegard of Bingen

Meditation

In the spirit of celebration, you can magnetize each day.

Your capacity for joyful response will transform your sorrows.

Your feelings of celebration unwrap the gifts of divine love.

Musical Keynotes   Hildegard of Bingen, *Feather on the Breath of God* (Hyperion; Musical Heritage). This early music brings in the voices of serenity and joyfulness. The music is restful and continuous—no sudden changes or shocks.

> In the praise of God
> a person is like an angel.
> But it is the doing of good works
> that is the hallmark of humanity.
> Hildegard of Bingen

Leo Delibes, *Coppelia* (Ormandy—Columbia). These invigorating tunes bring a dance-like joyfulness and a spirit of celebration.

February 22   ## *Patriotism*

Focus   Everyone must work for his country...without regard for profit and glory, because we are here.
Bedrich Smetana

Meditation   Each country offers its culture and colors in God's great pageantry.

Today you can feel the richness of your national heritage.

Imagine the many crossroads of brotherhood—the music of humanity contributing streams of song.

You can enjoy your own country and the varied unity of all nations of the planetary family.

Musical Keynotes   *Himnos Nacionales*, Central and South America (De Arriba—Montilla); *National Anthems of the World* (Everest); Georges Bizet, *Patrie (Country)*

(Munch—Nonesuch); Bedrich Smetana, *My Country* (Kubelik—DGG); William Schuman, *American Festival Overture* (Bernstein—DGG); Kate Smith, *God Bless America* (RCA); Sir Edward Elgar, *Land of Hope and Glory* (Davis—Philips); Frederic Chopin, *Grand Fantasy on Polish Airs* (Rubinstein—RCA). All of these pieces offer fervent expressions of love for one's country. The music emanates good energy.

February 23   ## Proclaim

Focus   I did think I did see all Heaven before me—and the great God Himself. Where I was, in my body or out of my body, as I wrote it [Messiah], I know not. God knows.

George Frideric Handel

Meditation   Consider these lines today:

O world, as God has made it! all is beauty: And knowing this is love, and love is duty. What further may be sought for or declared?

Clara Codd

Behind all outer appearances or testings, you can proclaim divine order.

Its glory shines upon us.

You can feel the glory and proclaim attunement with that power.

Musical Keynotes   George Frideric Handel, *Messiah* (Willcocks—Arabesque; Marriner—Argo). Celestial presences filled his room when this music came to Handel. Particularly powerful selections that proclaim the infinite glory include:

Ev'ry Valley Shall Be Exalted,
And the Glory of the Lord,
Hallelujah,
I Know That My Redeemer Liveth,
The Trumpet Shall Sound,
Worthy Is the Lamb,
Final Amen.

February 24   # Gratitude

Focus   In the White of the fire. . . how can I express the
               excellence I have found, that has no color but
               clearness; no honey but ecstasy; nothing wrought
               nor remembered; no undertone nor silver second
               murmur that rings in love's voice.

                                              Robinson Jeffers

Meditation   Now is a good time to count your blessings.

               Consider today the abundance of goodness in your
               life.

               Gratitude is the embrace of the heart.

               Make a list of those persons, property, pets, health,
               opportunities and the all-inclusive divinity that
               shines through all that you are and all that you
               have been given.

Musical   Giuseppe Verdi, *Te Deum* (Giulini—EMI;
Keynotes   Solti—London). This mighty music of praise, com-
               posed for full choir and orchestra, is filled with
               grandeur and glory. Its melodies and the high
               energy will empower you.

               Land of Heart's Desire (Pearce, Watkins—
               Meridian). Love and gratitude come through
               strongly in these beautiful songs of the Hebrides.

February 25   **Nothing Is Lost**

Focus   The person knows that he will carry everything on
that he makes; that from life to life he will take
with him the treasures that he has accumulated;
that if he finds a deficiency and only partly fills
it, still it is filled to that extent, that part of the
work is done. If he makes for himself a power, that
power is his forever more, a part of the Soul never
to be taken away, woven into the texture of the
individual, not again ever to be separated from
him.   Annie Besant

Meditation   Nothing is lost in Spirit.

You can feel today how life is progressive.

You are becoming more as you discover who you
were created to be.

The errors and ignorance of yesterday are
transformed in the sunbursts and light of character
you show forth today.

Through lessons well earned and learned, you can
master how to live out what you know each day.

Musical   Ludwig van Beethoven, Piano Concertos 1 and 3,
Keynotes   Second Movements (Perahia, Haintink—
Columbia). Both of these slow movements take the
listener into an interior, meditative landscape and
spiritual searching for the roots of what you are.

Jacqueline du Pré, Recital (Angel); a. Maria
Theresia von Paradis, *Sicilienne;* b. J. S. Bach,
Adagio; c. Felix Mendelssohn, *Songs Without
Words.* These are wonderful, inward, reflective
pieces of music. They lead one to the center of life
and in the natural direction of self-examination.
The music is played by an artist with great
courage, and could be heard as an elegy.

February 26   ***Immensity of Light***

Focus   Thou who liveth within my heart,
                 Awaken me to the immensity of thy spirit,
                 To the experience of thy living presence.
                 Deliver me from the bonds of desire,
                 From the slavery of small aims,
                 From the delusion of narrow egohood!

                 Enlighten me with the light of thy wisdom,
                 Suffuse me with the incandescence of thy love,...
                 Let me be the seed of thy living light!
                 Give me the strength to burst the sheath of
                     selfhood,
                 And like the seed that dies in order to be reborn,
                 Let me fearlessly go through the portals of death,
                 So that I may awaken to the greater life:
                 The all-embracing life of thy love,
                 The all-embracing love of thy wisdom.
                                        Lama Govinda
                            "To the Buddha of Infinite Light"

Meditation   The immensity of infinite Light cleanses you from
                 the slavery of smallness.

                 Today, you can let the greater light suffuse you and
                 give you strength.

                 Fearlessly, you can open yourself to the immen-
                 sity of light.

Musical   Cho-Ga, *Tantric and Ritual Music of Tibet* (Dorje
Keynotes   Ling, Box 1410, San Rafael, CA 94902); Gyuto
                 Monks, *Tibetan Tantric Choir* (Windham Hill);
                 The Music of Tibet: Tantric Rituals (Anthology
                 Record and Tape Corporation, 135 W. 41st St.,
                 New York, NY 10036). Whether or not you are
                 familiar with teachings of Tibetan Buddhism does
                 not matter as these chants carry their own univer-
                 sal power and influence. Some arise out of deep

"bowels" of earthy sounds, while others are performed in a higher key and pitch.

Hymns Triumphant, arranged by Lee Holdridge
(Birdwing-Sparrow Records). In the Western
tradition these musical renditions of great hymns
are particularly inspiring.

February 27	## Sublimation

Focus	Whatever your fault may be, in time it will become your primal strength, the basis upon which all the other God-qualities flow to you with swifter wings. *Words of the Strong*
Meditation	Transmutation is a key to progress.
	You can redirect and refine destructive habits.
	Your own process of spiritual alchemy means finding ways to change what is crude or distorted in you by lifting it and reshaping it into some expression that is more beautiful, wholesome and helpful to the totality.
	Consider today the areas in yourself that you might wish to refine.
	Redirect these energies in yourself so that they can be released more constructively.
Musical Keynotes	Ludwig van Beethoven, Piano Concerto No. 1 in C (Ashkenazy, Solti—London). There is vitality in this strong music for piano and orchestra, and a sense of purpose and direction. The energy of the music points the way forward.
	Sir Hubert Parry, *I Was Glad; Jerusalem* (Wicks—Argo). Both of these great choral masterpieces emanate an inner strength and power. Parry

was inspired by the words of Psalm 122 and these lines from William Blake's *Jerusalem:*

> Awake! Awake! O sleeper of the Land of
> Shadows,
>   wake! expand!
> I am in you, and you in Me, mutual in Love
> Divine,...

February 28	*The Shift*

Focus

It really is extraordinary how the shift is already taking place. In this (new) age, hopefully, we will continue to do things voluntarily, not because we are forced to by fear or greed.... As Mother Teresa says, "We can do no great things, only little things with great love."

Alice O. Howell

Meditation

Today you can consider times in your life when you were forced, and others when you acted from seeing—from a sense of what had to happen.

A shift is taking place when you start living increasingly with love and compassion, not from being forced or dominated.

When you make the shift, the way becomes clear—you are more willing, unforced and unaggressive.

Little things, done with great love, move mountains.

Musical Keynotes

Elias Parish-Alvars, Harp Concerto (Zabaleta—Angel). This is a mellow, yet very convincing piece. The harp solo, accompanied by full orchestra, plays many nurturing melodies.

Adam Geiger, *Valley Mist* (Lura Media, 10027

Autumnview Lane, San Diego, CA 92126). This solo piano music is very expansive and gentle yet brings good energy with flowing melodies. It is excellent for refocusing, away from stress and tension.

February 29   ## *Interdependence*

Focus

God's peace prompts service among brothers and sisters. In that way one creature sustains another. One enriches the other, and that is why all creatures are interdependent.

Meister Eckhart

Meditation

The power increases and the time shortens when persons cooperate in the spirit of interdependence.

Today you can find new ways to sustain and enrich those around you.

You can deepen service and friendship as you develop the skill of relating interdependently as equals.

Musical Keynotes

Gioacchino Rossini, Sonatas for Strings (Nonesuch or Philips). These pieces are light and free-flowing, filled with delightful melodies. They insure harmony and a cooperative spirit.

Jim Chappell, *Dusk* (Music West). This music, for solo piano, is easy and light and puts you in a relaxed mood. Lovely melodies flow expansively.

Openings

Focus   Instrumental music has a broader spectrum . . . and it suggests a wider variability . . . than does the voice. A full orchestra, many types (timbres and colors) of instruments all playing together, offers infinite possibilities for complexities of tension-release; it presents a wide range of emotional tone, intricate rhythms, and varied structures in musical themes, textures, colors, harmony-melody combinations, etc. . . . In the work of a skilled composer, the possibilities for a TOTAL OPENING of the listener's sensibilities are enormous.

Helen Bonny

Meditation   Today feel yourself outside, open, clear, perhaps in a beautiful meadow. The air is fresh, the fragrance full, and the flowers beautiful in all their colors.

You can let the breezes blow through you, as you breathe naturally, in and out.

In the clear meadow everything is fresh and open; all staleness can now be released.

Feel the openings in the beautiful meadow; the color and music of the meadow allow you openings now.

Musical   Wolfgang Amadeus Mozart, Horn Concerto No.
Keynotes   2 in E-flat Major (Tuckwell, Marriner—Angel).

The music for horn and orchestra is spacious and bright. Beautiful melodies and vivid clarity make this music ideal for openings. The horn is especially stimulating and energizing.

Dyveke Spino, *Meadow Vista* from *Morning Dance* (Dyveke Spino Prod.). This beautiful song, for solo piano, brings an immediate openness and has a freeing quality. Barriers break down, fog clears and horizons appear.

March 2   **Affection**

Focus   Every sign of affection is doubly dear and precious to me....I do not forget any kindness, from whomsoever it comes.

                                        Bedrich Smetana

Meditation   You can feel the warmth of affection, perhaps a smile, an act of kindness—or a loving touch, an embrace or joyful hug.

                   How do you express affection? How do you show the love you feel in your heart?

                   Today, let out your ability to show affection and let others feel your warmth.

Musical   Gabriel Fauré, *Cantique de Jean Racine*
Keynotes   (Rutter—Conifer). The music is gentle and caressing. Fauré's text, translated from the Roman breviary, includes these words:

>   We break the silence of the peaceful night:
>   Presence divine, cast your eyes upon us....
>   Receive our hymns offered to thy endless glory;
>   May we go forth filled with thy gifts.

                   Alex Jones, *Kali's Dream (Art of Relaxation)*. This

is warm and nurturing music, composed for piano and flute.

March 3   *Festival*

Focus   You shall have a song as in the night, when a holy festival is kept; and gladness of heart as when one goes with a flute to come into the mountain of the Lord.   Isaiah 30:29

Meditation   This is a good time to feel the spirit of a festival occasion.

Remember a time of gaiety and conviviality, the music, the dancing, the joy of the occasion. Remember those who were with you.

Today, in the spirit of festival, you can feel again the banquet of life.

Musical   Joaquin Rodrigo, Concerto for a Festival (P.
Keynotes   Romero, Marriner—Philips); Frederico Moreno-Torroba, *Iberia Concerto* (Romero, Marriner—Philips); Rieder and Roberts, *MoonFlower Ascending* (Message Box Music Co.). This is sunny music, composed for guitar and orchestra. The mood is festive.

March 4   *Progress*

Focus   Any event can precipitate enlightenment:

                 - a crisis
                 - a voluntary sacrifice of the lower
                   in favor of the higher
                 - an unselfish deed

- a beautiful morning
- an elevated state of consciousness.

                                              Anonymous

Meditation   Your life is a spiral, not just a circle.

Your life is a spiral, not just a circle.

You can observe certain moments that seem to recur, but never in exactly the same ways.

Your life can go forward; progress is always possible.

Moving in the currents of progress, your life will always be new—always interesting and productive.

Musical   Antonio Vivaldi, *The Four Seasons* (Galway—
Keynotes   RCA); Flute Concertos (Rampal—Columbia).
                Vivaldi represents one of the most therapeutic of all composers. His music is friendly, warm and lively. To listen to Vivaldi is to begin the day focused and directed.

Schawkie Roth, *Dance of the Tao* (Heavenly Music). Lyrical and rhythmical music for flute and other sounds brings energy and newness.

March 5   **Heartbeat**

Focus   How dignified! How splendid!
                Let's set up and beat the drums;
                Let them roll and let them rumble
                To charm our great ancestors. . . .
                Hear the drums roll and hear them rumble!
                Let's play the pipes and oboes—
                Sweet and soothing—
                To the accompaniment of the chime.
                Strong descendants of T'ang
                Sing your joyful and mellow songs!

The bells and drums roll and rumble;
Graceful and vigorous are the dances.
Here we have honored guests and fine—
Rejoicing they are with us all.

The Book of Songs (Chinese)

Meditation   The currents of life keep on flowing.

The gates of divine love are open, inviting you to
live in the spirit of the great heartbeat.

Now come opportunities to give and receive in
abundance.

Share yourself with rejoicing; today expands
beyond measure.

Musical   Heitor Villa-Lobos, *Bachianas Brasilieras* (Villa-
Keynotes   Lobos—Angel). These are all beautiful, untamed
musical outpourings, exuberant with the florid
landscapes of the great forests of South America
and tropical lifestreams. The exotic qualities make
this music a unique experience.

Amampondo, *Heartbeat of Africa* (Amampondo,
40 Washington Street, Langa Cape Town, South
Africa). Voices, marimbas, drums, rattles and bells
make this music a unique expression of joy and
celebration.

March 6   # Communion

Focus   Where all words end, music begins; where they
suggest, it realizes; and hence the secret of its
strange, ineffable power. Music reveals us to
ourselves; it represents those modulations and
temperamental changes which escape all verbal
analysis; music utters what must else remain
forever unuttered and unutterable. Music feels that

deep, ineradicable instinct within us of which all
art is only the reverberated echo—that craving to
express, through the medium of the senses, the
spiritual and eternal realities which underlie them.

H. R. Haweis

Meditation   It is a magnificent feeling to be in communion with
life.

Life can be a sacrament in which the passing
moments are all beautifully relating.

Your day can be a communion; your tasks and con-
tacts can flow in smoother rhythms, expressing a
deeper, natural order.

Today you can feel the divine appointment, the
rightness of experiences, the communion with life.

Musical   George Frideric Handel, *Water Music* (Menuhin,
Keynotes   Eminence—EMI); (Kubelik—DGG). This con-
genial music is filled with sprightly, joyful
melodies. It is especially good for combatting
lethargy and for opening the feelings.

Patrick DiVietri, *Invocation* (Teresiana Records).
This music, for solo guitar, is in honor of the Pope
and is very beautifully performed.

March 7   **Faith**

Focus   He who sees farthest has the most faith. The
spiritual values and the progressive but slow advance of humanity cannot be destroyed even if current developments were to obliterate them.

Ernest Bloch

Meditation   The reach of your faith allows you to proceed in
the spirit of trust, for whatever lies ahead.

Faith opens the doors for advancement, and the gates of learning reveal the lessons of opportunity.

You can let your faith feel the essential divine goodness intending and attending you throughout your life.

Musical
Keynotes   Tomaso Vitali, *Chaconne* (Orion). This is a quiet, introspective piece, good for deep centering. The quality of faith and deep feelings of hope are present. In this recording, it is performed on the violin and organ. The music recalls the faith of St. Thomas Aquinas who is remembered on this, his feast day.

Ray Lynch, *Sky of Mind* (Music West Records). This deep music is composed in the New Age idiom—flowing and spatial, cosmic and open. There are some beautiful melodies, and the tone is devotional.

March 8   **Heights of Power**

Focus   Mountains are symbols, like pyramids, of man's attempt to know God. Mountains are symbolic meeting places between the mundane and spiritual worlds.   Alan Hovhaness

Meditation   Feel yourself, in total safety, looking out over a high mountain.

The view is clear and expansive.

Littleness and pettiness disappear. Your fears or worries are released into a larger order and perspective.

You can breathe freely now, as the great wind blows through you, clearing and empowering you on mountain heights.

Recall the composer Mieczyslaw Karlowicz's words: "Atop a high mountain I became one with the surrounding space. I cease to feel individual. I can feel the mighty everlasting breath of eternal being."

Musical
Keynotes

Richard Strauss, *Alpine Symphony* (Kempe— EMI; Hatink—Philips; Karajan—DGG). This is a magnificent symphony which emanates the many moods of the high Alpine reaches. It is composed for full orchestra, with organ. Great power streams from the music.

Alan Hovhaness, *Mysterious Mountain* (Reiner— RCA). This deeply meditative music takes the listener into secret grottos and landscapes. A sense of mystery and inner journey fills the atmosphere. Hovhaness has these words to say about heights of power:

> The Mysterious Mountain may be the phantom peak, unmeasured, thought to be higher than Everest, as seen from great distances by fliers in Tibet. To some it may be the solitary mountain, the tower of strength over a countryside—Fuji-yama, Ararat, Monadnock, Shasta, (Egmont, Tatvas), or Grand Teton (or Mount Cook).

March 9   **Good Will**

Focus

Unity and right human relations—individual, communal, national and international—can be brought about by the united action of men and women of good will in every country.

Alice Bailey

Meditation

How often have you felt the thrill of participating with others in a mutually shared project or purpose?

You can feel your energy accelerate as you unite with others in constructive action.

In the spirit of good will, enjoying the camaraderie, you can join with others to build the spirit of service and brotherhood.

Musical   Samuel Barber, Violin Concerto, Movements 1 and
Keynotes   2 (Kaufman and Goehr—Orion; Oliveira, Slatkin—Angel). This serene concerto for violin and orchestra radiates goodwill and nobility. Heartfelt melodies and landscapes unfold, emanating power, intimacy and the reach of vision.

Rick Erlien, *Ascending Colors* (Rick Erlien, phone 1-619-235-8171). This music, for solo piano, radiates peace and harmony. It is relaxing and good for instilling unity and productive relationships.

March 10   **Building Bridges**

Focus   The highest mission of music is to serve as a link between God and man. It builds a bridge over which angelic hosts can come closer to mankind.
                                              Corinne Heline

Meditation   Bridges connect energies.

As the vibrations of music can bring persons together in greater harmony and receptivity, so can you help to make links interpersonally.

You can forge new directions while also making connections.

You can build bridges, not chasms.

Musical   Pablo de Sarasate, *Spanish Dances* (Rosand—
Keynotes   Turnabout; Perlman—Angel). These dances, for
               violin, are lively and filled with energy and
               warmth.

               Max Highstein, *The Healer's Touch* (Search for
               Serenity). The beautiful, friendly music promotes
               harmony and increased cooperation.

March 11   *Mercy*

Focus   God will give each of us a white stone at the end
               of the world. The secret name of each of us will
               be written there, the name he gives us, and only
               the man himself will be able to read it. I can't tell
               what your name will be. But I think in my own
               mind it will be "Mercy"—not just the mercy he
               shows to you, but the mercy as well that you show
               to others.   James K. Baxter

Meditation   Mercy implies kindness and charity to others,
               especially those who are vulnerable.

               At times when we could use the upper hand to be
               dominant and powerful, an act of mercy is called
               for.

               Consider today the times when you could have
               been and can now be merciful. Remember times
               when others have shown you mercy—times of
               weakness when divine grace has been kind.

               Mercy does not take advantage; it is generous in
               meeting the needs of others.

Musical   Gabriel Fauré', *Pie Jesu*, from *Requiem* (Rutter—
Keynotes   Conifer); Maurice Duruflé', *Pie Jesu*, from *Re-
               quiem* (Davis—Columbia); John Rutter, *Pie Jesu*
               from *Requiem* (Rutter—Collegium); Andrew
               Lloyd Webber, *Pie Jesu*, from *Requiem*

(Maazel—London). These lovely, gentle pieces, for soprano and orchestra, bring in the quality of mercy.

Paul DiVietri, *Partita Teresiana* (Teresiana Records). This recording, for solo guitar, was done inside a mission. It carries a meditative and contemplative quality.

March 12	*The Flow of Feelings*
Focus	Music has the ability to elicit pure emotion, deep feeling without personal association. Manfred Clynes
Meditation	In this meditation you can use the musical selections just to feel. Pure feeling itself, without any particular psychological connection, can be awakened within you.
	Just the capacity to be sensitive to your own feelings and emotions can be very valuable.
	Emotional response shows you have ability to respond—to life, to persons, to sounds, to nature, to love and to all of human experience.
	Let your feelings come forth: use the music today just to feel.
	You may wish to record feelings or impressions in your journal after the music has ended.
Musical Keynotes	Thomas Arne, Overtures (Hogwood—Oiseau). These bright pieces for orchestra stimulate the flow of feelings.
	Kim Robertson, *Moonrise* (Invincible Recordings). These pieces for Celtic harp are light and airy. They offer clarity, joy and vitality.

March 13   ## Rejoicing of Angels

Focus   The consciousness of the angels, from nature sprite to archangel, is laughter-filled joy. . . . If you would become aware of the angelic presences, listen to the music of the trees, the way the firs and pines and beeches live, swaying to the wind and singing all the time—till you can see yourself in every tree, in every flower, in every blade of grass, in every passing cloud.   Geoffrey Hodson

Meditation   Your breathing expands as you feel angelic presences filling you with peace and joy.

Breathe in the spirit of light, hear the rejoicing of angels, "the beauty that is the soul of all natural things."

Musical Keynotes   Giovanni Gabrieli, *Jubilate Deo, Jubilation to God* (Vail—Noran Records). This music, recorded in a great cathedral, carries the spiral feeling of expansiveness and joy that is suggestive of angelic presences.

Jean Sibelius, *Karelia Overture* (Ormandy—RCA). There is tremendous energy in this music, a dance of devas and angelic forces in nature.

Iasos, *Elixir* (Interdimensional Music). *Procession on the Horizon* describes in New Age fashion a ceremony of legions of angels, as they soar in the vast reaches of cosmic light.

March 14   ## Attraction

Focus   One who strives to keep his mind steadily attuned to faith, joy, peace and goodwill discovers that his consciousness attracts the blessings of the inner and outer worlds.   Flower A. Newhouse

Meditation   Your consciousness is like a magnet. Your feelings, attitudes, thoughts and deeds create an energy field that attracts corresponding experiences to you.

Today meditate upon the many unseen presences and forces for good that surround you. Blessings wait for you as your consciousness attracts them.

Cultivate your consciousness, like a garden, so that your highest good may come to you.

Musical Keynotes   Georg Philipp Telemann, Trio Sonatas (Nonesuch). The music is light, sweet and attuning. Seemingly effortless melodies fill the listener's ears with joyfulness and good energy.

César Franck, *Praise Ye the Lord,* Psalm 150 (Mormon Tabernacle Choir, Ormandy—Columbia). The great power and exhilaration in this music for choir and orchestra magnetize one's attraction to the "blessings of the inner and outer worlds." Words include the following:

> Praise the Lord with the sound of the trumpet;
> Praise the Lord with the lute and harp.
> Praise the Lord with the timbrel, the timbrel and the dance;
> O praise Him with the organ and instrument of strings.

March 15   ## The Beautiful

Focus   In beauty we are united, through beauty we pray, with beauty we conquer.

                                          Nicholas Roerich

Meditation   It is one thing to experience the beautiful; it is another to share it.

To touch another person's life in beauty, is to see the beautiful grow.

You can find a new way today to share the beautiful.

Musical   Robert Schumann, *Cathedral Scene*, 4th Move-
Keynotes   ment from Symphony No. 3, *Rhenish* (Muti—
               Angel). This is a very beautiful musical experience.
               The orchestra plays a melody, signaled by trom-
               bones and horns, and the music then quietly opens
               out in majesty, disclosing the view of the expan-
               sive cathedral overlooking the river.

               Pietro Mascagni, *Easter Hymn* from *Cavalleria
               Rusticana* (Levine—RCA). This is a marvelous
               moment of exalted beauty and worship. Chorus
               and orchestra open one up to a beautiful dawn,
               filled with a sense of prayer and beauty.

March 16   **Peace**

Focus   The life that is centered in God or All-Good
               possesses an inner feeling of security, peace and
               well-being which all the inharmonies and confu-
               sions of the outer world can never take away. This
               peace is the peace that passes all understanding.
                                                 Corinne Heline

Meditation   You can rest in the ocean of divine peace, as the
               Earth rests in space.

               Geoffrey Hodson reminds us: "Peace is a princi-
               ple in nature: it belongs to the essence of all things.
               Behind all movement there is rest; behind all sound
               there is stillness, that power of divine equipoise
               which nothing in the outer world can shake."

               Feel the peace of divine Presence, always with you
               throughout the day and night.

Musical *Keynotes*	J. S. Bach, *Largo* from Concerto for Two Violins in D-Minor (Lautenbacher, Vorholz—Allegro). An extended melody brings peace and upliftment. The violins soar in their serenity, bringing feelings of reassurance. The orchestra is totally supportive. One person has called this piece "a wholly unique and transfiguring experience." Daniel Kobialka, *Path of Joy* (Li-Sem Enterprises). This extended version of Bach's *Jesu, Joy* brings a sense of great peace and inner well-being. It is ideal for relieving stress and tension.

March 17	**The Highest**
Focus	Let this be the motto for you all—THE HIGHEST— and let all who join our ranks pledge themselves to that motto. We, too, pledge ourselves, and every time this inward pledge is uttered by a person, an angel shall repeat his pledge and bear it like a torch to add to the great reservoir of power apportioned for our work. <div align="right">Geoffrey Hodson</div>
Meditation	THE HIGHEST! You can always aim to live in the spirit of the highest that you have touched. With an upreaching heart you can live your life to the fullest measure. You can sense that which is beyond you. Living in dedication to the Highest, what is greater comes into view. As you do what is before you to the best of your ability—in the spirit of the Highest—the doors of

the Infinite open wider, and you are empowered
from beyond yourself.

Musical   Philip Green, *Saint Patrick's Mass* (RCA). This is
Keynotes   a contemporary rendition of the mass, in honor of
                 Saint Patrick on his feast day. It is a wonderful
                 work, melodic, joyful and filled with devotion.

                 Josef Rheinberger, Concerto in F-Major (Biggs,
                 Peress—Columbia). This work is exulting, filled
                 with strength, melody and vitality. Organ, horns
                 and string orchestra burst forth with power and
                 praise to the Highest.

March 18   *Universality*

Focus   Great art is universal, for everyone.... Great art
                 and music are for all humanity and forever....
                 The first element in performance is life and love.
                 Then I think it is important to have much ex-
                 perience and knowledge.

                                          Carlo Maria Giulini

Meditation   Consider how your sensitivity enlarges.

                 Watch a pebble dropping into a pond. From the
                 center you can see the circles moving out.

                 Your attention moves from the center outward, ex-
                 panding to larger circles.

                 Today your feelings of love can move outward—
                 to one other person, to family and groups, reaching
                 to all humanity, the full family of mankind, and
                 then to all living things.

                 Expand your reach today; your center moves in the
                 infinite spaces of limitless universality.

Musical   Ludwig van Beethoven, *Ode to Joy* from Sym-
Keynotes   phony No. 9 (Furtwangler—EMI; Stokowski—
London). The finale of this great symphony speaks
of universal brotherhood. The vision of a
brotherhood of all nations and peoples, united
under one heaven in the love of a common God,
and the joy of each individual taking part in it—
this is the vision imparted by chorus and orchestra.

Daniel Kobialka, *Sun Space: Ode to Joy* (Li-Sem
Enterprises). This is a contemporary extended version (without voices) of Beethoven's great hymn to
universal brotherhood. The atmosphere is one of
extended cosmic peace and serenity. The music
flows into unlimited space.

> O ye millions, I embrace you,
> With a kiss for all the world.
> Brothers and sisters over the starry sphere,
> Where there surely dwells a loving Father-Mother
>   God.
> O ye millions, kneel before Him.
> Feel thy Maker near. Adore Him!
>
> Johann von Schiller

March 19   **Direction**

Focus   At times when you are very quiet and when desire
and emotion have become stilled, you can observe
the quiet shaping of yourself from within—can see
the form you are intended to take, the work you
should do—your function in the environment and
the scheme of things. It is very important to see
this. This is not forecasting as the astrologers and
soothsayers do it; it is a deep and intelligent obser-
vation of your own nature and propensities.

Virginia Burden

Meditation   It is a good time to balance feeling and thinking.

Sometimes direction comes after you have weighed a problem. How do you feel about something, and what do you think about it?

You can let your feelings and your thoughts come up. After looking at them, you can just let them be.

And without forcing anything, a deeper You will know what to do.

In a moment of silence, your heart and mind will touch to open the doors to guidance.

Musical   J. S. Bach, Suites for Orchestra (Marriner—
Keynotes   London). This stirring music is filled with clarity, good spirits and energy that can give one direction. It is especially good for overcoming lethargy and passivity.

Patrick Ball, *Secret Isles* (Fortuna). The music, played on the Celtic harp, brings in a bright, motivational kind of energy. The tunes are clear and good for focus.

March 20   **Relationships**

Focus   All relationships are formed from three essential rhythms: similarity, complementarity and opposites.   Anonymous

Meditation   Consider three types of relationship: similar, complementary, and opposite.

Sometimes you feel close to others because you share the same interests; or you may think and feel alike.

Other persons have different interests and feelings, but they enhance your energy.

There are those who think and feel in ways opposite to you, but these opposite views may be stimulating and catalytic. Or there may be "unfinished business" in a relationship.

Today, consider the kinds of relationships that you most need in your life and how to cultivate them.

Musical
Keynotes

Antonin Dvořak, String Quartet in F, *American* (Quintessence). This melodic, mellow work is good for finding focus and calm.

Larry David, *Peace Offerings* (Eastern Gate Pub.). This is very beautiful music for piano and guitar. The atmosphere is calm and relaxing.

March 21   *Inspiration*

Focus

To strip human nature until its divine attributes are made clear, to inform ordinary activities with spiritual fervor, to give wings of eternity to that which is most ephemeral; to make divine things human and human things divine: to reach the heart of every noble thought...

Pablo Casals, speaking of the music of Johann Sebastian Bach

Meditation

There is a great cosmic order and nobility at the heart of life.

Today you can feel the meeting of the earthly and celestial worlds.

"As above, so below" is the ancients' way of expressing this basic union in the cosmos.

You can aspire to great heights, and you can open in attunement to the energies of divinity, already feeding and sustaining you.

Musical   Christopher Parkening, *Bach* (Word). This is
Keynotes   peaceful, ennobling music for solo guitar. The
               album is ideal for inspiration and focus.

               Daniel Kobialka, *Sleepers Awake* and *Sheep May
               Safely Graze*, from *Daniel Kobialka Performs* (Li-
               Sem). This is good music for creativity and stress
               reduction. The music flows continuously, without
               any sudden shocks.

March 22   **Concentration**

Focus   I stand face to face with the Eternal Energy from
               which all life flows, and I draw upon that infinite
               power. To contact this Eternal Energy, I must con-
               form to certain laws, two of the most important
               being SOLITUDE and CONCENTRATION. A
               composer must sit in the silence and wait for the
               direction from a force that is superior to the in-
               tellect.   Max Bruch

Meditation   Concentration is the magnet for contacting the in-
               finite power.

               The deepest creativity comes in times of aloneness.

               Today, in the quiet of your own solitude, open to
               the divine.

               In relaxed concentration, let the power of the
               Presence vibrate through you.

               In relaxed receptivity, let the direction and the in-
               spiration come through.

Musical   Antonio Salieri, Sinfonia in D (Märzendorfer—
Keynotes   Musical Heritage). This music is pleasant and good
               for focusing. There are many beautiful melodies
               and its rhythms bring a baroque regularity.

Patrick Ball, *From a Distant Time* (Fortuna). The music, played on the Celtic harp, is good for focus and concentration. It is melodic and pleasant, without being demanding.

March 23   **Sound and Tone**

Focus   The capacity of music to arouse feelings which induce emotions is quite evident....The power of sound can heal and reinvigorate an organism—mental, emotional and physical....

Dane Rudhyar

Meditation Music can change your energy and can change the order (or disorder) of your being.

Today focus on music as a means of creating vibrations that can alter the tone of your life and yourself.

Become sensitive to how certain pieces of music affect you: where do you feel the vibrations in your body?

How do you feel as you listen? Do you feel happier and more alive after the music has finished?

You can become more conscious and alert to the music you hear.

Musical   Dane Rudhyar, *Sinfonietta* (Varese—Sarabande).
Keynotes   This lyrical and haunting work has some beautiful melodies. A mysterious tonal landscape makes the piece appealing and continuously interesting.

Franz Schreker, *Prelude to a Drama* (Gielen—Schwann). A marvelously kaleidoscopic piece of music, joyful and strong.

Paul and Brenda Neal, *New Leaf* (Blue Ash Records). This music is performed on Troubadour harps, which are approximately three-quarters the size of concert harps. The music delivers a variety of tones.

March 24　　　**Attention**

Focus　　Every morning when I go for an early stroll in the woods, I think upon my Maker.

Franz Joseph Haydn

Meditation　Through attentiveness you can always feel the radiance of love.

As your mind searches and considers, your heart can open in gladness.

Relationships grow in whatever area you give attention to.

Today consider your interests, where you give the most attention.

In the center of your deepest attention, there you will find your divine essence.

Musical Keynotes　*Brother James' Air,* sung by St. Paul's Cathedral Boys' Choir (K-tel). This music radiates love and warmth. It is a beautiful setting of the Twenty-Third Psalm, orchestrated by Gordon Jacob, composer. The high sopranos of the boys' choir lift the spirits into glory.

Joel Andrews, *Celestia* (Joel Andrews Productions). This sparkling and flowing music is played on the solo harp. There is less melody here and more emphasis upon relaxation and a lilting kind of music.

March 25   **The Eternal Star**

Focus   The perfection, the potentiality of the loveliness
which is in everything, is inevitable. The eternal
star...brings all processes to their appointed end,
and presides over our voyage through life.

N. Sri Ram

Meditation   Your life can be seen as a continuous voyage across
infinite horizons.

In time you move through many conditions and
residences.

In the midst of your travels, the eternal star abides
in the center of your life.

You can draw upon the radiance—the loveliness
of the starry light, always shining through the
night, leading you into increasing loveliness and
completion.

Musical   Felix Mendelssohn, *And Then Shall Your Light
Keynotes*   Break Forth*, from *Elijah* (Corboz—Erato); *There
Shall a Star from Jacob Rising* (Mormon Taber-
nacle Choir—Columbia).These inspiring choral
works are highly elevating and devotional.

David Storrs, *Sedona Sunrise* (Valley of the Sun,
Box 38, Malibu, CA 90265). *Night in the Vortex*
on side 2, for synthesizers, presents a striking,
quietly radiant starscape experience.

March 26   **Dedication**

Focus   Make every rehearsal a performance, and every
performance a debut.

Arturo Toscanini

Meditation   In life nothing is really wasted.

You keep on playing the music, rehearsing until you play it right.

Your dedication makes every moment full and more beautiful.

Lived in the spirit of dedication, every day is new, and you play the music of your life for the first time.

Musical Keynotes   Charles Marie Widor, *Toccata* from Organ Symphony No. 5 (Jane Parker-Smith—Classics for Pleasure). This is powerful, highly energizing music for solo organ. The notes fly off the pipes with drama and sparks.

Peter Michael Hamel, *Organum* (Kuckuck—West Germany). This powerful New Age organ music is like a ceremony of devotion and strength. Especially striking is Part One, suggesting the harmony of the divine creation.

March 27   **Resonance**

Focus   The love of music is a continuous life of enjoying beauty and sound.

All music is composed of three dimensions:
— frequency
— intensity
— duration
Mine has been a continual effort to make music more alive.   Leopold Stokowski

Meditation   You can let the music of your life sound through you.

According to your opportunities and lessons, the

Great Plan is helping you to compose your life themes.

You can welcome the conditions of your life.

If you are deeply interested and intense about life, you can stay in love with life.

Consider today how you resonate with the persons and events of your life.

Musical
Keynotes

Vincent d'Indy, *Symphony on a French Mountain Air*, First Movement (Casadesus, Ormandy—Columbia). This marvelous, evocative music is redolent with melody, suggesting high Alpine vistas and open air.

Kevin Setchko and Janet Bray, *Cloud Etchings* (Crystal Wind Pub.). Some of the music here is ethereal and quite beautiful. Instruments are flute and Tibetan bells.

March 28   # Awake

Focus

Gloria be sung to Thee by tongues of men and angels, with harps and cymbals. Twelve pearls are the doors of thy city; we stand as consorts to the angels by thy throne. No eye has seen no ear has heard such joy. Therefore are we glad, forever in dulci jubilo, in sweet praise.

J. S. Bach, *Sleepers Awake*

Meditation

Awake and alert, you begin a new day.

To be awake implies being ready and prepared.

Today you can awaken to the divine glory surrounding you: in nature, your home, your work, on the road, in company or alone.

You can awaken to the inner glory.

Musical *Keynotes*	J. S. Bach, *Sleepers Awake* (Ormandy—Columbia); George Frideric Handel, *Dettingen Te Deum* (Preston—DGG Archive). Both selections are wonderfully alive and bright. Chorus and orchestra sing energetically in praise.

Johannes Brahms, Trio for Horn, Violin and Piano (Nonesuch). The Boston Chamber Players deliver a beautiful rendition of this lovely work that really awakens and attunes the listener. One writer, Gál, in speaking of the first movement, says: "It is a reflection of the noblest perfection that human endeavor can fashion."

March 29   *To Be an Instrument of God*

Focus   The goal is to be an instrument of God. The more confident we are, the more intuition works through us.   Paul Neary

Meditation   Your greatest enjoyment is to live as an instrument of God.

In confidence and receptivity, your life will become harmonious and useful.

The Light of God shines through you, and empowers you to be an instrument of the Infinite.

Musical   Sir William Walton, Violin Concerto (Haendel,
Keynotes   Berglund—EMI). There are many haunting melodies here and also sections that suggest the thorns one meets with the roses on the life journey.

John Michael Talbot, *Troubadour* (Sparrow). This is a contemporary statement of how to be an instrument of God in service. There are many simple, beautiful tunes—vocal and instrumental.

March 30	**Stream**

Focus

The mystery of love is not held within one's heart, but is a stream of feeling toward the loved one.

J. Rosemergy

Meditation

Today let love from your heart center stream outward toward those you meet.

You can see and hear and feel a stream, gurgling and moving onward until it finally flows into the great ocean. So let your love flow like a stream, reaching those that it touches, moving onward to join in the divine love at the heart of the universe.

Musical
Keynotes

Bedrich Smetana, *The Moldau* from *My Country* (Karajan—Angel). The sounds of the Moldau River begin with a trickle in the woods, then spread out, becoming larger currents of power, until finally the great river emerges, filling the landscape with its mighty roar. The music contains many lovely melodies and gathers toward increasing force and openness.

Aiki Domo, *Twilight Walk Along a Stream* (Mirror Image Labs). Just the quiet sounds of a stream in the woods are beautiful and renewing.

March 31	**Daily Routine**

Focus

I shall thank my Almighty God for having given me His blessing. And I shall remember all those to whom I could render some little pleasure.

Franz Joseph Haydn

Meditation

Your deepest experiences often come in the little moments of rendering good to others.

You can often rise to the occasion in larger testings, but remembering to render little pleasures to those in need is a magnet for divine blessings to flow through you.

Today, in the midst of your schedule and routine, remember to render little pleasures to others.

Musical Keynotes

Franz Joseph Haydn, *Choruses from the Creation* (Willcocks—Argo); *The Heilig Mass* (Marriner—Argo). This joyful strong music is good for focus and empowerment.

Patrick Ball, *Celtic Harp* (Fortuna). This music for Celtic harp is lively in a way that focuses the mind and centers activities and learning. There is a regularity to the music that is refreshing and stimulating to routine.

Invocation

Focus   With a joyful face, sing the sweet name of God,
Till, like a wind, it churns the nectar sea;
Drink of that nectar ceaselessly,
Drink it yourself and share it with all.
If ever your heart goes dry, invoke God's name,
If it goes dry in the desert of this world,
Your love of God will make it flow again.

Ramakrishna

Meditation   A joyful face sings of inner light.

Today you can decide how you will express joy,
invoking your divine essence with the song of your
heart.

You can let your heart and voice be filled with
divinity as you sing your song.

Musical   Sergei Rachmaninoff, *Vespers* (Sveshnikov—
Keynotes   Quintessence; Rostropovich—Erato). In his
Vespers Rachmaninoff used nine chants from the
sacred music of the Russian Orthodox Church. The
composer's personal favorite was the fifth hymn,
"Lord, now lettest Thou Thy servant depart in
peace" (Luke 11:29). The devotional work is like
a mantra. Many parts are deeply mystical.

Ravi Shankar, *Miscellaneous Ragas* (DGG). Especially beautiful are ragas with their fixed melodic
material plus embellishments, marvelously played

here by Shankar. I particularly like the lyrical and
romantic piece called *Raga Gara*.

April 2   ***Integrating Opposites***

Focus   Aim for union and cooperation with the life force
                 at its source. Act in all things as though you were
                 bipolar—becoming in any given situation either
                 more active or more receptive: make of yourself
                 at will either the bow or the arrow; granite or wax.
                 Overcome anger with love; overcome evil with
                 good; overcome greediness with generosity and lies
                 with truth.   Claude Bragdon

Meditation   You can learn the power of balance by moving har-
                 moniously between the opposites within you.

                 You can gain strength by adjusting yourself to an-
                 tipathies coming from persons and environments.

                 What you do not integrate can eventually produce
                 a greater separation and split in you, almost like
                 becoming two persons.

                 You can bring together and harmonize your oppo-
                 sites; balance conflicts in attitudes and behaviors.

                 The more you integrate the opposites, the more you
                 build your strength.

Musical   Ralph Vaughan-Williams, *Sine Nomine: For All*
Keynotes   *the Saints* (Choir of St. Luke's Church, San
                 Francisco—Wilson Audiophile). Vaughan-
                 Williams included these words in this stirring
                 hymn:

                      And when the strife is fierce, the warfare long,
                      Steals on the ear the distant triumph song,
                      And hearts are brave again, and arms are strong.
                      Alleluia!

Daniel Kobialka, *Coral Seas, Vivaldi, Largo* (Li-Sem). This music is very relaxing, quite the opposite of the Vaughan-Williams which is more triumphant. The integrating peacefulness leads to increasing harmony of opposites.

April 3   ## *Wandering Not Alone*

Focus

Upon that Road one wanders not alone. There is no rush, no hurry. And yet there is no time to lose. Each Pilgrim, knowing this, presses his footsteps forward, and finds himself surrounded by his fellowmen. Some move ahead; he follows after. Some move behind; he sets the pace. He travels not alone.

       "The Rules of the Road," Anonymous

Meditation

You do not travel alone.

Always you are accompanied, whether you are leading or following, creating footsteps on the path.

You can feel the rhythms of your path, faster or slower, but never alone.

Enjoy the journey; welcome all fellow travelers.

Musical Keynotes

Mario Castelnuovo-Tedesco, Concertino for Harp and Orchestra (McDonald, Hull—Klavier); Concerto in D for Guitar and Orchestra (Williams, Ormandy—Columbia); Guitar Concerto No. 2, for Guitar and Orchestra (Oraison, Gatehouse—Etcetera). These melodic works give the sense of imagery, beauty and forward motion.

Ron Goodwin, *Drake 400 Suite* (Goodwin—Chandos). Commemorating the 400th anniversary of the circumnavigation of the globe by Sir Francis

Drake, this composition gives the sense of a journey. Especially lovely is the expansive section *The Eddystone Seascape.*

April 4   **Basic Needs**

Focus   Each Pilgrim on the Road must carry with him what he needs:

—a pot of fire, to warm his fellowmen
—a lamp, to cast its rays upon his heart
  and show his fellowmen the nature
  of its hidden life
—a purse of gold, which he scatters not upon
  the Road but shares with others
—a sealed vase, wherein he carries all his
  aspirations to cast before the feet
  of Him who waits to greet him at the gate.

The Pilgrim, as he walks upon the Road, must have the open ear, the giving hand, the silent tongue, the chastened heart, the golden voice, the rapid foot, and the opened eye which sees the light. He knows he travels not alone.

"The Rules of the Road," Anonymous

Meditation   Today you can remember your basic needs: enough to enjoy, not too much and not too little.

Consider what you desire and what is most essential. Move forward, without too much weight, but carrying enough to keep you anchored.

While fulfilling your basic needs, remember to offer a giving hand to others.

Musical   Ralph Vaughan-Williams, *The Pilgrim's Progress*
Keynotes   (Boult—EMI). This is a large, operatic work, based upon John Bunyon's classic *The Pilgrim's*

Progress. Especially beautiful is the closing section, *The Shepherds of the Delectable Mountains. The Pilgrim Reaches the End of His Journey* describes his welcome into the heavens: "Alleluia, Alleluia, Blessed are they that dwell in Thy house, they will always be praising Thee." A great trumpet sounds, and the Pilgrim's Way leads up through golden gates.

Gordon de la Sierra, *Duets for Sea and Guitar* (de la Sierra—L'aubade Prod., Putney, VT). Here the journey is described through several guitar tunes, with the seascape in the background. It is an evocative piece.

April 5	*Evocations*
Focus	Art is beautiful because it concentrates ancient evocations in contemporary forms and rattles the chain of centuries, causing the palpitation of eternal rhythms of love and harmony.
	<div align="right">Ramon del Valle-Inclan</div>
Meditation	Today in your meditation, consider memories and areas of your life that evoke something special for you.
	Perhaps a smell, a scene in nature, a particular country, a name, specific sounds—what evokes something in you?
	Evocations indicate pieces of your history. They remind you of all that you are and all that has been a part of you through many centuries.
	Let today bring back to you the sense of evocations.
Musical Keynotes	Albert Roussel, *Evocations* (Kosler—Supraphon). This is a powerful and evocative work. Particularly

striking is the final section, *On the Sacred River*. Soloists, chorus and orchestra combine to bring a sense of mystery and enchantment. Some of the words are as follows:

> The temples of the holy city...
> in the silence of the night,
> descend toward you....
> The immense army of stars
> and their passionate beauty
> reign alone over the ocean....

Alan Hovhaness, *The Holy City* (Lipkin—CRI). Within approximately seven minutes, the scene of a holy city is evoked and created by the orchestra. Mysteriously, it appears then recedes into silence.

April 6	*Loving Kindness*

Focus

Yea, I have loved thee with an everlasting love: therefore, with loving kindness have I drawn thee.
Jeremiah 31:3

Meditation

This is an especially beautiful passage, emphasizing cosmic compassion.

Today you can reflect again upon everlasting divine love.

Unlike most human love, it does not change or diminish according to our behavior. Genuine love does not alter when it "alteration finds."

Today, remember the loving kindness in the heart of the universe, in which you are always included for who you are now and who you are becoming.

Musical Keynotes

Johannes Brahms, Symphony No. 2, First Movement (Jochum—EMI). This is an essentially pastoral movement, beautifully unfolding and bringing a sense of warmth and assurance.

Amazing Grace, Traditional (Goodwin—Chandos; Judy Collins—Elektra). The piper opens this music and is then joined by full orchestra. There is a haunting sense of a cosmic loving kindness, and the music brings a sense of reverence. The Judy Collins version also brings deep feeling, and is done in a folk-like style.

April 7	## *Making Life Holy*
Focus	The true sanctification, which I came to perceive something of later, is the result of a process of endless patience and infinite delay, and the attainment of it implies a humility, seven times refined in the fires of self-contempt, in which there remains no smallest touch of superiority or aloofness.

A. C. Benson

Meditation Your spiritual growth requires much patience and daily self-examination.

Sanctification is a continuous process, not an overnight marathon.

Today you can center again upon the upward journey, feeling the joy of progress, the steps that form the sweep.

Complete honesty about yourself is needed, no self-condemnation, no feeling of superiority.

You can live today, eager to advance upon the journey, and you can enjoy each step of the trip.

Musical Keynotes Anton Bruckner, *Adagio*, From Symphony No. 7 (Karajan—DGG; Haitink—Philips). This is one of the deepest, most noble pieces of music ever composed. The music starts slowly and gradually builds to a tremendous climax, then recedes. It is the music of a soul's journey in cosmic reaches of eternity.

Dmitri Bortnyansky, *Hymn of the Cherubim*, No. 7 (Yurlov—Melodiya). This contemplative hymn breathes an intimate, secret dream of happiness. It is a movingly serene work.

April 8	## *Resolution*
Focus	Indeed we are called by the music of the universe to reply, each with his own pure and incommunicable harmonic.
	Teilhard de Chardin
Meditation	Your life is always asking you to reply.
	You contain a particular soul's wealth, an interweaving complexity of experiences.
	Your own harmonic is uniquely you; nobody else makes exactly the same music.
	Today you can accept and enjoy yourself as a music-maker in life, connected to all, yet uniquely yourself in your inner essence.
Musical Keynotes	Giuseppe Tartini, Concerti for Flute and Strings (Rampal—Columbia). This music is filled with vitality and a sense of order. Within the baroque frame of stability, the music is highly charged.
	Born Free, Soundtrack (MGM). In John Barry's wonderful score, expansive melodies are grounded by the recurring drums and percussion suggesting

the African landscape. Flow and focus are integrated in the music.

April 9   **Arise**

Focus   The sound of a distant nightingale, a last tremulous echo of earthly life. The gentle sound of a chorus of saints and heavenly hosts is then heard: "Arise, yes, you will arise." Then appears the splendid glory of God. A marvelous light penetrates us to the heart—all is quiet, blissful....A feeling of overwhelming Love envelops us with understanding and illuminates our souls.

                                        Gustav Mahler

Meditation   Today you can remember the light as it penetrates, warms and feeds the earth.

               Distance melts away—there is always connection in the heart of Spirit.

               Remember, in the midst of crisis, "an overwhelming love envelops you," understands you and invites you "to ARISE."

Musical   Gustav Mahler, Symphony No. 2, *Resurrection*,
Keynotes   5th Movement (Price, Fassbaldner, Stokowski—RCA).

               You will lose nothing. Yours is what you desired, yours what you loved, what you fought for.... What was created must pass away, arise! With wings that I have won for myself in fervent, loving aspiration will I soar to the Light that no eye has ever seen. I shall die that I may live. Arise, yes, you will arise, my heart, in a moment! What you have borne will carry you to God.
                                        Klopstock and Mahler

This powerful music is a towering statement of Mahler's credo. It also offers every listener a "resurrection" experience. Choir, full orchestra and organ scale the heights of glory.

April 10   *Your Life Painting*

Focus   We are painting our lives on the canvas of living, Each moment a brush stroke of the whole, the finished picture to mankind giving the final portrait of our soul.   Wilfred Peterson

Meditation   Imagine your life as a large canvas, and you are painting it with shape and color.

                 What are the brush strokes that you most wish to add to your work of art, which is your unfolding life?

                 Today consider the colors of character, the shapes and contours of life experiences in the landscape you wish most to describe.

Musical   Sir Arthur Bliss, *A Color Symphony* (Groves—
Keynotes   EMI). Every piece of music emanates its own colors and shapes into the atmosphere. Bliss describes here his musical feelings about various colors in the spectrum. It is an active piece, filled with various rhythms, melodies and impressions.

                 Paul Horn, *Inside the Powers of Nature* (Golden Flute). This is a contemporary impressionistic work: surf, forest sounds, rain and children playing create the soundscape background that accompanies the flute music against another element— space. No electronic sounds are used.

April 11	# *Hope*

Focus   And in the night of death, hope sees a star, and
              listening love hears the rustle of a wing.
                                        Tennessee Williams

Meditation In this moment go to your favorite place—a place
              of peace and hope.

              Visualize this place opening to you.

              It is a place of safety, quiet, and renewal. When
              you are tired or troubled, you can always come
              here.

              Even now, the energies here are helping to give
              you hope and great peace.

Musical   Jean Mouret, *Fanfares* (Birbaum—Turnabout).
Keynotes   These festive pieces for winds bring light and hope.

              William Byrd, *Mass in Five Parts* (Preston—Argo).
              This early music for unaccompanied choir is very
              beautiful and ethereal. It is deeply devotional
              music, engendering sensitivity and hope.

              David Naegele, *Sanctuary,* from *Temple in the
              Forest* (Higher Consciousness Music, Box 38,
              Malibu, CA 90265). Soft bells combine with sounds
              of birds and stream in a forest to make this a very
              gentle experience.

April 12	# *Nature*

Focus   All nature itself. . . is nothing but a perfect music
              that the Creator causes to resound in the ears of
              man, to give him pleasure and to draw him gently
              to Himself.   Jan Sweelinck

Meditation   Today enjoy the feelings and views you get from a favorite scene in nature.

You can let your own imagination take you where you want to be: high on a mountain trail, walking along a sandy beach, listening to the crickets in the desert, smelling the pine trees in a forest.

Let yourself go now to a scene of nature; feel the strength and the freshness.

Let this scene pour through you, drawing you back to the perfect music of the supreme Creator.

Musical   Anton Dvořak, *In Nature's Realm* (Kertesz—
Keynotes   London); Joseph Lanner, Waltzes (Boskovsky— Angel). The music combines impressions of nature with rhythms of the dance. Beautiful melodies carry the listener along, against a background of birds and nocturnal sounds suggested by the music.

Deuter, *Cicada* (Kuckuck—West Germany). A tropical background of animals and nature sounds, accompanied by sitar, makes this a unique experience.

April 13   **Glow of the Good**

Focus   Withdraw into yourself and look. And if you do not find yourself beautiful yet, act as does the creator of a statue that is to be made beautiful: he cuts away here, he smooths there, he makes this line lighter, this other purer, until a lovely face has grown upon his work.

So do you also: cut away all that is excessive, straighten all that is crooked, bring light to all that is overcast, labor to make all one glow of beauty. Never cease chiselling your statue, until there shall shine out on you from it the godlike splendor of

virtue, until you shall see the PERFECT GOOD-
NESS surely established in the stainless shrine.

                                        Plotinus

Meditation   Within every life there is the Godlike splendor.

You are the creator of your own statue. Consider
today what needs to be smoothed, cut away or
reshaped. In the spirit of Plotinus' words, consider
the edges and the center.

Your inner splendor is already emerging.

Musical   Johann Hummel, Mass in B-Flat Major (Wil-
Keynotes   helm—EMI). This work, for chorus, soloists and
orchestra, vibrates with the feelings of divine splendor. Hummel describes the music with these
words:

> Art judiciously combined with feeling and taste
> increases the charm of music, gives it importance
> and dignity and guides the artist to his true
> destination.

Ralph Vaughan-Williams, *The Springtime of the
Year* (Musical Heritage). These beautiful folksongs
help chip off the rough edges in ourselves.

April 14   **Life Commentary**

Focus   Think big.
Talk little.
Love much.
Laugh easily.
Work hard.
Give freely.
Be kind.
Pay cash.
   It's enough.
         Ralph Waldo Emerson

Meditation	Look at your life as a series of flash photos.

Imagine each moment as a snapshot describing your life. Each second is a microcosm of your life unfolding.

You can fill each moment of the day with pictures that make a pleasing commentary on your life.

Each moment counts as a new photo emerges.

*Musical
Keynotes*

Salli Terri, *Songs of the American Land* (Angel). These are beautiful arrangements, for voice and orchestra, of songs from American folk music. They fill the atmosphere with feeling and vitality. *My Old Kentucky Home* is especially well done.

John Williams, *The Guitar Is the Song* (Williams—Columbia). This is another beautiful collection of songs that form a life commentary. Folksongs from around the world are presented in this colorful program.

April 15   **Healing**

Focus

Ultimately, healing the physical form does nothing unless there is a complementary change of consciousness. . . . If this does not take place, the physical form will return rather rapidly to the state it was in. . . .

The secret of all healing is in the ability of the consciousness to relax and to flow and allow its fragmented parts to come back together again, which they will do quite naturally given half a chance.   David Spangler

Meditation

Think about healing and wholeness today.

As your perception grows and you relax deeply, necessary adjustments within yourself take place.

And as you change more at the center of yourself, natural changes begin to occur outside, in relationships and in the environment.

Healing begins deep in your consciousness, and flows outward to heal the fragmented parts.

Musical Keynotes   Wolfgang Amadeus Mozart, *Three Divertimenti,* K. 136, 137, 138 (Ristenpart—Nonesuch). This music is friendly and accessible. It is very lively, cheerful and full of good spirits.

Robert Beaser, *Mountain Songs,* for Flute and Guitar (Musical Heritage). The music is very melodic and rhythmically alive. On the other side of the tape are some beautiful pieces by Edward MacDowell, most notably *Woodland Sketches.*

April 16   **Serenity**

Focus   Lord, make me an instrument of Your peace.
Where there is hatred, let me sow love;
Where there is injury, pardon;
Where there is doubt, faith;
Where there is despair, hope;
Where there is darkness, light, and
Where there is sadness, joy.

O, divine Master,
grant that I may not so much
seek to be consoled as to console;
To be understood as to understand;
To be loved as to love;
For it is in giving that we receive;
It is in pardoning that we are pardoned;
And it is in dying that we are born to eternal life.
               Saint Francis of Assisi

Meditation   The prayer of St. Francis of Assisi redirects your

energy outward; you move toward others in peace
and the spirit of helpfulness.

You can use this prayer as an effective meditation:
St. Francis' words can reorient your consciousness—away from yourself, toward others.

Musical   Palestrina, *Pope Marcellus Mass* (Willcocks—Sera-
Keynotes   phim). This piece is filled with serenity, deep devo-
               tion and beautiful upliftment. There is a sense of
               upward spaciousness, and the vibrations lift like
               a spiral in a great cathedral.

Ludwig van Beethoven, *Pathetique Sonata*, Second
Movement (Kempff—DGG). This lovely, inward
piece of music, for solo piano, is filled with
moments of melody and serenity.

Riz Ortolani, *Brother Sun, Sister Moon* (Soundtrack). The life of Saint Francis of Assisi is beautifully portrayed in this music drawn from Franco
Zeffirelli's gorgeous film.

April 17   **Self-Conquest**

Focus   There are three deep cravings of the self, which
               only mystic truth can fully satisfy:

1. Craving that makes us a pilgrim and a
wanderer, longing for a lost home

2. Craving of heart for heart—the soul for its
perfect mate, which makes him a lover

3. Craving for inward purity and perfection—the
ascetic and saint.

Evelyn Underhill

Meditation   Today consider the three longings Evelyn
               Underhill pointed out, which are important for
               most persons.

Your earthly residence awakens a deeper need, perhaps a memory, for your eternal spiritual home.

Your closeness to God also can awaken a need for human closeness and a desire to express God's love in devotion to another human being.

Your desire to be the best you can awakens a need for continuing refinement in yourself, a journey in purity, toward greater completion that leads to sainthood and greater illumination.

Musical   Franz Joseph Haydn, *Sinfonia Concertante* (Ris-
Keynotes   tenpart—Nonesuch). The final movement of this marvelous and powerful piece is especially impassioned. It's good for magnetizing strength and self-conquest.

Hector Berlioz, *Te Deum* (Abbado—DGG). This music, filled with exaltation and joy, lifts and focuses the consciousness. There are moments of strong feeling, and the energy of choir, soloist and orchestra is very intense.

April 18   ## Infinite Space

Focus   Think of our solar system, its colossal size. I have the impression that there are many solar systems, that ours is a very big one, but that there are others which are much larger. And that their distance from other solid bodies floating in the atmosphere, this distance is enormous. I have also the impression that not only is there endless space and the endless mass of the solar systems that are in that space, but there is endless time and endless mental power, that there are great masses of mind which are ours, in this little earth that we live on, is only a small part. . . .

We are all under the same conditions, and it is our

privilege to make the best of these conditions—of the air we breathe, of the light we receive from the sun, THAT LIFE-GIVING LIGHT.

Leopold Stokowski

Meditation   Today reflect on cosmic immensity.

Sir James Jeans said that there are stars so immense that they could hold 25,000,000 stars the size of our sun. For every human being on earth, there are 5,000,000 stars.

Feel the tremendous reaches of infinite space.

In the great sweep of endless time and mass, you are held by the divine order, which also directs and sustains all galaxies and the starry regions of creation.

Consider today the infinite spaces and the intimate reach of God and creation.

Musical   J. S. Bach, Toccata and Fugue in D (Orchestral
Keynotes   version by Leopold Stokowski—Seraphim; London). I include this selection a second time in the book because of its magnificent spatial, cosmic and mystical power. It reaches deep into infinity.

Richard Wagner, *Parsifal: Symphonic Synthesis* (Stokowski—Everest; Stokowski Society). This is a wonderful revelation of power and vision. Stokowski takes the outstanding moments of the opera *Parsifal* and weaves them into a continuous soundscape. (Also *Liebestod-Tristan and Isolde*.)

April 19   **_Explorations_**

Focus   The driving force is one of "Praise" and a firm belief in "One God." My journeys are always exciting.

African music is fascinating, weird, and wonder-ful....I wrote "African Sanctus" to record and preserve tribal music and to create my music around it, thus adding many more colors and variations which would express my adventures and love of people. The African music, African songs and dances, religious recitations and ceremonies would live within the heart of a work conceived along "Western" lines in the form of a Mass.

David Fanshawe

Meditation   It is important to expand your impressions and your understanding of the peoples of the earth.

You can read books and magazines, such as *National Geographic* and *Horizon*. You can explore world music (Nonesuch and Lyrichord).

You can read the great literature, drama and poetry of the world's peoples.

And the music, paintings, arts and religions reveal mankind in a great variety and an incredible richness.

You can always continue your explorations.

Musical   David Fanshawe, *African Sanctus* (Fanshawe—
Keynotes   Philips). Voices, instruments and the sounds of nature all join to celebrate the mass. The music contains many moods and an unforgettable mix-ture of ancient and modern history.

A Persian Heritage: Classical Music of Iran (None-such Explorer). A variety of rhythms, sounds and tones makes this a rich musical experience, very expanding for one's sense of exploration.

E. Koestyara and Group Gapura, *Sangkala* (Icon Records/Tapes, New York). *Sangkala* means "a rhythm." This tape of Indonesian music contains many such rhythms and colorful melodies and sounds.

April 20	**Resting Place**

Focus   Our life is an allegory to convey something which, whatever form it is given, can never be adequately expressed. . . . That which draws us by its mystic force, what every created thing, perhaps even the very stones, feels with absolute certainty as the center of its being—the RESTING PLACE, in opposition to the striving and struggling towards the goal. This resting place can be called LOVE.

Gustav Mahler

Meditation   At the center of all storms, there is always the stillness.

The resting place within you finds its natural complement in outer places of rest, such as mountains, gardens, cabins or private rooms.

Today spend some time in your own particular resting place—inside or outside.

Remember the divine center of being—find and visit your inner resting place.

Musical Keynotes   Ludwig van Beethoven, Symphony No. 2, Second Movement (Jochum—EMI). A searching quiet leads the listener to a place of rest and renewal.

Nikolai Miaskovsky, Symphony No. 27, Slow Movement (Melodiya). This is an inspired movement by one of the great Russian symphonists of our time. Some beautiful melodies unfold in a quiet and mystical atmosphere.

April 21	**A Living Flame**

Focus   All fine art is a symbol leading to a shrine of golden fire. Pause and prepare to pass through the

beautiful gate of symbol into the starry world
beyond.   Paul Brunton

Meditation   Today, as a symbol of beauty, visualize and feel
a flame of golden fire.

Let the flame come into you as it is purifying and
clearing you.

You can open the gate to the golden fire of cleansing power and love.

Musical   Randall Thompson, *Alleluia* (Vail, U.S.C.
Keynotes   Choir—Noran Records, 27 S.E. Molino Ave.,
Pasadena, CA 91101). This strong choral piece
gradually rises to a crescendo. The music is highly
devotional and also ennobling.

Frank Perry, *New Atlantis* (Celestial Harmonies,
Box 673, Wilton, CT 06897). The composer's own
mystical experience of an angelic visitation inspired
him to write this unique music, for "petalumines,"
or bells of metal invented by Mr. Perry. The piece
is very spatial and expands the consciousness.

April 22   **Fruition**

Focus   Blessing and glory and honor and power be unto
Him that sitteth upon the throne, for ever and ever.
Blessed are they that dwell in Thy house; they will
always be praising Thee.

John Bunyon

Meditation   After a job well done, it is good to experience a
period of fruition.

The gates of divine grace open mysteriously when
fruition is appropriate.

There have to be many risks taken in order to reach greater fulfillment.

Today, you can renew your own efforts to move forward—toward fruition.

Musical Keynotes

Ralph Vaughan-Williams, *The Pilgrim Reaches the End of His Journey* from *Pilgrim's Progress* (Boult—Angel). This is the trumpeting final section of an opera. I especially like this release at the end of the journey—the pilgrim's welcome home into the heavens: "Alleluia, Alleluia, Blessed are they that dwell in thy house. They will always be praising thee."

Guiseppe Torelli, Concerti Grossi (Faerber—Turnabout). These pieces are welcoming and nurturing. They provide a friendly focus and a sense of well-being.

April 23

A Greater Strength

Focus

There is an entirely different kind of force, a far greater power, which of course, is not measured by its victories over others: the strength to recognize one's own weakness and rely upon God, the strength to respect others, and help them become stronger, instead of taking advantage of their weakness.   Paul Tournier

Meditation

Your strength comes from a higher power working through you.

Today you can realize and feel the power that helps you to be strong.

When others are weak, you can inspire them to be stronger.

You can open yourself for help through vulnerability.

As you reach out to those who are needy, you will be empowered to help.

Musical   Franz Schubert, Symphony No. 9, *Great* (Boult—
Keynotes   EMI). This humanitarian work combines strength and playfulness. A certain child-like quality pervades the music, but in the end the trombones "lead away from pastoral enjoyments to speak with the tongues of archangels" (Burnett James).

Eugene Friesen, Paul Halley, *New Friend* (Living Music). Warmth and energy emanate from *New Friend*, for piano and cello.

April 24   **Sharing**

Focus   May the Forces of Light bring illumination
                  to mankind.
              May the Spirit of Peace be spread abroad.
              May the Law of Harmony prevail.
              May persons of good will everywhere meet
                  in a spirit of co-operation.
              So let it be and help us to do our part.
                                      Michal J. Eastcott

Meditation Today can be a time for sharing.

Music you can share your substance with others, and even more important, you can share of yourself.

You can consciously share your energy in the spirit of cooperation.

Today find new ways to share.

Musical   Max Bruch, Concerto for Two Pianos and Or-
Keynotes   chestra (Herbig—Turnabout). This is a very "sharing" work, composed for two pianos and orchestra. Many lovely tunes are to be heard in this cheerful music.

Paul Halley, *Pianosong* (Living Music). There is a wide range of emotions and moods in this friendly and easy-flowing music. An organ accompanies three of the ten selections.

April 25   *Guidance*

Focus   It has always been the policy of the Higher Beings I have worked with on other levels not to tell us what to do but to share perspectives with us and help us to help ourselves.

David Spangler

Meditation   As you learn how better to attune yourself to the universal life energy, lessons come to you about decision-making: what to do and how to do it.

Guidance often comes in the form of a larger perspective.

You can visualize your intuition, imagination and knowledge working together, much like a triangle surrounding you, with energies that help you to make the choices you need to make.

The process of attuning to inner guidance helps you by enlarging your perspective.

Musical   Enrique Bossi, Concerto for Organ and Orchestra
Keynotes   (Mace). There is a sense here of dynamism; it is not an inward-looking piece. But the power opens out and there is much inspiration.

Gustav Mahler, *Adagio*, from Symphony No. 10 (Haitink—Philips). This is a very personal statement from Mahler—a spiritual journey in itself. Mahler never finished, although it has been "reconstructed" effectively by Deryck Cooke. The music of the *Adagio* opens doors into higher worlds.

April 26   *Improve the Quality*

Focus   There is an unlimited ability to improve the quality
of anything.   Thomas Peters

Meditation   Today focus on your ability to improve the quality
of whatever is a part of your life:

You can improve the quality of your relationships.

You can improve the quality of your work performance.

You can improve the quality of your life.

Can you think of other ways in which you can in
some way improve the quality of your life and its
contents?

Musical Keynotes   J. S. Bach, *Trio Sonatas* (Alain—Erato). These
sonatas, played on the organ, are filled with
vitality and good spirits and are highly inspirational.

Ann Williams, *Summer Rose* (Art of Relaxation).
Harps, flutes, autoharp and bells bring a sense of
joy and relaxation and contribute to the richness
of this music. Paracelsus' words are recalled:

> The closer our communion with the Angels, the
> deeper will be our realization of the spiritual ministry of the world of flowers.

April 27   *Clearance*

Focus   Music washes away from the soul
the dust of everyday life.
       Auerbach

Meditation   You can feel beautiful music as it washes over you.

Like a healing waterfall, the sparkle and freshness
of music can rinse you clean.

Today listen to a favorite piece of music and allow
its vibrations to flow through you.

In this way you can use music and your imagination for release and clearance.

Musical   Francis Poulenc, *Concert Champêtre—Rustic
Keynotes*   Concerto* (Van de Wiele, Pretre—Angel). A rare
freshness and sparkle accompany this fine piece.
The energies help the listener drop tension and
staleness, especially the harpsichord, which re-
juvenates one.

Frank Perry, *Temple of the Stars* (KPM Music, 21
Denmark St., London, WC2H 8NE, England).
These zodiacal pieces were inspired by the
Himalayan paintings of Nicholas Roerich. Oriental bells, gongs and Tibetan "singing bowls" contribute to the variety of sounds. This is a rare
experience that clears and heightens the consciousness.

April 28   # Welcome

Focus   Riches in another need a welcome before they can
appear.

                                                 Unknown

Meditation   A beautiful jewel shines at the center of every
person.

Look for this treasure in yourself and in others.

You can help it emerge if you inspire trust and
openness that are not judgmental.

Welcome and receive the best that you and others

may be able to offer now, remembering the best
is yet to come.

Musical   Hermann Suter, Symphony in D-Minor, Op. 17
Keynotes   (Hans   Münch—CT   Records,   Lausanne,
Switzerland). This ebullient work, filled with high
spirits, also has searching moments. The style is
romantic, and the Adagio is particularly lovely.

Jean Pierre Rampal, *Carnaval de Rampal*
(Rampal—RCA). Several pieces for flute and piano
offer a pleasing, varied program. Especially
beautiful is the Doppler work, *Fantasy on a
Hungarian Pastorale.*

April 29   ## Addressing the Needs

Focus   Nobody was going to pay me for my work, but I
knew if I were doing what God wanted to be done,
I would get on. Since I have committed myself to
others, only the impossible has happened.
                                    Buckminster Fuller

Meditation   Today commit your energies to whatever needs to
be done, with gladness and love of service.

You can begin at home by observing the immediate
needs of persons and lives around you.

By doing what needs to be done, now, you can
begin to accomplish what at first seemed impossible.

Musical   Wallingford Riegger, *Romanza* (Antonini—CRI).
Keynotes   This is quite a lovely little piece—very lyrical and
not as dissonant as some of this composer's works.
There is a strong individuality in the music.

Rod   McKuen,   *The   Balloon   Concerto*

(Greenslade—Stanyan). This music is a twentieth century masterpiece—strong yet extremely expansive. There are many beautiful melodies, some spatial and others suggesting heraldry. The closing combines pipe organ and synthesizer—a beautifully mystical moment where the Presence shines in.

April 30   ## Sing in Exaltation

Focus   Beauty of line and color can go only so far; the joy of fragrance can go a little further; but MUSIC touches our innermost being and in that way produces new life, a life that gives exaltation to the whole being, raising it to that perfection in which lies the fulfillment of man's life.

                                        Hazrat Inayat Khan

Meditation   Today tap into feelings of exaltation and upliftment.

                 When you are feeling the gladness of life, you come into balance, and all your energies flow together.

                 Joyful exaltation is a key to releasing the deeper energies of fulfillment in you.

                 Today play those pieces of music that fill you with jubilation and exaltation.

Musical   Wolfgang Amadeus Mozart, *Coronation Mass*
Keynotes   (Ristenpart—Nonesuch). A sense of exaltation pervades the various movements and joy is evident in this splendid choral work.

                 Ellen Taffe Zwilich, *Celebrations* (Nelson—New World). Powerful sonorities and orchestral colors make this piece joyful.

Angels of Music

Their sound is as of a million harps..., their voice is like the surging of the sea. Order after Order answers to the Word of God. As the angels sing, they glow with the color of their song. The mission of the Music angels is to bear this radiance of a million prisms, this surging of a million planets, downwards to the ears of man, outwards into material worlds, that even tree and plant and mole beneath the earth may hear the Voice of God and, hearing it, obey.

Geoffrey Hodson

Meditation Today choose a favorite piece of beautiful music. Feel the vibrations and the colors of the song.

You are surrounded by the music, the streams of color that fill the spaces of creation.

As you listen, you can open up to the angels of music, "radiance of a million prisms."

Musical Keynotes Hugo Alfven, *The Lord's Prayer* (Sjökvist—Bluebell, Sweden). A marvelous gift for melody is revealed in this music. Great spaces open, allowing the sense of the higher worlds to come into our presence.

Paul Horn, *In Concert* (Golden Flute). Some music is enhanced greatly through the sonic ambience of a great cathedral. The music here is played in the

111

St. Mary's Cathedral in San Francisco. Especially
expansive and open to the presence of angels are
the pieces *Amazing Grace, Siciliano*, and *Jesus'
Sweet Memory*. The flute rises in the open air atmosphere.

May 2   **Unseen Companions**

Focus   Recall frequently every day that behind the screen
of the invisible are those who love you and who
are your friends, beyond any friendship you
understand on earth. Your strength, your happiness, your growth, can be quickened by a
recollection of this reality.

                                                    Anonymous

Meditation   You can remind yourself today that you are always
accompanied.

In the divine Presence are many of those who care
about you and quicken you throughout life's
journey.

Along with human companions, others accompany
you, and you are empowered.

Musical   Alessandro Scarlatti, *Stabat Mater* (Németh—
Keynotes   Hungaroton). In this choral work with orchestra
the sense of invisible presences is clearly to be
heard.

Alain Kremski, *Prayer and Secret Meditation*
(Auvidis, 14, r. Jean-Baptiste Potin 92170
VANVES, France). This is very special inner music
for bells and gongs. The sounds are extremely delicate and transparent producing a calming, inner
experience which also reminds the listener of the
higher worlds.

May 3	**Hearing**

Focus   Today everything is visual. The young generation places too much emphasis on the eye, on what they can see, not enough attention on words and music.

Carlo Maria Giulini

Meditation   Today, as you close your eyes and come to peacefulness, listen to a piece of great music.

The sounds approach you. The music is warm and friendly.

Feel yourself breathing into the music, breathing out all fears and worries.

Through the sense of hearing, welcome the energies of the music. Feel the currents now filling you.

The music washes over you, bringing new power and peace.

Musical *Keynotes*   Antonio Vivaldi, *Gloria in D* (Willcocks— London). The *Gloria* is a sparkling work that exudes joy and praise, exhilarating and uplifting to the spirit.

Daniel Kobialka, *Moonglow* (Li-Sem). These are contemporary arrangements of two classics, Pachelbel's *Chorale and Variations* and Mozart's Piano Sonata in A (K. 300). The music is beautifully flowing and moves inside the listener to provide warmth and assurance.

May 4	**Triumph**

Focus   I remember the world of beauty and peace from my best days of childhood. . . . I have always believed in the triumph of Good over Evil . . . and in love—the magic word that this planet is often forgetting.   Marisa Robles

Meditation   There is always a better way.

Consider today how the spirit of love and goodness brings triumph over distortion and destructive tendencies.

Can you remember one experience in which you were able to release love in a way that brought triumph to a difficult situation?

Let your love overcome evil or disharmony with good. In such a moment you will feel the spirit of triumph.

Musical   Marisa Robles, *The Narnia Suite* (EMI). The
Keynotes   music, for harp, flute and piccolo, awakens a sense of enchantment. Beautiful scenes stimulate your imagination, and there is also strength in the melodies which empower you with a feeling of triumph.

Kim Robertson, *Wind Shadows II* (Invincible). This music for solo harp is empowering and stimulating. Lovely melodies and clear tones sweep through the listener with freshness and openness.

May 5   *Lift Your Spirits*

Focus   On earth there is no music
                To be compared with ours. . . .
                The angelic voices
                Lift up the spirits
                So that everything awakens in joy.
                                    Arnim and Brentano
                                Des Knaben Wunderhorn

Meditation   Today is Children's Day in Japan, so enter into the spirit of playfulness and good spirits.

Feel your spirits lifting you into joy of the heavens.

Angels are singing.

As you open to the awakening of joy and song, your heart opens.

Musical   Gustav Mahler, Symphony No. 4, Fourth Move-
Keynotes   ment (Blegen, Levine—RCA). The music describes a child's delight in paradise. Jingle bells, soprano and orchestra bring the feeling of joy and innocence.

Abraham Kaplan, *Psalm 23* from *Glorious*. I have mentioned this album before, but the *Psalm 23* needs to be highlighted. It is a very energizing piece that truly awakens the spirits.

May 6   *Lifebreath*

Focus   The light of thy music illumines
      the world.
The lifebreath of thy music runs
      from sky to sky.
The holy stream of thy music breaks
      through all stony obstacles and rushes on.
                  Rabindranath Tagore

Meditation   You have come into this lifetime to sing God's song.

The lifebreath is playing through you now, and you are singing your song.

You can let the holy stream flow through you.

In all that you do, you can draw upon the lifebreath and sing the music that runs from sky to sky.

Musical   *Evening Ragas from Benares*, Sitar and Tabla
Keynotes (Musical Heritage). In the Indian tradition, these
            meditative pieces are highly rhythmical in places
            and wonderfully melodic.

David Casper, *Birth Sight* (Hearts of Space). The
section with sitar is especially evocative of music
before the industrial age.

May 7   **Subtlety**

Focus   Music possesses much richer means of expression
            and it is a more subtle medium for translating the
            1000 shifting moments of the feelings of the soul.
                                     Peter Ilich Tchaikovsky

Meditation Your life expresses many subtle shadings of feel-
              ing and experience.

Today you can feel the great spectrum of colors,
feelings and gestures, the thousands of shifting
moments in the feelings of the soul.

You can feel the music of life's subtle moments,
shifting like the sparkle of diamonds in the glistening Light.

Musical   Peter Ilich Tchaikovsky, *Andante*, from Symphony
Keynotes No. 5 (Ormandy—Delos). The subtle shadings and
            longings of the heart emerge poignantly in this
            music. The horn leads with a deeply felt theme,
            and the orchestra answers.

Johannes Brahms, Piano Concerto No. 2, Third
Movement (Gilels, Jochum—DGG). This deeply
moving music describes an interior landscape.
Feelings and longings are expressed in the dialogue
of cello and piano.

May 8	## *Nobility*

Focus   Music aims to fill the heart with noble feelings.
                                                          Li-Ki

Meditation   Today feel how life seeks to raise you upward and higher in your consciousness.

Now, in the silence or rising through the music, see a ladder of golden light lifting you, leading you higher, into Light.

As you breathe in and out, smoothly and calmly, you can feel yourself rising. Let yourself move easily, clearly.

As the light glows through you, you feel empowered, ennobled.

Musical   Oscar Hammerstein, *Prologue* from *The Sound of*
Keynotes   *Music* (RCA). The cleansing, lifting effect of this music always helps the listener to breathe in the nobleness and radiance of life's finest qualities.

Wu Hai-lin, *Singing at Night* from Violin Concerto (Hong Kong). A beautiful lyrical movement unfolds, which later leads into a dance-like section, introduced by the sheng, the Chinese reed mouth-organ.

May 9   ## *The Heavens Opening*

Focus   Music can be all things to all persons. It is like a great dynamic sun in the center of a solar system which sends out its rays and inspiration in every direction. . . . Music makes us feel that the heavens open and a divine voice calls. Something in our souls responds and understands.
                                                    Leopold Stokowski

Meditation   Today, from the center of the great heavens, music
                sounds through your silence.

                The heavens open and great power emanates into
                your atmosphere, bringing you energy and the
                divine music.

                You live in a universe that resounds with inspira-
                tion and music.

                And there is the music waiting in you that hears
                the cosmic spheres now opening with music.

Musical   Dietrich Buxtehude, *Magnificat* (Turnabout). This
Keynotes   is earlier music, for chorus and orchestra, which
                in its own way is full of reverence and devotional
                fervor.

                Franz Joseph Haydn, *Lord Nelson Mass* (Davis—
                Philips). This music is strong, devotional and
                joyful. It is for soloists, chorus and orchestra.

May 10   **Holy Expectancy**

Focus   In life, as in music, we need the great theme as
                well as all the motifs. The only thing that brings
                lasting contentment is the service of God. In ser-
                vice, apart from any mere outward results, we are
                one with God and that brings its own inspiration,
                strength and inward contentment.

                                                        Unknown

Meditation   Today consider the great theme of your life.

                As an instrument of God, how do you see the most
                important ingredients and direction that your life
                is expressing?

                In an attitude of holy expectancy, you can recall

frequently the great theme of your life and how your expression of service takes many turns and different paths along the way toward greater fulfillment.

The great theme contains all the motifs.

Musical Keynotes   Rodgers and Hammerstein, *Climb Every Mountain* from *The Sound of Music* (RCA). This music is wonderfully motivating and inspirational. One writer was moved by the music to write the following:

> You have the mountain of self-mastery to climb in your incarnation; be busy and see that every hour is filled with love and the incentive of joy in the climb.

Ned Washington and Leigh Harline, *When You Wish Upon a Star* (Mormon Tabernacle Choir—Columbia). This is another very uplifting piece that emphasizes the theme of holy expectancy.

May 11   **Being Pliable and Unbiased**

Focus   Conformity leads to mediocrity. It is in the understanding of ourselves that fear comes to an end. If the individual is to grapple with life from moment to moment, if he is to face its intricacies, its miseries and sudden demands, he must be infinitely pliable and therefore free of theories and particular patterns of thought.

J. Krishnamurti

Meditation   You can be free of fears as you gain more insight.

By gaining understanding, you can reach greater perspective.

You can be firm without becoming rigid.

Free from the enslavement of theories, you can feel and freshly perceive the moment, and do what needs to be done.

Musical   William Grant Still, *Ennanga* (Orion). The name
Keynotes   of this beautiful piece comes from a native African harp, and it is composed for harp, piano and strings. Appealing melodies, especially in the more meditative second movement, provide refreshing energy.

Irving Berlin, *Give Me Your Tired and Your Poor* from *Miss Liberty* (Kostelanetz—Columbia). This song was inspired by Emma Lazarus' poem engraved on the Statue of Liberty. It sings of hope for a better future, and proclaims America's destiny as a friend to all races.

May 12   **Bells**

Focus   Almost unconsciously, the very old memory of a ringing of bells came to me when, in evening during my childhood, this sound wafted across from the west, from a village called Cadirac. Musing on this, I began to dream. But it would be difficult to describe this vagueness in words.

Isn't it often that an exterior event fills us with these kinds of thoughts, so imprecise that in reality they are not thoughts but something in which we take pleasure. Perhaps the desire for things that do not exist. And that is really the domain of music.

Gabriel Fauré

Meditation   The sound of bells—can you hear them now?

Listen to them ringing and let a joyful memory surface.

Bells, singing high in a tower; bells, streaming across the meadow; bells of a troika, jingling with the snow.

The sounding of the bells recalls the kingdom of light and the music calling from eternity.

Musical Keynotes Gabriel Fauré, *Sanctus* from *Requiem* (Rutter—Conifer). Soaring soprano voices highlight this music which reaches to the heavens.

Edvard Grieg, *The Sound of Bells* (Drew—Unicorn). Mysterious and suggestive, these short pieces for orchestra carry the mysterious sounds of bells and awaken the imagination.

Sergei Rachmaninoff, *The Bells* (Previn—Angel). This beautiful choral-instrumental music describes bells in all their timbres. Large-scale energy.

May 13   *On Time*

Focus Wasting time must be the greatest prodigality. Lost time is never found again; what we call time enough always proves too little enough; let us then up and be doing, and doing to the purpose. By diligence shall we do more with less perplexity.
Benjamin Franklin

Meditation Today you can tune in to the sense of time, the space of opportunity.

You have been given the gift of time. Each moment is precious, each day valuable.

Since timing is everything, also focus upon the sense of timing—the rhythm, the pace and movement of your life.

Musical Keynotes Sir Arthur Sullivan, *The Irish Symphony* (Groves—Musical Heritage). The symphony is filled with beautiful melodies which give one the sense of the richness of life's moments.

Spencer Brewer, *Emerald* (Narada). A strong folk-like quality is to be found in this happy music. Especially uplifting and energizing is the piece *Fisherman's Dream*. Various instruments play the music: guitar, oboe, cello, flute, Celtic harp and synthesizer.

May 14   **Contacting Inner Depths**

Focus   The end of all good music is to affect the soul.
             Claudio Monteverdi

Meditation   Your life has a depth, like a deep wellspring in the currents of eternity.

Music, like clear water, runs deep inside you, nourishing and affecting the lifeline of your soul.

Musical Keynotes   Claudio Monteverdi, *Vespers: 1610* (Corboz—Erato). *The Vespers of the Beloved Virgin Mary* is highly inspirational and reduces stress by its mystical, devotional tones. This unique work is one of the true landmarks of sacred music.

Do'a, *Ornament of Hope* (Friends of Do'a, Box 128, Dover, New Hampshire 03820). "Music that nourishes a hungry soul" is performed on a flute, guitar, chimes, piano, ocarina, xylophones, kalimba, etc. International, cross-cultural music, beautiful and appealing.

May 15   **Kinship with All Life**

Focus   Wherever a man, woman or child cares for creatures, this person becomes a guardian of the welfare of these vulnerable lives. Where there is active love expressed for all creatures, there to some extent is the Kingdom of God realized on this earth. A new dimension of love has been entered. Through its activity the stage of "kinship with all life" has been realized.

Flower A. Newhouse

Meditation   Today is a good day to consider your relationship with nature's creatures.

Animals can offer you a new dimension of love. It is estimated that animals give us ten times more love than do other humans.

Albert Schweitzer helps us feel our kinship with the creatures in this beautiful prayer:

Hear our prayer, O God, for our friends the animals. Especially for animals who are suffering; for any that are hunted or lost or deserted or frightened or hungry; . . . Make us, ourselves, to be true friends to animals and so to share the blessings of the merciful.

Musical   John Lanchbery, *Tales of Beatrix Potter*
Keynotes   (Lanchbery—Angel); Francis Poulenc, *The Model Animals* (Pretre—Angel); Camille Saint-Saens, *Carnival of the Animals* (Pretre—Angel); *Black Stallion* (Coppola—Liberty). All of these selections help the listener become more attuned and sensitive to themes connected with animals.

May 16   **Radiance**

Focus   As he prayed, the fashion of his countenance was altered. His face did shine as the sun.

Luke 9:29; Matthew 17:2

Meditation   Today, waiting in the quiet, you can feel the great energy surrounding you.

Even now, you are being bathed in the radiance of light.

You can look into yourself from above, feeling God's radiance and power entering through the crown of your head, swirling down, filling all the spaces and cells inside and around you.

From head to toes, you can let divine radiance illumine your countenance and your consciousness like the radiating light in Rembrandt's paintings.

Musical Keynotes

Alexander Gretchaninov, *Holy Radiant Light* (Ottley—Columbia). The Mormon Tabernacle Choir sings this inspired Slavic music, which emanates white light into the atmosphere. It is highly charged and radiant.

Eugene Friesen, Paul Halley, *Cathedral Pines* (Living Music). Cello and pipe organ combine to produce a beautiful, radiant piece of music.

May 17

Self-Mastery

Focus

Sometimes all that is required for the attaining of the open door into the Kingdom of Light is for a man or woman to be able in deepest dedication to say "No" to his appetite—to say "Be gone from me forever!" to the animal magnetism of personal attractions that appeal to the sensual nature of human beings.   Gamaliel

Meditation

Today look at your appetites. Are your desires healthy or are they limiting you?

Your desires can be refined, lifted and beautified.

You can find ever more loving and helpful ways to relate to whatever you desire.

Mastery means being in charge of appetites.

Musical   Ludwig van Beethoven, *Choral Fantasy for Piano*
Keynotes   *and Orchestra* (Barenboim, Klemperer—Angel).
              A strong will and sense of self-mastery come
              through this music. In the finale, piano, chorus and
              full orchestra affirm boldly the strength of self-
              mastery.

              Modeste Mussorgsky, *The Great Gate of Kiev*,
              from *Pictures at an Exhibition* (Giulini—DGG;
              Liebowitz—Quintessence). A sense of struggle and
              triumph comes through this musical selection. It
              is a great statement of triumph and helps the
              listener to try harder to reach self-mastery. The
              music concludes with a powerful crescendo by full
              orchestra, gongs and cymbals.

May 18   **Moments Remembered**

Focus   There are moments you remember
              All your life.
              There are moments you wait for
              And dream of all your life.
              This is one of those moments.
              I will always remember this chair,
              That window,
              The way the light streams in.
              The clothes I'm wearing,
              The words I'm hearing,
              The face I'm seeing,
              The feeling I'm feeling,
              The smell, the sounds, will be written
                 on my mind,

Will be written in my heart as long as
    I live.
No time can wear [them] away.
          Alan and Marilyn Bergman

Meditation   Consider today the most precious memories in your life.

Each memory, like a jeweled moment, illumines your path through life.

Which moments have you enjoyed the most? Which moments have taught you the most?

The most meaningful moments of your life connect you to the eternal river of God.

Musical   Karl Goldmark, *In the Garden*, from *Rustic Wed-*
Keynotes   *ding Symphony* (Previn—Angel). The music, for full orchestra, unfolds with a romantic tone that helps the listener recall pleasing memories. There is warmth in this music, and the gentle intimacy suggests love and devotion between two persons, in this case a bride and groom.

Bearns and Dexter, *Golden Voyage I* (Awakening Productions). Especially conducive to memories are the pieces *Golden Voyage* and *Timeless Love*. This new music is performed with synthesizers and bells, plus fountains and streams.

May 19   ***Spiritual Signposts***

Focus   Remember the spiritual verities:

—Let your mind reach stillpoint.
—Reverence God and holiness.
—Live better each day.
—Study the great teachings of the ages.

—Serve and overcome your smaller self,
> through conscious knowledge.
—Give yourself.

> An Initiate

Meditation Today, in deep reflection, review these themes.

In the quiet you can feel the divine Presence shining through you.

You can do one thing better today than you did it yesterday.

Take time to ponder the great teachings of those wiser than you.

Find some way to serve others' needs and give yourself today, especially when it may be inconvenient for you.

Musical Keynotes Albert Hay Malotte, *The Lord's Prayer* (Burrows—London). "This glorious and inspiring piece emanates blue into the atmosphere, and gradually the archetypes of an altar and praying hands appear," one clairvoyant so reported. You also can feel the deep devotion of this music and the power to raise your consciousness that comes through. Notice the special moment of power that is released with the words, "Thy Will be done."

Sir Arthur Sullivan, *The Lost Chord* (Burrows—London). This highly charged piece, for soloist and orchestra, lifts the consciousness and strengthens resolve.

May 20 **Sound as Intermediary**

Focus There is an intimate connection between Sound and all other expressions of life. . . . Sound is the intermediary between the "abstract" idea and the "concrete" form. Sounds mold the ether into shapes, and through these shapes the corresponding Power is able to play and make its impress on physical matter.

                                        Vera Stanley Alder

Meditation   Today you can consider sound as an intermediary between form and the inner life.

Beautiful music can connect you to divine archetypes and shapes waiting to find concrete form.

Today you can build the bridge and be the carrier to help give form to seeds of divine possibilities and archetypes.

Musical   Frederic Chopin, Nocturne, Opus 9, No. 2
Keynotes   (Ormandy—Columbia). This piece, played here by strings, suggests the accompanying presence of a larger love, linking with the longings of the heart for human love.

Alfredo Ortiz, *Harp for Quiet Moments* (Alfredo Ortiz Recordings, Box 911, Corona, CA 91718). *A Light in the Sea* and *Quiet Moments* are especially beautiful and provide the "intermediary" moment between the visible and invisible.

May 21   ## The Beautiful

Focus   Beauty is a necessity. . . . Beauty is a power which, if we associate with it, ennobles us.

                                        Manly Palmer Hall

Meditation   Beauty uplifts; ugliness degrades.

Consider what is beautiful in your life.

What are the ingredients of your life that help to connect you and associate you with the beautiful?

How can you cultivate the beautiful?

Musical   Richard Wagner, *A Siegfried Idyll* (Marriner—
Keynotes   London). A beauty emanates from the music, sug-
              gesting landscapes that are intimate and warm.
              Wagner wrote this lovely piece for strings as a pre-
              sent to his wife Cosima.

              Radhika Miller, *Within the Wind* (Radhika Miller,
              Box 185, Sebastopol, CA 95472). A variety of
              music, for flute and chamber orchestra, is pre-
              sented here. Especially beautiful are *Irish Lovesong*
              and *Soul of the Sea*.

May 22   ***Presence of Angels***

Focus   Only a shadow divides us from eternity. The light
              of God flows into receptive angel hands and the
              angel is ever ready to pour it into our hearts if we
              hold them open. Can we on earth not overhear the
              angelic praises? Perhaps we find an echo of them
              in our deepest silences.

                                          Lothar Schreyer

Meditation The angels' presence is always near. You can
              deepen your attunement with the angels.

              Your life and all of earth is enriched by the love
              and blessings of angels.

              Listen carefully today; the music of angels echoes
              through the silence.

Musical   Richard Wagner, *Lohengrin*, Prelude to Act 1;
Keynotes   *Parsifal*, Prelude and *Good Friday Spell*
              (Haitink—Philips). This is some of the most
              ethereal, angelic music ever composed. The sounds
              are transparent, highly charged and transcendent.
              The music moves in stillness.

César Franck, *Panis Angelicus* (Kilbey—EMI).
The music of the "bread of angels" never fails to
awaken a deeper sense of the presence of celestial
beings.

Pablo Casals, *Song of the Birds* (Munroe,
Kostelanetz—Columbia). This unique music, for
cello and orchestra, opens the door to the presences
of angels.

May 23	## Song of Life

Focus   I sing the song of life, with the smile of the sun
and the dance of the twilight. I float in the sky in
rhythm, with the free spirit and joyous heart.

                                            Paramananda

Meditation   You can let the song of life flow through you.

With a free spirit you can find the rhythms of life's
dance.

You can break free of limiting habits that are no
longer necessary.

In the smile of sunshine, find the open road that
leads joyously toward discovery and fulfillment.

Musical   Gustav Mahler, Quartet for Strings and Piano
Keynotes   (Erato). This youthful work brings joyful feelings
and enthusiasm. At points the music rises into
rhapsody and free-flowing melody.

John Rutter, *The Beatles' Concerto* (Rostal and
Schaefer, Goodwin—MMG). The song of life
comes through this music, for pianos and orchestra,
which is a marvelous arrangement of the Beatles'
best tunes. The music is woven into a full-fledged
concerto that carries impact and exuberance.

Jean Francaix, Piano Concerto (Turnabout). This
pleasant piece is quite songful in sections.

May 24	### *Sharing Blessings*

Focus
    Peace be with you, O ministering angels,
        messengers of the Most High
    The supreme King of Kings, the Holy One, blessed
        is He.
    Enter in peace, O messengers of peace,
        messengers of the Most High,
    The supreme King of Kings, the Holy One, blessed
        is He.
    Bless me with peace, O messengers of peace,
        messengers of the Most High....

                Martin Kalmanoff, *Sholom*
                Aleichem (The Joy of Prayer)

Meditation
    Wherever you are, you can extend a friendly blessing.

    The ministering angels sing the praises and the peace of God to all lives.

    You too can share the peace and blessing of friendship and love.

Musical
Keynotes
    Martin Kalmanoff, *The Joy of Prayer*, concert setting of Sabbath liturgies (Milnes, Westenburg—2MMG). The peaceful aspects of this music, for soloists, chorus and orchestra, are especially evident in the beautiful prayer: Yih'yu L'Rotzon (Let the Words of My Mouth); As the person who has prayed has opened his heart to God, may God open His heart to the prayer's petition.

    Daniel Kobialka, *Softness of a Moment* (Li-Sem). This beautiful setting of Rameau's *Le Cupis*, one of the selections offered here, comes as a lullaby of peace. This music, for violin and synthesizers, was composed by Rameau as a present to a friend whose wife had given birth to a son.

May 25   **Talents and Calling**

Focus   Each man has his own vocation: the talent is the
              call. There is one direction in which all space is
              open to him....Every person has this call of the
              power to do something unique, and no person has
              any other call.
                                    Ralph Waldo Emerson

Meditation   Your vocation is more than just a job. A vocation
              is a calling to express your particular purpose this
              lifetime.

              No two people have identical vocations. Everybody
              has unique talents, experiences and perspectives.

              Find your talents and the sense of your vocation.
              Enjoy your real calling. As you sense the direction,
              openings occur; your talents will begin to flower.

Musical   Gustav Mahler, Symphony No. 7, First Movement,
Keynotes   *Song of the Night* (Haitink—Philips). In this move-
              ment of the large symphony, you can hear the
              soul's journey through the veils of night and the
              sense of seeking in the midst of uncertainty.

              Adam Geiger, *Evening Songs* (Lura Media).
              Beautiful, soothing melodies flow from electric
              piano, acoustic piano and synthesizer. Especially
              beautiful is *Lullaby of Mist*.

May 26   **Source of Ideas**

Focus   The basic idea never leaves me: it rises, it grows,
              and I see and hear the picture in its entire range
              as if molded in one; from where do I get my ideas?
              That I cannot with certainty say. They come un-
              called, directly, indirectly, I could grasp them with
              my hands: in the open, from nature, in the forest,

in the quiet of the night, in the early morning.
Sometimes moods...come to me in tones: they
ring, storm and roar until they finally stand before
me in notes.   Beethoven

Meditation   Inexhaustible seeds of delight fall into the soil of
your temperament, and new ideas find birth on
earth.

Today you can see yourself as a field, ready and
fertile for planting and harvest.

The Source of all ideas is filling you now; the entire range unfolds across your horizons.

Let the new ideas take shape.

Musical   La Mantovana, *Italian Baroque Dances* (Tyler—
Keynotes   Nonesuch). These instrumental dances are
energetic and cheerful with many beautiful tunes.

G. I. Gurdjieff, *Sacred Hymns* (Jarrett—ECM,
Warner Brothers). There is a quality of solemnity
to some of these pieces, played on the baroque
organ. A sense of mystery comes through in other
sections.

May 27   **Accepting Yourself**

Focus   It seemed impossible to leave the world until I had
produced all that I felt called upon to produce, and
so I endured this wretched existence—an excitable
body which a sudden change can throw from the
best into the worst state. Patience I must now
choose for my guide, and I have done so.

Divine One, thou lookest into my inmost soul, thou
knowest it, thou knowest that love of man and
desire to do good live therein.
                                                Beethoven

Meditation	The more you feel the sense of purpose, the clearer the meaning of your life becomes.

In patience you can now feel the divine light revealing your soul and heart to you.

As you can accept your imperfections and efforts to refine in all that you are doing, you will always be enfolded in divine love.

Musical Keynotes   Joachim Raff, Piano Concerto in C (Ponti, Kapp—Candide). This piece is filled with beautiful, vibrant melodies. There is a tone of joyful acceptance in some places, and a more reflective tone in others.

Daniel Kobialka, *A Whiter Shade of Pale,* from *Fragrances of a Dream* (Li-Sem). This long, flowing melody is based upon J. S. Bach's *Air on a G String.* There is a wonderful quality of acceptance and receptivity here to the larger, all-encompassing Presence of God so typical of Bach's own outlook.

May 28   **Unfoldment**

Focus   For every step you take in the pursuit of hidden knowledge, take three steps in the perfecting of your own character.   **AE**

Meditation   Genuine unfoldment combines discovery with the perfecting of your character.

Insights lead to self-cleansing. Use your inward openings to refine and expand your character.

Light pours in, empowering your inner work; clarity in action yields greater unfoldment.

Musical Keynotes   Sir George Dyson, *Hierusalem* (Rennert— Hyperion). The music describes the Heavenly City, first in foggy mists; then as the soprano enters, the longing and the vision grow. The burdens of the soloist are lifted into the transcendent song of the choir, and eventually the gates of gold are flung open, as harp, organ and full orchestra combine in glory.

The Psalms of David, King's College Choir (Willcocks—EMI). These Psalms, accompanied by organ, are rendered in a deeply devotional and reverent tone.

May 29	## *Keynote*
Focus	If you are able to discover your own keynote or chord and play it over gently to yourself, you will revive as if by magic. Your keynote can be ascertained by listening to some good orchestral music. When the note is played it will send a thrill right through you. Vera Stanley Alder
Meditation	Certain tones and sonorities of music will center and empower you.
	Let yourself resonate to the music. Listen for your keynote.
	You can feel certain vibrations and musical patterns opening up areas within your body, emotions and mind.
	The greatest music brings you connection with and openings into your soul.
Musical Keynotes	Isaac Albeniz, *Legend*, from *Suite Española* (Segovia—RCA). Here the keynote is mystery. A fragrance and an aura envelop the exotic tune and the tones surrounding it. The music is intoxicating.
	Christopher Breen, *Of Eve* (Zen Song—Wilkinson,

651 W. 7th Ave., Escondido, CA 92025). A wonderful, gentle piano tapestry brings its own heart-warming keynote.

May 30	# *A Hobby*
Focus	In order to balance work with fun, it is important to have both a vocation and a hobby.

Unknown

Meditation	Work and fun are valuable allies.
	After you focus for long hours, you need to draw back into light-heartedness and playfulness.
	Your hobby does not have to be more work or a task.
	Today, along with work, you can also experience wholesome fun. Work and play—the alternating rhythms—provide renewal and health.
Musical Keynotes	Ignaz Moscheles, Concerto in G for Piano and Orchestra (Ponti, Maga—Candide). The music, filled with good energy and fine romantic tunes, is fun to listen to because it is exciting and varied.
	Kim Robertson, *Wind Shadows* (Invincible Recordings). The open air sounds of the Celtic harp make this music come alive. Its good energy rejuvenates the listener.

May 31	# *The Cosmic View*
Focus	On the beach at night, alone, As I watch the bright stars shining, I think a thought of the clef of the universe and of the future.

A vast similitude interlocks all,
All distances of space however wide,
All distances of time,
All souls, all living bodies though they be ever
    so different,
All nations, all identities that have existed
    or may exist,
All lives and deaths, all lives and deaths,
    all of the past, present, future,
This vast similitude spans them,
    and always has spanned,
And shall forever span them and shall completely
    hold and enclose them.

Walt Whitman

Meditation   Look at your present situation in terms of the
larger, cosmic view.

Feel your place in the great span of lifetimes.

Remember the great similitude: All lives are interconnected as they move in the infinite.

Find your place in the moment and in the great
spaces ahead.

Musical   Ralph Vaughan-Williams, *A Sea Symphony*, First
Keynotes   Movement (Boult—EMI). The music for soloists,
chorus and orchestra is a proclamation of space and
openness. The words and vistas of Walt Whitman
inspired Vaughan-Williams:

> Behold the sea itself,
> And on its limitless, heaving breast, the ships;
> Thou sea that pickest and cullest the race in time
>   and unitest the nations.

The music ebbs and flows, sounding the majestic
sweep across the waves of time and space.

Quiet Moments at the Chapel of the Holy Cross
(Box 1181, Sedona, AZ 86336). This is strong, open
music that carries the resonance of majesty in a
great cathedral.

Moving Ahead

Focus   Any credit you give yourself is not worth having.
                                                Irving Thalberg

Meditation   It is advisable to enjoy your successes BRIEFLY.
                 Extended self-congratulation is not productive.

                 In the moment there is great joy, and it cannot be
                 protracted or brought back.

                 Enjoy the triumph of this moment, and then move
                 on. More awaits you.

                 The past can be released into expectancy for what
                 is ahead.

Musical   Mikhail Glinka, *Bellini Variations* (Schwann). This
Keynotes   highly enjoyable music, for piano and orchestra,
                 is strong and filled with pleasing melodies.

                 Heartdance (Song of the Wood Music, 203 W.
                 State St., Black Mt., NC 28711). Especially haunt-
                 ing among these folk pieces is *The Forest Path*, a
                 beautiful and mysterious musical journey. The
                 dulcimer sounds are especially evocative.

June 2   *Relationship*

Focus   I want to be in the thick of people who are feeling
                 and living. Whether I like them or their life does

not matter so much. I want to find out what there is in human hearts. . . . When I have had my fill of being this tumultuous being, then I want one place for reflection and creation. Finally, alone.

Baudelaire

Meditation Today you can feel the rhythm of contact and drawing apart.

You can deepen the sense of how to be close to another, then draw away to be alone with God, happy in your own space.

In company and apart—the human mingling and the divine communion in solitude.

Musical Keynotes Sir Edward Elgar, *The Dream of Gerontius* (Boult—Musical Heritage). This is a great choral and orchestral work, filled with mystical moments and overtones. Elgar drew the text from the poem by Cardinal Newman. Especially beautiful are songs of the angelic choirs:

> Praise to the Holiest in the height,
> And in the depth be praise:
> In all His words most wonderful;
> Most sure in all His ways.

Marvin Hamlisch, *Sophie's Choice*, soundtrack (Southern Cross). This music is uniquely intimate and warm. The orchestra weaves beautiful melodies. A solo piano selection of Mendelssohn adds to the beauty.

June 3   **Frontier of Beauty**

Focus The greatest activity of which man is capable is opening up yet another fragment of the frontier of beauty.   Albert Einstein

Meditation   You can open new fragments on the frontier of beauty.

Today look for ways to enjoy something beautiful—a sunset, a painting, a piece of music, a place in nature. Also express beauty in some way—in how you dress, in a flower arrangement, in a well written letter. You can explore the endless frontier of beauty.

Musical   Felix Mendelssohn, *Calm Sea and Prosperous*
Keynotes   *Voyage,* Overture (Maag—MCA). It is a memorable experience to listen to this seascape. The listener can move across open vistas and broad horizons. The energy mounts to a crescendo with full orchestra, then recedes into calmness.

Schawkie Roth, *You Are the Ocean* (Art of Relaxation). This is "celestial water music," good for relaxation and reverie. It is composed for harp, zither, bamboo flute, alto flute, and cello—accompanied by sounds of ocean and stream. A beautiful experience awaits you.

June 4   *Integrity*

Focus   The goods of this world are most dear to me, but much dearer are peace of mind and my own honor.
                                          Claudio Monteverdi

Meditation   Examine your feelings today concerning your own integrity.

Behind all outer successes arises your need for peace of mind.

As you live each day with integrity and act to the best of your ability, your feelings of peace of mind will bring joyful connection with the larger divine peace.

That peace is sustaining you now.

Musical Keynotes Claudio Monteverdi, Franz Liszt, *The Legend of Saint Elizabeth* (Supraphon). This stirring music describes the spiritual journey in service of Saint Elizabeth—her testings and her triumphs beyond suffering. The integrity of a life journey emerges.

Shayla, *Vision Seeker* (Yansa, Zensong—Wilkinson, 651 W. 7th Ave., Escondido, CA 92025). An inner awakening is connected with this mysterious music for synthesizers. *Water Dance* is especially memorable.

June 5 ## *Be Not Submissive*

Focus My God, how good, how fine you are!
Your eyes, your spirit
Wide open to the last small star....
Your loveliness yet lingers warm,
A glowing ember....
Though all that fate has brought me through
Is past redeeming,
Still my pure songs in flocks to you
Go teeming, streaming.
Down on each heart, down on each year,
My seeds incisive:
Be not submissive, Never fear.
Be not submissive!

Mikhail Dudin

Meditation All your fears today require you to overcome undue submissiveness to others.

The divine spirit, wide open to the last small star,

is the inner fire in you that will not allow you to
give in to what is lesser in you.

Today, with confidence, express your real self in
your life. Let others know who you truly are.

Musical   Adolf Wiklund, Concerto No. 2 for Piano and Or-
Keynotes   chestra (Westerberg—Caprice). The music is
melodic and rhythmical, suggesting vitality and
feeling that set you free to express yourself.

Susan McDonald, *World of the Harp* (Delos). Scintillating harp sounds make Albeniz' Sonata
memorable and strengthening.

June 6   ## *Robed in Light*

Focus   O God, our merciful Father (and Mother),
I'm wrapped in a robe of light,
Clothed in your glory
That spreads its wings
Over my soul.
May I be worthy.
Amen.

                                         Barbra Streisand

Meditation   Today you can feel God's garment of glory surrounding you.

Wrapped in a robe of light, you can feel the call
toward greater clarity and purity.

When your desire for the divine is deep and heartfelt, understanding is quickened accordingly.

Along the way, you are always robed in light.

Musical   A *Mass from the Monastery of Keur Moussa,*
Keynotes   *Senegal* (Musical Heritage). The twenty-one strings

of the kora and the choir of monks provide a glorious paean of praise.

Barbra Streisand, *Yentl* (Bergman and Legrand—Columbia). This stirring music blazes with the sense of being robed in light. A magnificent performance by Streisand lifts the music into the realm of the androgynous expression of ecstasy and the mystical.

June 7   *In Silence the Open Door*

Focus

Keep thyself in this silence and open the door so God may communicate Himself unto thee, unite with thee and then form thee unto Himself. The perfection of the soul consists not in speaking, not in just thinking much in God, but in loving Him sufficiently.

Miguel de Molinos

Meditation

Today you can open the door in silence.

God communicates through the silence of divine love, uniting himself with you, thinking through your mind and loving you in himself.

Musical Keynotes

Wolfgang Amadeus Mozart, Symphony No. 39 (Szell—Odyssey). This is one of the great, inwardly searching works of Mozart. Maestro Szell was a master with Mozart's music, and this version brings out the inner silences and spaces.

Akasha: In the Cosmic Flow (Vision-Reality Radio, Box 16265, San Francisco, CA 94116).

Come, come, come, O moon, O stars,
O sun of the blue-vast sky.
Come to hear the flute of Immortality in my heart,
To watch the smile of Infinity in my life.

These are among the words that form the texts for
this group of devotional songs. They are open and
flowing, able to lead one into the silence.

June 8	## *High Standard*
Focus	There is just as high a standard to be reached in practical life as in art. Robert Schumann
Meditation	You can keep living in the spirit of your high standards. High standards apply to your love of creativity and fun, but also to the daily routine. Today you can replace whatever is mediocre in your life: higher standards bring transformation to whatever is dull and half-hearted.
Musical Keynotes	Robert Schumann, *Paradise and the Peri* (Czyz—EMI). This is a very unusual oratorio based on Thomas Moore's *Lalla Rookh*. It is a mystical work, with a Persian quality. The music describes the soul's journey from darkness into redemption and light. An excerpt from the text, set to music, includes the following words:

> And now behold, in humble prayer,
> The Man kneels there beside the child,
> While a sunbeam shines on both,
> The sinner and the guiltless boy,
> And hymns of joy ring out in Heaven....
> There fell a purer, lovelier ray
> Than ever shone from sun or star
> Upon that tear.

Robert Schumann, Piano Concerto (Argerich,
Rostropovich—DGG). Beautiful melodies and
strong lyricism describe the soul's journey.

JUNE 9   145

Holy Places

June 9

Focus

That I might often see
  The face of the ocean;
That I might see its heaving waves
  Over the wide ocean,

    . . . .

That I might bless the Lord
  Who conserves all,
Heaven with its countless bright orders,
  Land, strand and flood;
That I might search the books all
  That would be good for my soul;
At times kneeling to beloved Heaven;
  At times psalm singing;
At times contemplating the King of Heaven,
  Holy the Chief...

Saint Columba

Meditation

A few places in the world are to be held holy, because of the love which consecrates them and the faith which enshrines them. Their names are themselves talismans of spiritual beauty. Of these is Iona.   Fiona MacLeod

"A small isle..., with the spray of an everlasting wave," Iona vibrates with the energy of the "bright orders." It is a power center of spiritual energy in Scotland—a world chakra point.

Consider today the places you have visited that have been special to you: the places filled with the bright orders.

Reflect on the places where you have felt a greater Presence and power.

Musical Keynotes

Sir Arnold Bax, *The Tale the Pine Trees Knew* (Thomson—Chandos). This mysterious piece for full orchestra suggests the west coast of Scotland and its mystical energies.

Ossian, *Dove Across the Water* (Finnebar). This simple music honors Iona. It is from the soundtrack of a movie about Iona and St. Columba.

June 10   *The Great Staircase*

Focus

As we extend our aid to those whom we can help, so will those who have already attained be able in their turn to help us. From the lowest to the highest, we... on the Path are bound together by one long chain of mutual service; none need feel neglected or alone; though the lower flights of the great staircase may be wreathed in mist, we know that it leads up to happier regions and purer air, where the light is always shining.

C. W. Leadbeater

Meditation

Even as you bend to help another up the great staircase of unfoldment, others are lifting you toward the light.

Invisible helpers surround you; mutual service is the great connection.

Through the mists of uncertainty, you can be assured of eventually reaching the upper flights where light is always shining.

Musical Keynotes

William Mundy, *Vox Patris Caelestis, Voice of the Celestial Father* (Tallis Scholars—Angel). Certain pieces of music, often composed to be sung in the great cathedrals of Europe, unfold like a spiral, lifting the listener as though he were ascending a great staircase into the heavens. Other examples of such music, in addition to the Mundy work, include Palestrina's *Pope Marcellus Mass*, anthems by Thomas Tallis, especially *Spem in Alium*, and the Masses of William Byrd. This type of music, although not good for grounded work, is excellent for meditation and visualization. The energy rises to the higher chakras.

Alessandro Scarlatti, *O Great Mystery* (Norrington—Argo). This music, for double choir, is serene and beautiful. The final Alleluia section rises into majesty.

June 11	*Deliverance*

Focus   From the heavenly spaces come sounds mightily to greet you with deliverance from the world and transfiguration of the world. Your passing..., and then all is peaceful.

                                                    Richard Strauss

Meditation   There is a magical time of transition—from moment to moment and from life to life.

As you move from old patterns, deliverance comes to you, offering new solutions, new choices and new, appropriate action.

Today welcome the heavenly spaces that come to you at these times of change.

Musical Keynotes   Richard Strauss, *Death and Transfiguration*, for orchestra (Previn—Angel); *Four Last Songs*, for soloist and orchestra (Norman, Masur—Philips). These works, both in their exquisite ways, describe earthly transition and deliverance into the greater light of God.

> O broad, still peace,
> So deep in the sunset,
> how tired of wandering are we—
> could this perhaps be death?
>   Joseph von Eichendorff

June 12   **Divine Delight**

Focus   Love, Joy and Beauty are the fundamental deter-
                   minates of the Divine Delight of Existence.... One
                   who loves God finds the object of his love every-
                   where; the spiritual man, the intellectual, the sen-
                   suous, the aesthetic all do this in their own fashion
                   and must do it if they would find embracingly the
                   Knowledge, the Beauty, the Joy or the Divinity
                   which they seek.   Sri Aurobindo

Meditation   Finding delight in God leads to a fruitful life.

                   Today, in the spirit of love, joy and beauty, sense
                   the delight of God that fills the universe.

Musical   Werner Josten, *Concerto Sacro I-II* (Stokowski—
Keynotes   CRI). This beautiful, florid work, for piano and
                   orchestra, is filled with melodic tunes and good
                   energy.

                   Dawn Chorus, Birds of Morning, Pro Musica (Sine
                   Qua Non). Just birds, many different birds, sing-
                   ing their joyous songs. This music is presented as
                   background to the program "Morning Pro
                   Musica," with host Robert J. Lurtsema.

June 13   **The Steadfast Heart**

Focus   Whoever praises God, sings. If you do not sing, you
                   are not deeply affected. Gregorian chant is a
                   perfect form of expression for the steadfast heart.
                   "My heart is steadfast, O God, my heart is stead-
                   fast! I will sing and make melody."
                                              Gerardus van der Leeuw

Meditation   Today, in whatever forms are comfortable for you,
                   sing and make melody.

You can sing at home, on the way to work, on your break, or wherever you are.

The song you sing vibrates through you, activating your inner divinity, making you steadfast in your spiritual journey.

Musical Nicanor Zabaleta, *Baroque Harp Music*
Keynotes (Zabaleta—DGG). Selections from J. S. Bach, Handel and Viotti mark this album as a joyful expression of steadfastness.

Music of the Weston Priory: Listen (Weston Priory, Weston, VT 05161). Sacred songs sung by the monks of the priory bring the qualities of joy and steadfastness.

June 14   # Childhood

Focus The things which the child loves remain in the domain of the heart until old age. The most beautiful thing in life is that our souls remain hovering over the places where we once enjoyed ourselves.
                                                Kahlil Gibran

Meditation Take the time today to look back in imagination to a favorite place. When you were a child, you visited this place and felt happy there.

You can go there again, now. Feel the happiness, the joy, the peace.

You can always return to the beautiful place you remember and be strengthened by touching roots and pleasing memories of childhood.

Musical Jean Cras, *Scenes of Children* (Stoll—Cybelia).
Keynotes This orchestral music describes the movements, the feelings and the world of children.

Steven Halpern, *Lullabies and Sweet Dreams* (Halpern Sounds). Side 2 is especially lovely since it plays the children's songs against a background of a rippling stream. Many of the children's traditional favorites are included here, and they are the stronger pieces: *Rockabye Baby, Beautiful Dreamer, Blue Danube, Frère Jacques, Twinkle, Twinkle, Little Star.*

June 15	## *Reminiscences*
Focus	Every one of my reminiscences—insignificant or sentimental—contributed largely to my personality.... Every one of them was significant and important. Edvard Grieg
Meditation	Today, for a few minutes, reminisce. Recall those memories that are most significant.
	Feel the mingling of joys and sorrows, the ways that everything counted, moving together to shape your life.
	Often what seems insignificant at the time later plays its part and becomes an important thread, linking your past and present.
	Today, as you reminisce, let the memories surface, then move forward.
Musical Keynotes	Edvard Grieg, Piano Concerto in A-Minor (Lupu, Previn—London). This concerto is a powerful and lyrical description of nature. From the opening cascade of notes to the dramatic conclusion, this great work will evoke many reminiscences.
	Guy Ropartz, Symphony No. 3 (Plasson—EMI). "I love beauty...in whatever form it presents itself.... The essential is to have strength of

soul...and to give oneself completely to one's work." So reads the testament of Guy Ropartz, a follower of César Franck and a deeply imaginative composer. This symphony is a creative statement of a composer whose music is filled with reminiscences.

June 16	# *Light*

Focus

As each person spiritualizes his life, he becomes more transparent; the radiance of Light begins to fill his cells, until the body appears open and clear. Then the eyes are filled with light, like a luminous vortex surrounding the flesh and shining through it.   Unknown

Meditation

As every soul advances, there is greater light shining through.

Today you can see yourself becoming increasingly light-filled.

The more you can harmonize areas of your being, the more light shines through you.

For each challenge met and overcome, you will be that much more filled with light.

Musical Keynotes

Alexander Gretchaninov, *Holy Radiant Light* (Ottley—Columbia). In the mystical Russian tradition, this beautiful and compelling anthem resounds with light and power. As though rising up from the bowels of the earth, the music continues to expand in radiance. You can sense how the atmosphere becomes increasingly filled with white light.

Gabriel Fauré, *Sanctus* and *In Paradise*, from *Requiem* (Willcocks—Seraphim). Radiance and light

open up from the celestial worlds as this luminous
music unfolds, quietly and expansively.

June 17   **Valor**

Focus   Unfold, ye portals everlasting,
              With welcome to receive Him ascending on high.
              Behold the King of Glory.
              He mounts up through the sky,
              Back to the heavenly mansions hastening.
              Unfold, unfold, for lo, the king comes nigh.

              But who is He the King of Glory?
              He who Death overcame, the Lord in battle
                 mighty.
              Of Hosts, He is the Lord, of angels and of powers;
              The King of Glory is the King of Saints.
                                           Charles Gounod

Meditation You can show inner strength and valor in difficult
              outer circumstances, even old age. Gounod said,
              "What ages in us is the dwelling, not the tenant."

              Let your weaknesses lift into strength as you feel
              the transformations of divine power working
              through you.

              In the spirit of valor, you can see how all ill for-
              tune can become the power of understanding and
              lightness of heart.

Musical   Charles Gounod, *Sanctus*, from *Saint Cecilia Mass*
Keynotes   (Norman, Gibson—Philips); *Unfold Ye Portals of
              Creation* (Mormon Tabernacle Choir,
              Ormandy—Columbia). The resounding power of
              these pieces for chorus and orchestra releases
              blocks. You can feel the mightiness of this music,
              awakening the sense of valor and strength.

Mario Castelnuovo-Tedesco, Violin Concerto No. 2, *The Prophets* (Heifetz, Wallenstein—RCA). This music, for violin and orchestra, brings a sense of strength and searching. It describes the spirit of great Hebrew prophets, such as Jeremiah and Isaiah.

June 18   ## Great Expectations

Focus   It is more glorious to expect a better, than to enjoy a worse.   Henry David Thoreau

Meditation   Great expectations can always see improvement while tending to current problems and conditions.

Conditions change. Your expansive attitude magnetizes change, and what you can imagine will some day be.

Take one problem that is before you: see the temporary conditions, then surround them with a picture of how you want them to change.

Picture the changes you feel to be most constructive: draw them, sing them or write about them.

Avoid sharing your expansive attitude with negative people. Certain persons' responses can dilute your energy to envision improvement.

Keep your expectations alive and vivid.

Musical   Eduard Tubin, Symphonies No. 2 and 5 (Järvi—
Keynotes   Bis). The Estonian composer Tubin delivers energetic, deeply moving works. Power and rhythmical electricity make this a musical experience of great expansiveness. Strong timpani makes Symphony No. 5 very visceral. Symphony No. 2, *Legendary*, is more lyrical and inward.

Sunazaki and Koga, *Moon at Dawn* (Fortuna Records). In a very different way, these pieces for koto and Shakuhachi flute are also expansive. Michio Miyagi's *Sea of the Spring* is an especially lyrical and deeply felt work.

June 19   ## Toward the Future

Focus   The mystic is more particularly the builder of the future because he loves. Love is the most powerful energy in the universe. It is love that builds the earth and carries forward the thrust of evolution. Love brings together great traditions in a union which cross-fertilizes even when it differentiates. Love leads on. . . to the point of convergence which is also "the mountains, the solitary wooded valleys, strange islands. . . SILENT MUSIC."

                                                    William Johnston

Meditation   Your capacity to love builds your future.

Love brings healing to every situation and carries life forward.

Love emerges from the silence and forms the music of your life.

Today, in the giving of love, you create the silent music that harmonizes the world.

Musical   Ludwig van Beethoven, String Quartet No. 15 in
Keynotes   A-Minor (Smetana Quartet—Denon). Aldous Huxley described this masterpiece as follows:

It was as though heaven had suddenly and impossibly become more heavenly. . .;ineffable peace persisted;. . .it became an active calm, an almost passionate serenity. The miraculous paradox of eternal life and eternal repose was musically realized.

This great music leads the listener into sublime regions.

New Troubadours, *Winds of Birth* (Lorian, Box 1095, Elgin, IL 60120). Simple, lovely songs move the listener into future consciousness.

June 20   **Homeland**

Focus   We come from distant heights, and to a far-off land we make our homeward journey. Yet is all distance near when it is fully comprehended. Build your temples, all you who walk the Earth today, build your mansions, fill them with light. And remember: Midnight is past and the morning is come.

                                                    Manfred Kyber

Meditation   The feelings of security are remembrances of the heavens.

               The mansions of light await you and accompany you on the journey homeward.

               The far away is also near and at hand.

               Receive your challenges in a spirit of joy and welcome.

               Make your testings become stepping stones to overcoming.

Musical   Sergei Rachmaninoff, Piano Concerto No. 2
Keynotes   (Richter, Wislocki—DGG). This famous music describes a great composer's inspiration and his efforts to overcome depression and melancholy. The final movement rises out of the depths with a great surge of joy and energy. The music radiates the sense of the eternal homeland and the way to overcoming and return.

Daniel Kobialka, *Shenandoah; Goin' Home* (Li-
Sem). These timeless pieces are relaxing and bring
openings into larger vistas of an eternal homeland.

June 21   **True Beauty**

Focus   See what is lovely, graceful and delicate.... A
gleam from the eternal Sun of Beauty can shine
through a universe; persons seeing it, and dazzled
by the sight, think that they see the whole, though
the whole can never be seen by angel or by man.
But the fragment grows, the radiance of the gleam
increases, as more and more the universe embodies
it. More and more the Self and Beauty appear as
one in manifested worlds, as they are one in worlds
unmanifest. True beauty is ever new.

Geoffrey Hodson

Meditation   Today look for what is lovely, graceful and
delicate.

You can notice the sun shining through all lives;
a stream of light clarifies and opens the beauty in
everything before you.

Today, you can see the radiance increasing, uniting
all worlds, the light shining through, filling God's
universe.

Musical   Johannes Brahms, *Hungarian Dances* (Dorati—
Keynotes   Mercury; Rolla—Erato). This series of dances
brings a variety of energies and many beautiful
tunes. It is a very good way to enjoy the various
tones and colors of "the beautiful."

Daniel Kobialka, *Pavane*, from Fauré; *Afternoon
of a Faun* (Li-Sem). This is an extended, peaceful
work. Calm melodies unfold gradually, never
rushing.

June 22   *Keeping Your Center*

Focus   I must try to be alone for part of each day, even for an hour or a few minutes in order to keep my core, my CENTER, my island quality. Unless I keep the island quality intact somewhere within me, I will have little to give husband, children, friends or the world at large.

      Anne Morrow Lindbergh

Meditation   You can take your place in the world, yet it is important to keep your center.

Through centeredness, you are able to draw continuously from the island of God's power while spreading out to the mainland of life's challenges.

Today try to keep centered in the midst of testings and stressful situations.

Musical Keynotes   Jan Sibelius, *The Bard* (Berglund—EMI). There is a haunting quality to this music. A wonderful middle section rises to a powerful velocity, then recedes into stillness. It is a great piece for getting back into the privacy of your own space, and it recalls the bards of old.

Alain Kremski, *Christ on the Mount of Olives* (Auvidis). Serenity pervades this radiant piece for bells and gongs. It is transparent and vibrates through the listener in a peaceful, nonintrusive way. The music is also uplifting and inspirational.

June 23   *Spreading Worlds*

Focus   Lo! what a world I create for my own..., the beauty of the trees along the forest glades—the hushed soft masses of light and darkness, the

mysterious depths, the thousand faerie outlines—
all merged and blending in one serene Presence.

And I wait of you that in time you also spread
worlds equally beautiful, more beautiful for me,
in words. . . , in the sound of voice or look of a face,
the limb and brain and heart, and in the beauty
of deed and action, and in a thousand ways. Thus,
dear ones, building up these spheres of ourselves
continually for the joy of each other, it shall come
about that at length we shall need no other world,
no other worlds.

Edward Carpenter

Meditation   Today is your opportunity to spread more beautiful
worlds of feeling, thought and activity.

As you find sudden beauty in everyday sights and
persons, your world becomes more beautiful.

The beauty you feel will spread and beautify the
worlds of others.

Musical   Carl Reinecke, Flute Concerto (Galway, Iwaki—
Keynotes   RCA); Harp Concerto (Michel, Froment—
Turnabout). Both of these works exude good spirits
and strong melodic and rhythmical sections. They
are very appealing and expansive.

Paul Horn, *Inside Russia* (Inside Music). *Song for
Friendship* and *Song for Love* are especially
beautiful among a variety of pieces celebrating
cooperative contact and "spreading worlds" of
brotherhood.

June 24   ***Consideration***

Focus   It is better to live in peace than in bitterness and
strife.

It is better to believe in your neighbors than to fear
and distrust them.

The superior man does not wrangle; he is firm but
not quarrelsome, sociable but not clannish.

He sets a good example to his neighbors.

He is considerate of their feelings and their
property.

Consideration for others is the basis of a good life,
a good society.

Feel kindly toward everyone.

Be friendly and pleasant among yourselves.

Be generous and fair.

Confucius

Meditation   Today be considerate of the thoughts and feelings
of others.

Confucius points out that fairness, kindness and
generosity are ingredients of consideration. Do you
see why? Can you think of other ingredients?

When it is easier to quarrel or retain bitterness, you
can rise above these feelings with a greater perspective and the sense of consideration.

As Hildegard of Bingen said, "God has arranged
all things in the world in consideration of
everything else."

Musical   Antonin Dvořak, Cello Concerto in B (Fournier,
Keynotes   Szell—DGG). This humanitarian work is a masterpiece. Many nuances of feeling and consideration
can be found in this treasure chest of beauty and
radiance.

Jiang Wen-ye, *A Confucian Ceremony* (Zhong-
jie—Hong Kong). This is a fascinating work, composed in honor of the memory of Confucius (Master
Kung-Fu). The origin of Confucian ceremony goes
back to the Zhou Dynasty, 256 B.C. Today's theme
of consideration is enhanced by this festive music.

June 25	***Remain Empty***

Focus
Riches, material or spiritual, can suffocate you if they are not used in the right way. . . . Follow your calling. Remain as "empty" as possible, so that God can fill you. God does not impose Himself on us. Even God cannot put anything into what already is full. . . . Fill the world with the love God has bestowed on you.

Mother Teresa

Meditation
God always fills an empty vessel.

Likewise God will not impose, especially when "the house is already full."

Today empty yourself and become receptive.

Find spaces and moments where God can enter; allow God's love to flow through you; let the power of God fill your empty spaces.

Musical Keynotes
Samuel Barber, *Adagio for Strings* (Schippers—Odyssey). Out of a quiet background the strings build to an intensity of outpouring and release, then recede into complete stillness. This music is good for letting go of past sadness and disappointments. It is timeless and opens up deep feelings.

Orthodox Prayers of the Russian Church (Evetz—Philips). The whole record provides a continuous mantra of spiritual feeling. All the pieces flow together, and a continuous mood of devotion and reverence is maintained. This is a spiritual masterpiece. Especially beautiful is Rachmaninoff's *Ave Maria*.

June 26	***Success***

Focus
Life's greatest achievement is the continual remaking of ourselves until at last we learn how to live.

Winifred Rhoades

Meditation   Your greatest reward comes from continuous re-creation of yourself.

Refinements and adjustments begin to reveal the latent art form gradually emerging and manifesting daily.

You can learn to live successfully according to the higher capacities within you.

Musical Keynotes   Paul Hindemith, *Symphonic Metamorphoses on Themes of Carl Maria von Weber* (Ormandy—Columbia). This is a high-energy piece of music that releases much power and active rhythms. The finale is especially activating.

Jan Sibelius, Symphony No. 6 (Ashkenazy—London). This orchestral music of nature describes many moods and changes, which eventually lead to peace.

June 27   *Returning Good for Evil*

Focus   The purely spiritual person who has a superb reliance on divine Law to justify and sustain him will return good for evil, will endure all things without anger, and will not take to the sword because he believes he is throwing into the scales something which will outweigh all physical powers.   AE

Meditation   The supreme challenge is to learn how to return good for evil.

When you are feeling angry or anger is being directed at you, it is possible to change that energy.

There is no formula, but you can always find the necessary response from your center.

There is a better way than an eye for an eye, "which leads to blindness."

Look for the divine power in yourself which is greater than evil, anger or destructiveness. Throw something on the scales which will balance evil with good.

Musical Keynotes

Gustav Mahler, Symphony No. 3, Final Movement (Bernstein—Columbia). This unfolding adagio is entitled *What Love Tells Me*. Amid sections where nothing seems to happen, a great transmutation of energy takes place. The music is oceanic, coming in like waves, then going out into the great Infinite. In the end there are resolution and triumphant release.

Anton Bruckner, Symphony No. 9 (Haitink—Philips; Furtwangler—EMI). Cosmic forces of light wield power that cuts through veils of darkness and doubt. The trumpets are especially strengthening.

June 28   *Climb*

Focus

And high and high
The sharpened hills—
Proud amethysts
That no man tills
Carve pieces from the sky.
                    Frances Blunt

Meditation

Today you can lift your consciousness to the heights and peaks of great hills and mountains.

Visualize a favorite height, perhaps a mountain top.

Feel the power emanating from the mountain, teaching you, inspiring you and cleansing you.

The climb is healing. It transforms the pieces of your life and penetrates the heavens.

Musical
Keynotes
George Lloyd, Symphony No. 11 (Lloyd— Conifer). This powerful symphony describes the soul's aspiring journey and closes with a burst of energy and power.

Kirsten Flagstad, *Norwegian Hymns* (Simax). These stirring devotional pieces are sung by a great artist, proclaiming this credo: "Love is the source of light and the root of life."

June 29   **Balance**

Focus
An important part. . . is to maintain balance. You get out of balance when there is only one thing in life.   Eileen Farrell

Meditation
Today consider balance. Balance means coordinating and avoiding extremes.

When there is only one important thing in your life, it often becomes overwhelming.

Balance means diversifying, putting different aspects of your life in appropriate proportions.

You can find a balance by not putting too much emphasis just on one thing or person.

You can live balanced and centered.

Musical
Keynotes
Bernard Herrmann, *The Ghost and Mrs. Muir* (Varese—Sarabande). This wonderful soundtrack contains a variety of moods and energies. It is a good tonic for balancing.

Gabriel Lee, *Another Paradise* (Narada). These

solo guitar pieces offer a refreshing tropical atmosphere. Especially lovely is the ocean fantasy.

June 30   ***Becoming an Instrument***

Focus   The marvels of God are not brought forth from
one's self.

Rather, it is more like a chord, a sound that is
played.

The tone does not come out of the chord itself, but
rather, through the touch of the musician.

I am, of course, the lyre and harp of God's
kindness.

                              Hildegard of Bingen

Meditation   What does it mean to be "the lyre and harp of
God's kindness"?

How can you be like a keyboard waiting to be
played?

Consider your response to the circumstances that
come to you.

You can make music today; in the tones that you
release, remember that you can be the instrument
of divine love and kindness.

Musical   Georg Benda, Harpsichord Concerto in F
Keynotes   (Faerber—Turnabout). The music, for harpsichord and orchestra, is straightforward and
beautiful in its baroque simplicity. The melodies
and rhythms provide an upliftment and buoyancy
that are very appealing.

Laszlo Lajtha, *Magnificat; Three Hymns for the
Holy Virgin* (Parkai—Hungaroton). These pieces,

for women's and girls' choir and organ, are a
marvelous blend of old and new. The older,
Gregorian style, often composed for the great
cathedrals, is fused with a modern, powerful
idiom. I especially like the contrast of the delicate,
gossamer-like sounds of the voices that mingle with
the mighty tones of the organ.

Genius

Genius, in our view, is a person of supreme
            usefulness. It is only when a person's life is
            recognized by others as having significance for
            them that we call that person a genius. The mean-
            ing expressed in such a life will always be, "Life
            means—to contribute to the whole." We cannot
            imagine a genius who has left no advantage to
            mankind behind him.   Alfred Adler

Meditation   Consider genius as connected to supreme
            usefulness.

            Everyone draws on latent gifts within to learn how
            to contribute to the totality of life.

            You can find increasing ways to fill the needs
            around you; in so doing your genius begins to
            emerge.

Musical   Franz Joseph Haydn, Symphony No. 6, *Morning*
Keynotes   (Marriner—Philips). This lively symphony is "like
            sparks flying off a spindle." Its fresh and vivacious
            energies are a good way to begin your day.

            Randy Newman, *The Natural*, Soundtrack
            (Warner Brothers). This strong and vigorous music
            was nominated for an Academy Award. You can
            hear overtones of Aaron Copland, but the sounds
            and rhythms are uniquely Newman's own vision.
            Beautiful melodies and a strong Americana flavor
            are present.

July 2   ## *Your Inner Abode*

Focus
When you have reached a new and higher plane of spiritual awareness, remember that with it comes the challenge to abide there. There is a profound sense that it has been a gift of the spirit, the inevitable reward of aspiration and holy intent. Your work is to guard it, like country newly won, so that it will not be retaken by enemies—within yourself—enemies that reach out for diversions, excitements or indulgences.

Letters of the Scattered Brotherhood

Meditation
Your inner abode is a powerful shrine of holiness.

Abiding and residing in your holy place, you will find the power to meet the enemies within yourself.

You can draw upon the power of your inner abode to center your scatteredness, to calm the hunger for excitement and to temper the desire for excess.

Musical Keynotes
Christoph von Gluck, *Dance of the Blessed Spirits* (Stokowski—Seraphim). This piece is angelic and brings in the energy and presences of angels. It is usually played for flute and orchestra, and it quickens your sense of an inner abode.

François Francoeur, *Adagio Cantabile*, from *Afternoon of a Fawn* (Daniel Kobialka—Li-Sem). Kobialka has rearranged this lovely 18th-century piece into a flowing meditation that helps one become aware of the spiritual home within.

July 3   ## *Eternal Light*

Focus
The Kingdom of the Father
was the starry dome,
The Kingdom of the Son

the happy, smiling Sun.
The Kingdom of the Spirit
shall be the eternal Light.

Leos Janáček

Meditation   Today, reflect upon the ways that you feel God's Presence.

Perhaps images of larger worlds emerge; or you might feel beautiful places, colors or sounds coming through into your atmosphere.

Let the Kingdom of the Spirit shine through.

Let God's Presence speak to you as it will.

Musical Keynotes   Leos Janáček, *Glagolitic Mass* (Rattle—EMI; Angel). This exhilarating and dynamic statement of faith radiates power and joy. Janáček wrote the piece to be performed outside in the open air. Especially moving is the Sanctus:

Holy, holy, holy!
Holy Lord God of the Sabbath.
Heaven and earth are full of Thy glory.

The word for "Holy" is also very similar to the word for "Light," and this ambience of God's Holiness as Light resonates through the work, especially in the mighty organ solo *Allegro*.

Ariel Ramirez, *Misa Criolla* (Philips—Sequenza; Argentina). The celebration of God comes through this interpretation of the mass in native folk-music. Ariel Ramirez has composed a florid piece which radiates joy and light.

July 4   **Liberty**

Focus   Liberty is as real as heaven..., but it must be earned and conquered, not by oppression, but by self-devotion; not by pillage but by generosity; not by taking life, but by bestowing it, in the moral as well as the material sense. Liberty is obedience to eternal and unchanging laws.

Charles Gounod

Meditation   Today is a day to celebrate liberty and independence.

Liberty implies being free, and freedom announces obedience and responsibility.

You can be free in the gift of liberty, and you can use independence to bestow life and generosity on others.

In true liberty there is respect, endowment and empowerment of others.

Musical   Lukas Foss, *The Prairie* (Foss—Turnabout). This
Keynotes   is a large, sprawling work which intones the American spirit and a glorious vision of the land and pioneers. The music is for chorus, soloists and full orchestra.

Mormon Tabernacle Choir, *Stars and Stripes Forever* (Condie—Columbia). This stirring choral and instrumental recording contains favorites such as *Eternal Father, Strong to Save* and *Battle Hymn of the Republic.*

July 5   **The Dawn**

Focus   Awaken my soul with the dawn upon the top of the Carmel facing the sea. Shalom!

Paul Ben-Haim

Meditation   Today you can awaken to the dawning of a new day.

Imagine an open landscape, or perhaps an ocean scene; you can feel the sea breeze, the freshness, the light arising.

Receive the new dawn. Be at peace. Shalom! Go forward!

Musical   Paul Ben-Haim, Symphony No. 1, Second Move-
Keynotes   ment (Alwyn—CBS). This contemplative prayer in music sounds like an ancient Eastern chant. Soaring strings lift the listener over underriding suffering into a greater faith and transcendence. Also beautiful and radiant is Ben-Haim's Symphony No. 2 (Jerusalem Records).

Max Bruch, *Kol Nidrei or Adagio for Cello and Orchestra* (Fournier, Martinon—DGG). Also deeply moving is this minor masterpiece—a romance on two contrasting Hebrew themes. One melody is a lament while the other sounds like an ancient hymn. The music suggests deep, inner reflection.

July 6   New Wine

Focus   Like grapes I was,
                   Pressed I am,
                   Like new wine I shall be.
                              Henry Suso

Meditation   Every moment you are changing. What is latent in you will appear in greater beauty.

The pressing may cause friction but like new wine, something different will emerge in you.

A new frontier for you already appears on the horizon.

Let it open into your consciousness.

Musical Alberto Nepomuceno, *Brazilian Suite* (Lima—
Keynotes Fiesta Polygram). In this exotic and magical evocation of nature, beautiful melodies mingle with the
force and power of forests and jungles.

Henry Mancini, *Meggie's Theme* and *The Thorn
Birds Theme* from *In the Pink* (Galway,
Mancini—RCA). These haunting themes describe
the heroine, Meggie, and her dreams for a new
dawn. The music stimulates the imagination.

July 7   **The Force of Love**

Focus   That which draws us by its mystical force; what
every created thing, even the very stones, feels with
absolute certainty as the center of its being...is
the force of love. Christians call this "eternal
blessedness." It is a necessity of man for growth
and joy.   Gustav Mahler

Meditation You can feel the magnetism of divine love moving
like a powerful current through the stones of nature
and through you.

The force of love moves the universe.

You can feel this power; to live in the orb with the
certainty of love's currents brings peace and eternal blessedness.

Musical   Gustav Mahler, *Adagietto*, from Symphony No. 5
Keynotes (Kubelik—DGG). This deeply devotional music
flows in the ambience of human and divine love.
A great tenderness and a longing come through.
It reminds one of the composer's words:

> In adagio movements, everything is resolved into
> quiet being. It is like the peak, the highest level

from which one can view the world. God can only
be comprehended as Love.

Ernest Bloch, *Abodah, God's Worship* (Mordkovitch, Gerhardt—RCA). There is an intense
mystical fervor here, and deep devotion.

July 8   *Sowing and Reaping*

Focus   Every person,
All the events of your life
Are there because you have
    drawn them there.
What you choose
To do with them is
Up to you.
                    Richard Bach

Meditation   "Local sowing, universal harvest."

The seeds you sow today yield the reaping of
tomorrow.

The more you can expand yourself today and find
ways to develop and share your talents, the larger
the harvests tomorrow.

Today you can realize how you build your tomorrows with the attitudes you live by today.

The more beautifully and willingly you do what
is put in front of you, the more tends to open for
you, in time.

Musical   Percy Grainger, *Danish Folk-Music Suite,*
Keynotes   *Youthful Suite* (Hopkins—RCA). Both of these
lovely suites show Grainger at his tuneful, melodic
best. Especially beautiful is the selection called *The
Power of Love*.

Kathryn Tickell, *On Kielder Side*, Northumbrian
Pipes and Fiddle (Musical Heritage). Continuing

in the folk vein, these jigs and reels offer power and excitement.

July 9   *Adoration*

Focus   Behold the Great Lord!
                 Bless the Lord!
                 Sing the Hymn to God!
                 Alleluia!
                         Ottorino Respighi

Meditation   Open yourself today to the majesty and grandeur of God.

                 Creation rings with bells and sounds of trumpets, as the organ resounds like the voices of Heaven.

                 Let the magnificent music of God's grandeur resound through you in whatever ways are open to you.

Musical   Ottorino Respighi, *Church Windows* (Simon—
Keynotes   Chandos). These four beautiful tone poems bespeak the grandeur of God. The music is scored imaginatively for full orchestra. In the last of the four pictures, a great organ erupts, blazing forth with the glory of the celestial hierarchies.

                 Ottorino Respighi, *Adoration of the Magi; Birth of Venus* from *The Botticellian Triptych* (Marriner—Angel). This music is fresh and alive. In its own way it inspires vitality and adoration.

July 10   *Universal Currents*

Focus   I am convinced that there are universal currents of Divine Thought vibrating the ether everywhere, and anyone who can feel these vibrations is inspired provided he is conscious of the process and possesses the knowledge and skill to present them in a convincing manner—be he a composer, architect, painter, sculptor or inventor.

Richard Wagner

Meditation Deep currents of divine thought surround you.

Inspiration and progress are possible to anyone who feels their vibrations.

Today take the time to open up to the pulsations: you can feel the energy descending, entering through the top of your head, swirling into you, filling you from head to toes.

Musical Keynotes Henryk Wieniawski, *Legend for Violin and Orchestra* (Friedman, Sargent—RCA). This impassioned, contemplative music expresses the currents and vibrations of God's Presence.

Carl Orff, *Carmina Burana* (Previn—Angel; Frühbeck de Burgos—Angel). These ancient monks' songs are clothed in powerful, dramatic melodies and rhythms. There is a strong, exciting quality to this music, as well as some introspective moments, such as *In trutina*.

July 11   **Flow**

Focus Rhythm in music creates a particular flow of energy. The vibrations of music can change your being. Music creates the tone of your life.

Dane Rudhyar

Meditation It is important to stay in the flow of life.

You can sense when you are going with the flow and when you are going against it.

Often an event or a piece of music or a new decision can help you find the center again, the central flow of energy leading and supporting you.

You can find the central current of your life and
move with it.

Musical   Franz Joseph Haydn, Concerto in D (De Larrocha,
Keynotes   Zinman—London). This sparkling piece, for piano
and orchestra, emanates excitement and a pleasing flow.

Tony Scott, *Music for Zen Meditation* (Verve).
This is another pleasing experience. The music is
easy and non-threatening, very relaxing.

July 12   **Rainbow**

Focus   Is not the rainbow a faint vision of God's face?
How glorious should be the life of man passed
under this arch? What more remarkable
phenomenon than a rainbow?
                                    Henry David Thoreau

Meditation In the rainbow you can sense the glowing colors
of a limitless spectrum.

The rainbow is completed into a circle—above and
below.

The arch we see reflects divine order into our
world.

The visible rainbow suggests your arch of triumph.

Musical   Janis Ivanov, *Rainbow* (Sinaisky—Melodiya);
Keynotes   George Butterworth, *Two English Idylls; The
Banks of Green Willow; A Shropshire Lad*
(Boult—HNH; Marriner—Argo). These are four
of the loveliest nature poems in English music.

They are orchestral pieces that offer a sense of rainbow as pastoral scenes unfold, some very gently and so appealingly.

Donald Walters, *Rainbows and Waterfalls* (Ananda Recordings). This quiet music takes the listener into the peace of nature. The sounds of streams, birds and outdoor landscapes fill the atmosphere. The sounds are non-electronic.

July 13   ## Remembering the Departed

Focus   Friendship requires a great waste of time and much idleness: creative thinking requires a great deal of idleness. So it is that leisure constitutes a serious challenge for (American) life.

                                        Jacques Maritain

Meditation   Today the Japanese celebrate the Feast of Lanterns and lanterns are lit for departed souls visiting earth.

In the Japanese spirit, recall the friendships of those who are now departed from earth.

From where they are now, the love continues, even as all of us grow in our own ways.

Today, you can light a lantern, play a selection of music, or intone a prayer on behalf of those with whom you once spent time in friendship.

Let their faces come before you now, and value the time you passed together.

Musical   James Galway, *Song of the Seashore* (Galway,
Keynotes   Iwaki—RCA). This melodic collection of Japanese folksongs is scored for flute, koto and string orchestra. Many moods fill the landscape: joy, festivity, longing, wistfulness and even melancholy.

Jim and Carla Roberts, *No Beginning, No End*
(Back to Life Music). A variety of instruments provides a unique musical experience. There are many
beautiful melodies in this meditative music, and
it has an international flavor.

July 14

Landscapes

Focus   There is a great resemblance between the static and
the ecstatic...like the angels—static from very
ecstasy. The still center of music, however rap-
turous..., brings [it] close to a mystical experience.
                              Gerald Finzi and Diana McVeagh

Meditation   Consider today the sights and feelings of a landscape.

Choose a scene that is especially clear to you.
Notice the polarity of movement and stillness.

As you watch the motions and the intermingling,
at the center of your scene there is that delightful
stillness—the dance of life and the peace.

Musical   Gerald Finzi, *A Severn Rhapsody; Intimations of*
Keynotes   *Immortality* (Boult—Lyrita). These sensitively
drawn landscapes give a sense of inner feelings,
along with some outer energy and movement.

Chen-Lei Shi, *Spring Night on a Moonlit River*
(Nonesuch). This music for the Chinese zither is
a haunting evocation of nature.

July 15

Caring

Focus   Love thy brother as thy soul; guard him as the
apple of thine eye.
                              The Gospel of Thomas

Meditation   Today is the birthday of Mother Cabrini, the first American saint.

Consider today the quality of caring. You may not be your brother's or sister's keeper but you ARE your brother and sister.

We are all interconnected. In caring for others, you enrich your own soul as well as theirs.

Musical Keynotes   *Deep River*, Traditional, from *Ebb Tide*, arranged by Robert Shaw (Chacksfield—London; Stokowski—RCA). In this deeply devotional selection, blue waves seem to flow out into the atmosphere, and an archetype of a "gleaming golden-domed city shining above azure waves" emerges. A vision of Paradise, a city in the interior worlds, comes near.

John Barry, *Somewhere in Time* (MCA). This gorgeous soundtrack describes a deep love between two persons. The music is flowing and filled with a sense of nostalgia and distant memories. The love theme from Rachmaninoff's *Paganini Rhapsody* is especially romantic.

July 16   **Self-Forgetfulness**

Focus   The life which forgets itself turns to its true immortality.   **AE**

Meditation   While it is important to live your life, it is also essential to feel the Divine Presence moving through you.

You can feel at times how much things happen through you, not just "by" you.

This is the spirit of self-forgetfulness—the sense of

a participation with a larger energy that empowers you.

Musical Keynotes Felix Mendelssohn, *Songs Without Words* (Barenboim—DGG). These miniatures for solo piano envelop listeners in their own world, and a sense of self-forgetfulness comes through the music. They are beautiful little cameos, shining with the light of a larger, infinite accompaniment.

Ludwig van Beethoven, Symphony No. 9, Third Movement (Furtwangler—EMI). This unforgettable musical experience is a testament of fervent devotion and the light inside solitude.

July 17   ## *The Cosmic Note*

Focus Each vibration fulfilling its mission—all equal in purpose, in importance. All vibrating to the Cosmic Note by which this world was brought forth.   Sydney Taylor

Meditation The great Om surrounds you with its sounds.

Celestial harmonies ring through the earth, attuning the minds and hearts of mankind.

Today, you can feel the great Plan and embracing purpose of all lives moving in the cosmic note.

Listen for your own particular tunes. Your contribution is important; what you have to give to the world is helpful for all.

Musical Keynotes Sir Edward Elgar, *The Music Makers* (Boult—Vanguard). Elgar sensed the mystery and the magical music as all lives interweave in song. His text from Authur O'Shaughnessy's poem contains these words:

We are the music makers,
And we are the dreamers of dreams...;
In our dreaming and our singing
It must ever be
That we dwell a little apart from ye.
For we are afar with the dawning
And the suns that are not yet high....
You shall teach us your song's new numbers
And things that we dreamed not before.

Rudiger Oppermann, *Santa Barbara* and *Journey to Harpistan* from *Journey to Harpistan* (Fortuna Records). This music, played on the Celtic and other harps, suggests the cosmic note in world music as it is drawn from Chinese, African, Celtic and Javanese gamelan traditions.

July 18   **Stillness**

Focus   Just as man requires time for sleep to refresh and renew his life energies, so too he requires quiet periods to regain mental and spiritual composure. At one time stillness was a precious article in an unwritten code of human rights. Man held reservoirs of stillness in his life to restore the spiritual metabolism. Even in the hearts of cities there were the dark, still vaults of churches and libraries, or the privacy of drawing room and bedroom.... The holy days were quieter before they became holidays. In North America, Sunday was the quietest day before it became Fun-day. The importance of these quiet groves and times far transcended the particular purposes to which they were put. We can comprehend this clearly only now that we have lost them.

R. Murray Schafer

Meditation   Where do you find quiet?

Where can you go today to be restored in the privacy of your own stillness?

Find a place, a time and space for stillness.

Each day in quiet, your energies will be renewed.

Musical Keynotes R. Murray Schafer, *Ko Wo Kiku*, "Pass the Incense" (Ozawa—Arcana Editions, Box 425, Station K, Toronto, Ontario, M4P 2G9, Canada). This is a wonderful, inventive piece, filled with sounds and silence in between. A certain kinesthetic quality comes through the music.

Georgia Kelly, *Sound of Spirit* (Heru, Box 954, Topanga, CA 90290). This music, for harp and chorus, carries a sense of stillness.

July 19   *Excellence*

Focus A love of excellence makes the small thing a source of satisfaction.

On the inner planes thorough work creates archetypes that ensoul the object as long as they exist.
Flower A. Newhouse

Meditation Feelings are important; they create energies around you and whatever you touch.

Excellence and a love of good quality help you to rise above mediocrity.

You can do just enough to get by, or you can live in the spirit of excellence—taking joy and care in whatever you do.

Musical Keynotes Padre Antonio Soler, *Six Concertos for Two Organs* (Biggs—Columbia). These joyful, majestic pieces, played antiphonally, proclaim the crown of excellence. A resonant quality provides openings in the energy field of the listener.

Richard Wagner, *Die Meistersinger*, Overtures and Preludes (Païta—Lodia). This stirring orchestral music inspires excellence and rises into a tremendous crescendo of overcoming.

July 20   # Order

Focus   We exist in a universe of relationships in which everything is bound together in an ORDER, so that the whole constitutes a unity. This order is in itself something actual. We find order in the atom..., in the constitution of man's body..., in the world of stars and planets. We find positive and negative charges and a third principle, ORDER.

                                              Maurice Nicoll

Meditation   As divine order guides the universe, so your life arranges itself according to order.

                 You can overcome inner disorder and find your place in the cosmic order.

                 Your life shows order when there is harmony and all ingredients are playing their proper parts.

Musical   J. S. Bach, *The Goldberg Variations* Landow-
Keynotes   ska—RCA). This music of great feeling helps to bring inner integration, order and harmony. The various pieces fit together, inspiring the listener to make better sense of the pieces of his or her life. This version is played on the harpsichord by one of the great musicians of the century.

                 Wolfgang   Amadeus   Mozart,   *Cassations* (Boskovsky—London). Van der Leeuw says, "This magical music contains the Divine Order of levity,

an unearthly gaiety, like whispered laughter of
stars sublime" in their own orbits.

July 21	## *With a Glad Heart*

Focus   Ye shall have a song... and gladness of heart, as
when one goes with a flute to the mountain of the
Lord.   Isaiah 30:29

Meditation   Ultimately, you yourself decide how happy you
feel.

In the midst of every experience, you can find your
song.

Remember the power of gladness when you sing
your song; the heights of strength that your music
will contact from the mountain of the Lord.

Musical   Isaac Stern, *Romance* (Columbia). This is an
Keynotes   album of miniatures for violin and orchestra. Isaac
Stern plays many melodies, and the music breathes
with various soulful, poetic moods. There is real
magic in these renderings of some of the world's
most beautiful cameos.

James Willson, *In Idyllwild* (Isomata Recording
Service, 2201 Burbank Blvd., Burbank, CA). This
beautiful choral music celebrates the beauty of
mountains and nature, specifically the scenes of
Idyllwild, California.

July 22	## *Creative Intuition*

Focus   Six Conditions for Creative Intuition:

1. Ability to be alone with oneself
2. Removal from excessive routine

3. Taking time to daydream
4. Remembrance and reverie (recalling the past as it surfaces)
5. Ingenuousness (being open within)
6. Alertness and ability to respond quickly.

Anonymous

Meditation   Take some time to be alone.

Break up rigid routine.

Get in touch with your dreams and hopes.

Let memories bring new insight.

Feel the sincerity of a child within you.

Be alert; when the opportunity comes, respond immediately.

In these ways you will reach new depths of intuition within yourself, and your life will be ever new.

Musical Keynotes   Georges Bizet, Symphony in C (Beecham—EMI; Martinon—DGG). This remarkable piece brings both a creative imagination that takes wing and a sense of classical balance.

Sergei Prokofiev, Piano Concerto No. 1 (Graffman-Szell—Columbia). Sparkling rhythms and beautiful melodies make this piece especially good for imagery. It is extremely visual.

July 23   ## Moments of Wonder

Focus   There are a hundred chinks of time every day in the busiest lives; into these chinks we can shoot flash prayers for all the builders of the new world.

Every day is tingling with the joy of a glorious discovery. That thing is eternal and undefeatable. You and I shall soon blow away from our bodies.

Money, praise, opposition—these make no difference, for they will all alike be forgotten in a
thousand years, but this spirit which comes to a
mind set upon continuous surrender, this spirit is
timeless life.   Frank Laubach

Meditation   Discovery is always possible; each moment holds
wonder.

Every day you can feel the tingle of discovery.

When one door closes, already the new direction
is becoming clear and waiting to be discovered.

Even in the busiest times of your life, you can live
in the joyful anticipation of continuous discovery.

Musical   Wolfgang Amadeus Mozart, Piano Concerto No.
Keynotes   25 in C (Fleisher, Szell—Columbia). Try to listen
to Leon Fleisher as piano soloist in this beautiful
music for piano and orchestra. A great artist
emanates spiritual power in this performance.
Fleisher's own life embodies the depth and devotion revealed in this music making. Many moments
of discovery await you.

Franz Berwald, *Play of the Elves* (Bjorlin—
Seraphim). Enchanting music opens up magical
moments and scenes to discover.

July 24   ***True Family***

Focus   The bond that links your true family is NOT one
of blood, but of respect and joy in each other's life.
Rarely do members of one family grow up under
the same roof.
                                          Richard Bach

Meditation   You are linked to a larger, spiritual family. Union
of the spirit surpasses the bonds of blood.

Today, reflect upon those who mean the most to you. Perhaps they are related to you by blood, but more so by a mutual spiritual attraction.

Your friendships grow, perhaps not under the same roof, but you will always live together in the home of the Eternal.

Musical   Ernest Bloch, *Sacred Service* (Berkman, Simon—
Keynotes   Chandos). This choral work, composed for cantor, soloists and full orchestra, is noble and dramatic, suggesting human and cosmic life. A warmth unites the listener with feelings of deep, abiding friendship.

Ernest Bloch, *Rejoicing* from *Baal Shem* (Mordkovitch, Gerhardt—RCA). Baal Shem was one of the founders of the Jewish mystical movement, Hasidism. The music is joyful and celebrational.

> Spiritual values can never die. The crucial idea...is the unity of man. My faith is...in the right of each person to live his own life decently and usefully and giving to the community what he can give according to his gifts and forces. This is the great idea of our great prophets—like Confucius, Buddha and Christ.
>
> Ernest Bloch

July 25   **Aspiration**

Focus   As is our aspiration,
                 so is our inspiration.
                                    AE

Meditation   Aspiration suggests "breathing toward." Whatever you can visualize or feel deeply, that you will be inspired to reach.

Today consider the inner dreams that you cherish.

You will find true inspiration in whatever you aspire to.

*Musical
Keynotes* Sir Hubert Parry, *Blest Pair of Sirens* (Boult—Vanguard). This classic of choral music expresses deep aspiration and joy:

> Wed your divine sounds and mixed power
>   employ...
> With Saintly shout, and solemn Jubilee,
> Where the bright Seraphim in burning row
> Their loud-uplifted Angel trumpets blow,
> And the Cherubim host in thousand choirs
> Touch their immortal Harps of golden wires....
> O may we soon again renew that Song,
> And keep in tune with Heaven....

Lee Holdridge, *Beauty and the Beast*, Soundtrack (Varese—Sarabande). The music is very haunting, suggesting love and aspiration—deep feelings of longing for what seems impossible to have.

July 26   *Reserve Power*

Focus   Reserve power is a gradual and constant revelation of strength within us to meet each new need. Each successive day has its new supply of strength. There is in the leaning tower of Pisa a spiral stairway so steep in its ascent that only one step at a time is revealed to us. But as each step is taken, the next is made visible, and thus, step by step, to the very highest.... Thus if we believe and do our best, the Angel of reserve power will walk by our side....   William Jordan

Meditation   If you take your life step by step, reserve power is released.

What may seem overwhelming can be handled, by

responding in the moment, just taking the next step.

No stairway is too steep if we take one step upward and continue to move forward. Reserve power is always there.

Musical Keynotes   John Field, Piano Concertos (O'Connor, Furst—Fidelio). These lovely works carry a strong melodic content, and they bring strength. They are composed for piano and orchestra.

Maurice Jarre, *Lawrence of Arabia*, Soundtrack (Arista). This strong, forceful music demands attention. After the massive opening with its dominant tone, there are some lyrical moments, especially those composed for the haunting sounds of the ondes martinot, which evokes the heat of desert sands.

July 27   **Summer Night**

Focus   Dim, lovely, blessed is the summer night.
                                        Henrik Visnapuu

Meditation   Imagine a summer night—the sounds of crickets, insects and night birds; the full moon and reverie, silvery silence inside the moments.

Tonight go outside and feel the dim and lovely blessedness of the summer night.

Musical Keynotes   Othmar Schoeck, *Summer Night*, full orchestra (Kletzki—Genesis). The music is redolent of night moods and the smells and fragrances of nocturnal hours.

An English Meadow (Environments—Syntonic Research). The sense of a quiet evening in a meadow is beautifully described in this nature tapestry.

July 28   ***Emergence***

Focus   Any event can precipitate enlightenment—a crisis, a voluntary sacrifice of the lower in favor of the higher, an unselfish deed, a beautiful morning, an elevated state of consciousness. Be in love with God-Light more than you are with yourselves, your appetites or your material interests. Release the bondage that the earth holds over you; become a citizen of the Kingdom of Light through illumination.   Anonymous

Meditation   Every event holds promise and meaning for your life.

               When you face a crisis, or respond unselfishly to the needs of others, feel the fullness of a moment. Let go of what is no longer necessary.

               A new area in you emerges, adding strength, fullness and finer shaping.

Musical   *The Flute of Sans-Souci* (Rampal—Quintessence).
Keynotes   Especially beautiful is the flute concerto by Frederick the Great—scintillating, fresh melodies.

               Lee Holdridge, *Splash*, Soundtrack (Cherry Lane Records). The music emerges with power and melodic imagination and is especially good for imagery.

July 29   ***Prudence***

Focus   Prudence takes the laws of the world, whereby man's being is conditioned, as they are, and keeps these laws, that it may enjoy their proper good. Prudence respects space and time, climate, want, sleep, the law of polarity, growth and death.

Ralph Waldo Emerson

Meditation Practical wisdom will teach you foresight and ways to take the most necessary steps.

Today, think of the value of caution. Prudence displays good judgment and does not rush impulsively into hasty reactions.

Prudence can help you to take your time instead of acting hastily. You can wait for the most appropriate space and time.

Your ability to use prudence keeps you in harmony with cosmic laws and open to greater guidance.

Musical   Alessandro Scarlatti, *Stabat Mater* (Mackerras—
Keynotes   DGG Archive). This is music of simplicity and devotion. Voices and orchestra offer reverent praises to God.

Kathi and Milenko, *Canticle* (Lorian). Simple melodic songs, especially *Canticle* and *Happy Song*, bring a sense of expansion and order.

July 30   **Awakening**

Focus   Christ is always walking the earth, but not in a physical body. . . . He could walk in the middle of crowds and they would still stone him. No, the truth must now come through the awakening of man's soul. But. . . he still walks the way with those who love him, and there are many people he will touch. His blessing reaches them no matter what or wherever his vibrations are.

Marjorie Aarons

Meditation The living Christ, larger than any religion, is a cosmic Presence that inspires us to awaken.

Your life is made richer and fuller by the Christ, and his blessing opens doors into each individual's deeper fulfillment.

Today you can awaken to this great source of truth and empowerment.

Musical Keynotes Antonin Reicha, *Te Deum* (Smetaček—Panton). There is splendor in this sacred work. A strong Slavic quality comes through, and the organ and kettledrums play an especially significant role.

Robbie Basho, *Twilight Peaks* (Art of Relaxation). This very bright music, for guitar, delivers a quickening impulse. The style is contemporary, and the clean chords and melodies awaken imagery and response.

July 31   **Laughter**

Focus He laughed and the sound was like music. Laughter is the pure sound of merriment. . . . It is the echo of all joys you have ever known. As a sweet rain will pass down a wind of spring, and the sun will shine out the clearer, your fears will cease and your laughter wells up.

J. R. R. Tolkien

Meditation Laughing releases your tensions. You can use laughter to break up tightness and rigidity.

The sound of your laughter can free you and expand you.

You can do whatever needs to be done with merriment and enjoyment.

Laughing at yourself helps you find humor in self-importance.

Musical   Richard Strauss, *Till Eulenspiegel's Merry Pranks*
Keynotes   (Furtwangler—DGG). This is an especially exuberant and perky piece. It is good for release and
tends to break up blockages.

Gerard Hoffnung, *Music Festivals* (Hoffnung—
EMI). These concerts all employ humor and ex-
aggeration, to the delight of the listener. I particularly like Malcolm Arnold's *Grand, Grand
Overture*, which calls for three vacuum cleaners
in the score.

Problem Solving

Focus   If a problem is considered in the light of what it
does to the hunger for God, this alone will put it
into a different context and a new perspective. It
will no longer be regarded merely as something
that annoys, frustrates or discourages, but rather
as something that stands squarely in the way,
blocking the pathway to God. Under such circumstances, fresh insight is apt to come, and even if
there is no immediate solution, one is now in a position to challenge the integrity of the problem by
raising his sights—looking at it from the other side,
from the point of view of what it obscures.

Howard Thurman

Meditation   Today you can begin to put your life in a larger
perspective.

The outlook from the mountain top will automatically enlarge your view.

Annoyances and interferences, if put in this light,
will appear to you in a greater clarity.

Your hunger for the divine will bring you strength
and insight to handle every challenge.

You will find better solutions to your problems
when God becomes the center of your perspective.

Musical   Benedetto   Marcello,   *Recorder   Sonatas*
Keynotes   (Clemencic—HNH). These chamber music works

bring "open air" and exude good spirits and lovely melodies.

Antonin Dvořák, Piano Quartet in D (Suk—Pro Arte). Bright and cheerful, this music activates problem-solving.

August 2   ***The Promise***

Focus   For man no rest and no ending...each must go on...conquest beyond conquest...and when you have conquered all the deeps of space and all the mysteries of time, still you will be beginning. A heroic finale among the stars. The universe—or nothing! Which shall it be?

H. G. Wells

Meditation   Today focus on the polarity between rest and progress.

Consider the promise—what lies ahead; the moreness of life, the endlessness of divine purpose.

You can find momentary refuge, overnight lodging, but then the journey continues. Everything comes to pass.

If you remember the triumphs, the greater promise will call you forward.

In the promise of the future, you will find empowerment.

Musical   Sir Arthur Bliss, Piano Concerto (Fowke,
Keynotes   Atherton—Unicorn). This magnificent concerto combines the power of contained and released energy. In places there is an almost uncontrollable build-up of raw power and force. Only in the majestic conclusion does the energy find adequate

release. (Also Bliss, *Things to Come*, Groves—
EMI.)

David Friesen, *Inner Voices* (Global Pacific). The
beautiful piece *My Toby*, dedicated to the composer's son, highlights this music of promise. It is
written for flute, shakuhachi, synthesizer and bass.
Paul Horn plays the flute.

August 3	## Song of the Earth
Focus	All is beautiful, All is beautiful, All is beautiful, indeed. Now the Mother Earth And the Father Sky, Meeting, joining one another, Helpmates ever, they. All is beautiful, All is beautiful, All is beautiful, indeed! Navajo
Meditation	This poetry expresses the Navajo feelings of unity among the forces of nature and the elements. Today, in your own way, you can sing your benediction on the world. Enjoy the earth, the seasons and the elements, seeing these as the beauty of the divine emerging.
Musical Keynotes	Richard Adler, *Wilderness Suite* (Ketcham—RCA). This powerful music highlights the Anasazi Indians of Utah and the Navajo. Joys and sorrows mingle through the music, and a reverence for life and nature is clearly present.

R. Carlos Nakai, *Changes; Journeys; Cycles* (Canyon Records). This Native American flute music is mysterious and compelling—filled with the mystical Presence of the Creator in the many changes of nature. Nakai, a Navajo Indian, is also the soloist in an American Indian flute concerto, *Tapestry II—Spirit Horses*, by James DeMars. A tape is available through Canyon Records.

August 4	# *Results*

Focus

Of course you don't know whether you'll turn it out if you do work: but you can be sure you won't turn it out if you don't work.

William Schuman

Meditation

It is important to produce results.

Your attunement to the divinity within automatically creates pathways of service in the world.

Today, focus on your work. You can find meaning through what you do.

It is inevitable that work, well performed, will yield constructive results.

Musical Keynotes

William Schuman, *On Freedom's Ground, An American Cantata* (Mehta—New World). This marvelous work is inspired by the highest ideals and the wonderful poetry of Richard Wilbur. It is highly motivational in its tones and energy.

William Aura, *Lovely Day* (William Aura Music). *English Meadow* is an especially activating, imaginative and focusing piece of music.

August 5   *New Arrivals*

Focus   Already the new men and women are dotted here
and there all over the earth. Every now and then
one meets them. Their very voices and faces are
different from ours. When you have recognized
one of them, you will recognize the next one much
more easily. And I strongly suspect. . .that they
recognize one another immediately and infallibly,
across every barrier of color, sex, class, age and
even creeds. In that way to become holy is rather
like joining a secret society.

C. S. Lewis

Meditation   You can identify persons of the future as follows:
— They feel directed; their life shows a purpose.
— They find joy in working for the good of others.
— They handle their problems well and show
  balance.
— They are willing to take risks. They don't have
  to know everything beforehand.
— They know they are not alone. They feel a
  Higher Power.
— They do not stay in rigid roles; they are flexible.
— They aim for transformation more than
  comfort.
— They can see the relationship between human-
  ity and technology.
— They are healthy in body, emotions, mind and
  spirit.
— They are their own persons, but also coopera-
  tive and not rebellious.
— They use power to empower others.
— They feel a continuous sense of discovery, and
  they love life.
— They are expectant and dependable.

Adapted from B. Hubbard

Think of these qualities as ideals to bring into your own character.

Musical Keynotes   Ambroise Thomas, *Mignon*, Overture (Fiedler—RCA). The music is melodic and carries charm and beauty.

Susan Drake, *Echoes of a Waterfall* (Hyperion). These selections, for solo harp, offer a variety of melodies and rhythms.

August 6   # Nurturing

Focus   He loved persons into goodness.

Said about Christ

Meditation   Sometimes your love will produce changes in others.

To love and be loved is a great blessing.

Consider today how you are touching other lives through love and caring.

You can find new ways to nurture and support the persons in your life—and those you haven't even met yet.

In caring you will always touch others' lives in some way.

Musical Keynotes   Gabriel Fauré, *Sanctus; Pie Jesu,* from *Requiem* (Hendricks, Plasson—EMI). This is music of a rare warmth and peace. It envelops the listener in a reassuring aura of nurturing.

Mike Rowland, *The Fairy Ring* (Sona Gaia). I mention this excellent tape again for its beauty and quiet warmth. In my own work I have found this music is especially good for release of past hurts and sadness. The music is extremely nurturing. The listener can combine this piece with ocean sounds to give added feelings of timelessness and depths of memory.

August 7   **A Quiet Place**

Focus   Return each day, a place is waiting: like a clearing in the woods there is the quiet center in the heart.

Find a place, make room for Light: in the reach of earth to heights of trees and peaks, all nature sings; and quietly will breathe its thanks until Grace meets every prayer on leaf and heart and human sod is quickened whole by reigning Love and streaming Light is glory.

                                                        Unknown

Meditation Make a place for yourself where there is room for light.

A private place in your home can become a shrine for God's nearness.

Or find a special tree, a quiet cave, nestling leaves, a fragrant garden, a peaceful lake or pond.

Go now and find your quiet place.

Make room for Light. Find the centering strength, the reach of glory.

Return each day to your own quiet place.

Musical   Sir Granville Bantock, *Hebridean Symphony*
Keynotes   (Boult, Nathan Brown—Sound Archives, Box 1112F, El Cerrito, CA 94530). In this lyrical nature symphony, the slow movement offers an especially relaxing musical experience.

Antonio Vivaldi, Daniel Kobialka, *Largo*, from *Coral Seas* (Li-Sem). This is definitely music of a quiet place—warm and intimate.

August 8   *Taking a Stand*

Focus   Lack of character—all too easily we confuse a fear of standing up for our beliefs, a tendency to be more influenced by the convictions of others than by our own, or simply a lack of conviction—with the need that the strong and mature feel to give full weight to the arguments of the other side. A game of hide-and-seek: when the Devil wishes to play on our lack of character, he calls it tolerance, and when he wants to stifle our first attempts to learn tolerance, he calls it character.

Dag Hammarskjöld

Meditation   Life often forces you to take a stand.

Being open-minded and fair does not mean living limply in impartiality.

There is a time to be undecided and receptive, and there is also a need to take a position.

You may change your mind tomorrow, in the light of new perception, but today you can take a stand with firm conviction.

Musical Keynotes   Ludwig van Beethoven, *Leonore Overture No. 3; Egmont Overture* (Karajan—DGG). These pieces are very strong and granite-like in their power. They build to a rousing climax and a great release of energy.

Cecile Chaminade, Piano Concert Piece, for piano and orchestra (Marciano, Froment—Turnabout). The music is vital and alive, with some beautiful moments.

Sacrifice

Focus   Remember the Law of Voluntary Sacrifice: whenever you are in serious danger, remember to give up something of yourselves. . .for the good of others and yourselves. The power from such pledging will be put to good use.

                                Flower A. Newhouse

Meditation   The root meaning of sacrifice is "to make holy."

                Often, by giving up the lesser, you open the doors to what is greater and more important.

                Especially in times of difficulty, you can give over a part of yourself—perhaps a habit, an excess, a talent—for the larger cause of service and the need of the totality.

                In this way sacrifice leads to transformation and illumination.

Musical   J. S. Bach, Motets (Willcocks—Argo). These are
Keynotes   highly reverent, devotional masterpieces emphasizing the keynote of surrender.

                Albert Ketelby, *In a Monastery Garden; Bells Across the Meadows; In a Chinese Temple Garden; The Sanctuary of the Heart* (Lanchbery—Angel). These are light and highly accessible pieces. There are moments that are quite transcendent in their simplicity. The music suggests peace and receptivity.

August 10   # *Taking Wing*

Focus   We are each of us angels with only one wing. And we can fly only by embracing each other.
                                Luciano de Crescenzo

Meditation   "Nobody rises so high as when he bends to help another."

Without martyring yourself, you can fly higher as you embrace another's needs.

By sharing another's weights and burdens, you become lighter, and new wings lift you.

Loving and giving, you will grow wings of light that touch the orbits of the angels.

Musical   Alexander Glazunov, *Suite from The Middle Ages*
Keynotes   (Svetlanov—Columbia). This is a magical and evocative piece of music, powerful and uplifting.

Bettine Ware and Elizabeth Turrell, *On Eagles' Wings* (Joy of Music). Flute and harp present classics such as *Clair de Lune* and improvisational, winged music:

> With love shall life roll on gloriously throughout eternity, like the voice of great music that has power to hold. The hearer's heart is poised on eagles' wings far above the earthly world.

August 11   # *Humility*

Focus   You will be able to forgive and make allowances; you will concern yourself with loving others, not with trying to improve them up to your own standard. You will wish them to be different, but you will not condemn them if they do not change. . . . Persons may slight and despise you, but their hearts will turn to you again and again, and yours will be the face they will remember when they come to die, as that of the one person who loved them truly and unquestioningly. . . . Your destiny may be one of utter obscurity and nothingness upon earth.

Yet each time, when you return here, your work will be higher and holier, and nearer to the heart of God. For you have seen God, as I too have seen Him long ago; and henceforward, our hope is the same.   Arthur Benson

Meditation   You can love others without the thought of changing or improving them.

Today, you progress along the path of holiness, which is to love and serve, without conditional demands or expectations.

The more you can love in humility, the more you will see the face of God.

Musical   Anton Arensky, Concerto in A for Violin and Or-
Keynotes   chestra (Rosand—Turnabout). This is an unspectacular piece of music that moves the listener with its pleasing melodies.

Climb Every Mountain, Mormon Tabernacle Choir (Condie, Harris—Columbia). This is a wonderful album of uplifting songs, including *Oh, What a Beautiful Mornin'*, *Born Free* and *You'll Never Walk Alone*.

August 12   **Caravan**

Focus   . . . Seeking to enter those vast spaces which at first give nothing, but demand of you a long wayfaring, step by toilsome step; arable lands with vast horizons, in which perhaps, did you but know the way of access, you might lose—and find—yourself forever; you must walk a great while in silence.
                                    Antoine de Saint-Exupéry

Meditation   Imagine today the great caravan of life.

You share the company of many travelers, all pilgrims on a long journey through deserts of life.

Feel the winds and thirst, the blazing sands and caravans, the heat and "red seething glow" of deserts—and at night stars spangling diamonds above in the cold dome of dark sky.

Today, remember the caravan: your life progressing, the thirst for access in the great horizon . . . vast spaces, filling you with the sweeping sands of silence.

Musical Keynotes   Alexander Borodin, *In the Steppes of Central Asia* (Ormandy—Columbia). This haunting music, for full orchestra, suggests deserts and open spaces with a small figure, like a grain of sand, appearing on an endless horizon.

Kitaro, *Silk Road Suite* (Canyon Records). This is a marvelously nostalgic album for orchestra, recalling the trade route of the great Silk Road, stretching for 2500 miles across inner Asia. It suggests the mystery and power of caravans embroidering the scorching sands like moving jewels. For a deeper meditative experience, listen to the pieces in *Silk Road Suite* in the following order: *Tienshan, Peace, Fragrance of Nature, Andante,* and *The Everlasting Road.*

August 13   ## *Praise and Service*

Focus   In the praise of God, a person is like an angel. But it is the doing of good works that is the hallmark of humanity.

It is in praise and service that the surprise of God is consummated.

Hildegard of Bingen

Meditation   A beautiful companionship exists between praise and service.

Your work can be uplifted if you do it in the spirit of service to the Highest.

Remember today to go about your work with a song in your heart.

Musical   John Ireland, *Te Deum in F; My Song Is Love
Keynotes   Unknown* (Nicholas—Vista). These are strong, beautiful works, suggesting in choral fashion the praise and service of God. Also powerful, in the non-choral instrumental mode, are Ireland's Piano Concerto (Lyrita) and *Concertino Pastorale* (Chandos).

Larry Morey and Frank Churchill, *Whistle While You Work* from Walt Disney's *Snow White* (Ottley—Columbia). This is such a joyful song and *Heigh Ho* is also. The tunes awaken new energy and carry you along with a sense of surprise and possible discovery each step of the way.

August 14   ***Healing Energies***

Focus   Certain kinds of music can be used to form the environment in which energies can flow most properly. What we are trying to do in most kinds of healing is to create a state of relaxation and release in patients so that they can attune to the healing energies that are normally within themselves.

David Spangler

Meditation   When you are relaxed yet alert, your energies flow together clearly.

Healing occurs when there is enough relaxation to allow for release of blocks and inner re-alignment.

Certain selections of music can enhance attunement and integration of your energy system.

Let the vibrations of great music regenerate you.

Musical Keynotes   Samuel Wesley, *Anthems* (Lumsden—Lyrichord). These devotional, uplifting pieces of sacred music are good for activating energy.

Wolfgang Amadeus Mozart, *Church Sonatas for Organ and Orchestra* (Chorzempa—Philips; Biggs, Rozsnyai—Columbia). These enlivening pieces bring stimulus and also the feeling of harmony and attunement.

August 15   *Acknowledging Others*

Focus   The true server takes pleasure in seeing others advance and finds joy in their good fortune.

Anonymous

Meditation   It is wonderful to take pleasure in the advancements of others.

If anybody truly gains, everybody benefits. Such is the nature of real advancement.

Today, acknowledge the success of others, and be happy for it.

Celebrating the good fortune of others opens the doors to your greatest good.

Musical Keynotes   Lukas Foss, *Renaissance Flute Concerto* (Foss—Pro Arte). In this energetic music lovely melodies embrace the listener. There is real joy in this piece.

Samuel Coleridge-Taylor, *Hiawatha* (Sargent—Arabesque). This tells the beautiful love story of

Hiawatha, based upon Longfellow's poetry. The choral singing is large, generous and embracing.

August 16	## No Secrets—No Favorites
Focus	There are no secrets—no favorites: Illumination comes when the atoms of each vehicle of consciousness have been clarified to a certain point of intensification, which is determined according to the initiation. The Strong
Meditation	The Highest within you helps you to advance toward the light of increasing illumination.
	"God is no respecter of persons"; nobody is favored over others. You advance according to your inner condition.
	Today feel the joy of progressing at your own speed. There is no competition, except with yourself of yesterday.
	Today and tomorrow, you can become increasingly more of who you really are.
Musical Keynotes	Gabriel Pierné, *Franciscan Pilgrimages* (Dervaux—EMI). This beautiful work is inspired by the lives of Saint Francis of Assisi and Sister Clare. *Saint Clare's Garden* suggests Saint Francis' church, Saint Damian, in the evening, as darkness comes on. Fragrances are in the air, and the fountain murmurs, mingling with the sounds of a cuckoo. Delicate bell-like sounds, perhaps suggestive of angelic presences, ring quietly.
	Tim Wheater, *A Calmer Panorama* (New World). Beautiful flutes, bird songs and water sounds combine to make this a very centering, relaxing experience.

August 17 — *Alert and Ready*

Focus

It is like sitting in the center of a clearing in the forest, knowing that ultimate danger is about to strike but not knowing what form it will take or from what direction it will come.

Flora Courtois

Meditation

Today the focus is upon alertness.

There are experiences on the Path which we can anticipate, and there are others which come upon us suddenly, without warning.

It is good to be ready—as prepared as possible for what may lie just around the corner, an unexpected happening.

The attitude of readiness and alertness can help you deal more flexibly with the unknown.

Musical Keynotes

Joaquin Rodrigo, *In Search of Farther Along* (Batiz—Angel). This is a marvelously evocative piece of music, filled with mystery and sudden inbreakings. A sense of longing comes through the music, and the journey is filled with surprises.

Claude Bolling, *Guitar Concerto* (Romero, Shearing—Angel). In this fun piece, music that is unexpected appears at every turn. There are some very quick rhythms, and the music releases blocked energy. It is more activating than quieting.

August 18 — *Song of Songs*

Focus

Flowers appear on the earth; the time of singing is come.

Song of Solomon 2:12; *Adagio*, Herman Berlinski

Meditation   Today you can celebrate the joy and power of love.

The feeling of being in love, with people and life itself, greatly expands you.

The beauty you know through the senses can help you to rise into greater contemplation of the Infinite.

Celebrate the song of songs, the gift of love and life in all its fullness.

You can feel your heart expanding as you listen to the music of love.

Smell the rose now blooming; sing the song of songs.

Musical   Giovanni da Palestrina, *Song of Songs* (Weselka—
Keynotes   Supraphon); Ralph Vaughan-Williams, *Flos Campi, Flower of the Field* (Boult—Angel). Each piece in its own way celebrates the Song of Songs and devotion to the beloved. The music combines the intimate and personal with the love that lifts the partners into God's transcendent love and the eternal.

Herman Berlinski, *Symphonic Visions, Adagio* (Korn—CRI). The beautiful, quiet adagio celebrates love and reminds us of this composer's words: "Music is communication and communion."

August 19   **Study**

Focus   My scant knowledge is the product of deep and constant reading, done without method or discipline.   Andrés Segovia

Meditation Today you can reaffirm the importance of study.

To study means to dwell in thought upon any area of interest. In this way your study is your meditation.

In your studies you begin to penetrate mysteries.

Your knowledge opens pathways into eternal truth.

Musical Andrés Segovia, *The Guitar and I*, Volumes 1 and
Keynotes 2 (MCA). Listen to any performance of the unique artistry of Andres Segovia, and you will be enriched. He was a true master of his instrument and the music he played.

Sir Michael Tippett, Concerto for Double String Orchestra (Groves—Classics for Pleasure). The slow movement of this piece is especially deepening, melodic and centering.

August 20   **Permeation**

Focus All that takes place in nature is permeated with a mysterious music which is the earthly projection of the music of the spheres. In every plant and in every animal there is really incorporated a tone of the music of the spheres.

           Rudolph Steiner

Meditation It is a wonderful experience to feel the vibrations of nature singing.

Every tree and stone and creature intones its notes in the cosmic song. Each organism is filled with mysterious music.

Today you can appreciate nature, not just visually, but musically.

Musical Keynotes	Joaquin Rodrigo, *Aranjuez Concerto*, Second Movement (Williams, Ormandy—Columbia). This is an evocative musical landscape with melodies that float like perfume in the air. There is a crescendo, like light and open air pouring in, then a return to melodic reverie. You can allow yourself to be permeated by this beautiful musical experience.

Evenson, D'Rachael, *Lifestreams* (Soundings of the Planet). Sounds of waterfalls, birds, wind and whales highlight this very relaxing, permeating music. |

August 21	***Individual Spirit***
Focus	What I believe is one aspect, one view of a work—mine—and it must be valid. You can admire what someone else does, but you cannot imitate. It's a very personal thing. I can't be someone else, only an individual spirit. Dame Janet Baker
Meditation	It is important to be yourself. You can learn from others, but only you can contribute your stone in the great cathedral of God's creation.

Today, reflect upon how your own expression and approach to life is individually YOU.

Without egocentricity, you must nevertheless respond from your own center of experience and understanding.

Centered in Spirit, you can only be YOU. |
| *Musical Keynotes* | Sir Edward Elgar, *Sea Pictures* (Soloist: Dame Janet Baker, Barbirolli—EMI). This music, for soprano and orchestra, is filled with moods and im- |

agery that can take the listener across oceans and broad horizons.

Antonin Dvořak, *Silent Woods* (Schiff, Davis—Philips). This is a quiet, introspective piece for cello and orchestra, beautiful in the ways that it leads the listener inward.

August 22   # Culmination

Focus

I wish to express in music the slow and arduous birth of beings and things in nature, then their gradual unfolding, culminating in an outburst of joy upon rebirth into a new life.

                                                Claude Debussy

Meditation

Throughout periods of latency, lives develop slowly.

Gradually in the miracle of convergence, roots come together, the bursting forth of life occurs, and there is the wondrous culmination of the cycle of new birth.

Consider today the periods of culmination in your life: after a time of new beginning and a stabilizing process, there is always the great culmination before the closing, and a new cycle begins.

What period are you in now: beginning, stabilizing, or culminating?

Musical Keynotes

Claude Debussy, *Sacred and Profane Dances for Harp and Orchestra* (Zabaleta, Kuentz—DGG). The music suggests the fragrances of open air, perhaps an ocean landscape, with contrasting moods and rhythms, which both calm and enliven the listener. There is a marvelous crescendo near the end.

Gabriel Lee and Riley Lee, *Oriental Sunrise* (Plumeria). This music, for koto and shakuhachi flute, is mysterious, open and flowing.

August 23	*Eclectic*

Focus

In a spineless age such as ours, where everything is left open to question, where the old values are crumbling and new ones do not yet exist..., the great privilege is to be eclectic—for better or for worse.   Ernest Bloch

Meditation

It is wisdom to choose only after investigating various sources.

It is narrow to choose the only possibility you know without acquainting yourself with a wider range.

Today, you can move toward clearer values by acquainting yourself with many possibilities.

You can base your choices upon a broad and solid foundation. You can be better informed by being interested in learning more about different approaches—by being eclectic.

Musical Keynotes

Moritz Moszkowski, *Spanish Dances* (Argenta—London). There is a wonderful vitality to these dances, and beautiful melodies serve to energize the listener.

Antonin Dvořak, *Slavonic Dances* (Szell—Columbia). The energy and melodic richness in these pieces are particularly varied and exciting and always new.

August 24   **The Great Choir**

Focus   True music is a temporary, physical expression of
               the sound of the ever-uttered "Word." Throughout
               creative Day, the Great Breath is breathed upon
               the Great Deep, which responds as an aeolian harp
               of myriad, vibrant strings. As creative Night draws
               near, the Great Breath is breathed in. Thereafter
               Silence reigns within the Great Deep.
                                            Geoffrey Hodson

Meditation   The Great Breath breathes upon the face of the
               deep, and the Great Choir sounds. The world
               awakes in a new day of creation in the great cycle
               of Being.

               Each moment of your day moves between the
               silence and music.

               Today, you can tune in to the Great Choir filling
               your creative day, sounding through your life and
               all your activities.

Musical   Theodore Dubois, *The Great Choir* (Björklund—
Keynotes   Concerto Records, Sweden). This is a compelling,
               mystical piece, for solo organ. A great surge of
               power emanates into the atmosphere from it.

               Cesar Franck, *Redemption* (Barenboim—DGG).
               Franck himself says of this music, "The joy of the
               world becomes transformed and blossoms through
               the word of Christ." Chabrier said: "This piece is
               music itself." It is a composition that translates high
               mysticism into music.

August 25   **Refinement**

Focus   The Christ

                   Relaxed
                   Graceful

Aware
Reverent
An Initiate

Meditation   A great soul has mentioned these four ingredients of the Christ consciousness: desirable qualities for every life.

You can relax into the divine Presence.

In the spirit of relaxation, you respond more gracefully, in a manner that is unstressed and unforced.

The attitude of awareness brings clarity and perception.

And in awareness you will always feel wonder and reverence for all living beings.

Musical   Richard Wagner, *Pilgrims' Chorus*, from *Tann-*
Keynotes   *hauser* (Mormon Tabernacle Choir—Columbia). This is deeply mystical and attuning music. Its vibrations lift the listener.

Leonard Bernstein, *Chichester Psalms* (Ledger—Angel); Symphony No. 1, *Jeremiah,* Final Movement (Bernstein and Tourel—Columbia; Bernstein and Ludwig—DGG). These choral pieces are among Bernstein's most striking sacred works.

August 26   **Resting Place**

Focus   Thou hast made us for Thyself, O Lord, and our hearts are restless till they find their rest in Thee.
                                          Saint Augustine

Meditation   Restlessness comes when you lose the feeling of resting in the divine Presence.

Your life can be active and yet centered in the peace of the Infinite.

All life is dynamic, full of changes and uncertainties, yet each moment finds its resolution in the undisturbed repose of God's eternity.

Musical   Felix Mendelssohn, *Choruses from Elijah*
Keynotes   (Corboz—Erato; Musical Heritage). Mendelssohn's music always feeds the listener, and the oratorio *Elijah* is one of the most exhilarating and deeply devotional compositions ever accomplished.

Andy Portman, *Music from the Wyld* (Dawn Awakening, Box 15, Newton Abbot, Devon, TQ 12 6XE, England). Nature sounds and acoustic piano combine to provide a very relaxing, meditative experience—a true resting place.

August 27   ***Victory Song***

Focus   In my life and death,
                    in my sweet dream,
                 In the pure heart
                    of the known and unknown,
                 I shall sing your victory song.

                 O Lord of sweetness and compassion
                    I shall see no more
                    the feeble heart of ceaseless tears.
                                              Sri Chinmoy

Meditation   Life brings many joys and sorrows, changes and transitions.

                 Today, you can focus upon the song beyond the laughter and tears—the victory song.

                 All joys and pleasures, all disappointments and sorrows pass.

                 The victory song yet remains.

Musical *Keynotes*	Sri Chinmoy, *In the Cosmic Flow*, *Akasha* (Vision-Reality Radio); Piano Improvisations by Haridas Olivier Greif (Vision-Reality Radio). Each of these enjoyable tapes presents a different side of the composer, Sri Chinmoy. *Akasha* rings with the ethereal tones of the girls' voices of a Swedish group. Guitars, harmoniums, the esraj, and xylophone come together to produce a feeling of devotion and serenity. Haridas' piano pieces are much more energizing, yet also beautiful and uplifting. Rosemary Rhea and Lon Bass, *Stella Maris* (Unity Village, MO 64065). Ocean sounds and calls of seagulls combine with guided imagery to produce a highly relaxing and empowering experience.

August 28	## *Living with Music*
Focus	The pattern of any sound form can have a profound effect upon health, psychology and spiritual viewpoint—if the sound is lived with long enough. Unknown
Meditation	Today, you can recall the pieces of music that affect you the most. Which music makes you feel good? Which music depletes your energies or makes you feel "less" instead of more? You can learn from living with sounds. You can find the music that benefits you, nourishes you—physically, psychologically, and most deeply in your heart of hearts.
Musical *Keynotes*	Luigi Boccherini, Concerto in E for Guitar and Orchestra (Segovia—MCA). This work is full of melody and song. Segovia plays it marvelously and with great spirit and genteel strength.

Evenson, D'Rachael and Kramer, *Whistling Woodhearts* (Soundings of the Planet). Cello, flute and harp create an ambient music as they combine with sounds of streams, birds and woods.

August 29   ***Echo of the Divine Concord***

Focus   Music is the harmonious voice of creation: an echo of the inner world; one note of the divine concord which the entire universe is destined one day to sound.   Mazzini

Meditation   Great music puts us back in harmony with the sound of divine concord.

You can feel the underlying harmony singing through clearly in particular persons, in musical selections, in certain relationships, and other connections.

Listen today for the divine concord in whatever ways are available to you.

Musical   Johannes Brahms, Symphony No. 3 (Jochum—
Keynotes   EMI Eminence). This is wonderfully radiant music, especially the final movement. It creates a spacious landscape in which the great abiding harmonies sound forth. Like great waves, the music finally recedes into the ocean of stillness.

Iasos, *Crystal Love* (Interdimensional Music). *How Deeply Do I Love You* is especially expansive and appealing. This synthesizer music is open and flowing.

August 30   ***Contrasts***

Focus   I consider that the principal emotions of the soul are these: ANGER, SERENITY and HUMILITY.

The art of music reaffirms this in these three terms:
agitated, soft and moderate. I am sure that CON-
TRASTS move our soul.

Claudio Monteverdi

Meditation   For genuine progress, it is important to experience
the dynamics of contrast.

A rich palette of feelings exists in subtle colors
within each person. Learn to appreciate the whole
range.

Contrasts often bring out a larger unity and
harmony.

Reflect today upon the value of contrasts and differences, not just similarities and sameness.

Musical   *In a Medieval Garden* (Nonesuch). This is a
Keynotes   treasury of sounds and melodies.

Ottorino Respighi, *Ancient Dances and Airs*
(Marriner—Angel). These beautiful selections are
rich in rhythmic contrasts and melodic flavor.

August 31   ***The Inner and the Outer***

Focus   When you make the two one, and when you make
the inner as the outer and the outer as the inner,
and the above as below, and when you make the
male and female into a single one. . . then shall you
enter the kingdom.

The Gospel of Thomas

Meditation   Grounding our ideals in daily life is an essential
part of being whole.

Today, you can consider how to apply the truth
and the ideals you most treasure.

How can you connect cherished dreams with actual behavior?

Today, you can work on blending the inner and outer, so that inside and outside of the cup of life are one.

Musical   Amilcare Ponchielli, *Dance of the Hours*, from *La*
Keynotes   *Gioconda* (Ormandy—Columbia). This work
                   combines melodic beauty with power and
                   rhythmical vitality.

                   Michael Jones, *Wind and Whispers* (Sona Gaia).
                   This solo piano music provides a unifying ex-
                   perience.

The First Shall Be Last

Focus   The more you know, then the more you actually know you are the servant. The less you know, the more you think you are actually God's gift to mankind.   Prabhupada

Meditation   All power and success come to you from on high.

Sincere efforts to serve attract new opportunities and openings.

Today remind yourself that the farther you advance, the better you can serve.

Everything that is truly gained can be channeled into service.

Musical   Johann Pachelbel, Canon in D (Paillard—Musical
Keynotes   Heritage); Engelbert Humperdinck, *Children's Prayer*, from *Hansel and Gretel* (Ormandy—Columbia). These are two of the most spiritual pieces ever composed. The Pachelbel Canon is a very quieting, centering and renewing experience. The Humperdinck music fills the atmosphere with the sense of the angels' presence.

Hare Krishna Chant (Hare Krishna Temple). This chant greatly inspired Prabhupada, founder of the Hare Krishna movement. It is devotional music in the mantric spirit, good for this approach to attunement.

September 2   **Sharing**

Focus   At that point in life where your talent meets the
                 needs of the world, that is where God wants you
                 to be.   Albert Schweitzer

Meditation   You are where you need to be.

                 You can find your talents and develop them by
                 coordinating them with the needs you see around
                 you.

                 You are already in your right place; now is the ap-
                 propriate moment.

                 Look for talents that will meet each need that you
                 observe.

                 Share your abilities and yourself.

Musical   Saverio Mercadante, Flute Concerto, Op. 57
Keynotes   (Rampal—RCA). In this bright, friendly piece the
                 flute and strings sound forth in appealing tunes and
                 melodies.

                 Melissa Morgan, *Gateways* (Melissa Morgan, Box
                 4024, San Diego, CA 92104). Beautiful, flowing
                 sounds for harp provide an experience that
                 engenders sharing and peace.

September 3   **Moreness**

Focus   We are constantly escaping from ourselves in our
                 very effort to possess ourselves. What we love in
                 the last resort in our personality is always "another"
                 ahead of us.   Teilhard de Chardin

Meditation   Today you can sense the "moreness" ahead of you.

                 You are moving forward, into your greater totality.

You are being completed, according to your ability to be taught and your readiness.

You can love what you are and what you are becoming.

Musical   Pietro Locatelli, *The Art of the Violin* (Lauten-
Keynotes   bacher, Kehr—Vox). These selections are filled
               with the freshening vitality of the baroque period.
               There are many lovely melodies, and the uplifting
               qualities of the music are especially rewarding.

               Jan Prine, *Magic Flute* (Findhorn). These New Age
               flute sounds emanate an open, spatial out-of-doors
               quality that is refreshing and free-flowing. This is
               music of nature.

September 4   **Righteousness**

Focus   As long as you love another person less than you
               love yourself, you will not really succeed in loving
               yourself, but if you love all alike, including
               yourself, you will love them as one person, and that
               person is both God and man. Thus he is a just and
               righteous person who, loving himself, loves all
               others equally.   Meister Eckhart

Meditation   Righteousness implies treating each person justly,
               according to what is for his or her highest good.

               Today reflect on how you treat others and yourself.

               As you are able to reach out to others with fairness
               and equity, sensing the need as best you can, so
               will you come to love and accept yourself.

               If you wait until you love yourself sufficiently, you
               may never reach out.

Musical Keynotes Anton Bruckner, *Adagio*, from Symphony No. 3 (Karajan—DGG); *Adagio*, from Symphony No. 8 (Haitink—Philips). These beautiful movements from Bruckner's symphonies will take you into private worlds of feeling. A love of God emanates from this music. The great conductor, Wilhelm Furtwangler, describes this music as follows:

> Bruckner's Adagios penetrate into the mystical stillness of Divine Light. His Allegros are the galvanic eruptions and mounting up of Divine Power.

Michael Jones and David Darling, *Amber* (Narada). Hammered dulcimer, piano, cello and other instruments play these clear musical pieces. *Rainfall* and *Sunshine Canyon* are especially memorable.

September 5 ## Rose of Mary

Focus There is Rosemary, that is for remembrance.
William Shakespeare

Meditation Today, you can consider the fragrant shrub, the warm fragrance of rosemary.

Rosemary is the emblem of loyalty and constancy. As such it describes two essential qualities residing in each person.

There is a particular beauty to rosemary: clarity, directness and the sincerity of love that is true.

Today reflect upon the gifts of rosemary, the beautiful rose of Mary.

Musical Keynotes Amy Beach, Concerto for Piano and Orchestra (Boehm-Kooper, Laundau—Turnabout); Sir Edward Elgar, *Rosemary* (Del Mar—Chandos); Frank Bridge, *Rosemary* (Boult—HNH). These haunting and charming works describe in music the rose of Mary.

Erich Korngold, *Garden Scene*, from *Much Ado about Nothing* (Sakonov—London). This delightful cameo, for strings, embodies the warmth and lyricism of the rose of Mary.

September 6	## *Loyalty*
Focus	Real love is the intimate participation together in the greater mystery; caring for each other we reach into Light. Unknown
Meditation	Today you can review your capacity for loyalty, honesty and supportiveness.
	It is easy to be a "fair weather" friend; more is required for a greater constancy and caring.
	How good are you at being there for others in the difficult as well as the good times?
	You can become a loyal friend to others, thus coming closer to them in your relationship.
	Loyal friendship opens the doors to greater mysteries of love.
Musical Keynotes	Wayne Barlow, *The Winter's Past* (Hanson—Mercury). This rhapsody for oboe and strings is a quiet piece, a bit restrained, but bringing warmth and calm.
	Eugene Friesen, Paul Halley, *New Friend* (Living Music). This lovely, friendly music for cello and piano inspires partnership.

September 7   **Tranquility**

Focus   Feeling nearer to God's intentions, nearer to nature; where in some respects we are free, where there is beauty and tranquility, where we sometimes long to be, quiet and undisturbed, free from the hubbub of life.

Anna Mary Robertson
(Grandma Moses)

Meditation   It is important to find time for tranquility.

You will feel renewed each day if you can find a few minutes of quiet time in a quiet place, perhaps in nature.

In the quiet you come nearer to your own indwelling divinity and your purpose in life.

Musical   Ralph Vaughan-Williams, Symphony No. 3, *A*
Keynotes   *Pastoral Symphony* (Boult—EMI). The Second Movement is especially entrancing as a quiet scene in nature, very much removed from crowds and noise. It is very therapeutic music. A haunting, wordless soprano closes the symphony as her voice recedes into silence.

Jules Massenet, *Meditation on Thaïs* (Karajan—DGG). This lovely cameo, for violin and orchestra, moves into deep tranquility.

September 8   **Discriminating Spirit**

Focus   The music of the people is like a rare and lovely flower growing amidst encroaching weeds. Thousands pass it, while others trample it under foot and thus the chances are that it will perish before it is seen by the one discriminating spirit who will prize it.   Antonin Dvořak

Meditation	Sometimes it is easy to miss the lovely flower in front of you, because your focus is on the weeds.

Meditation　Sometimes it is easy to miss the lovely flower in front of you, because your focus is on the weeds.

Sometimes beauty is fragile: you can prize it, while others might miss it.

You can discriminate and choose between what is elevating and beautiful or what is depleting and ugly.

Look for the diamond in the rough—in persons and places. At the center there is always the beautiful.

Musical Keynotes　Antonin Dvořak, Cello Concerto in D (Fournier, Szell—DGG). This music, for cello and full orchestra, is impassioned and noble. Melodies and tunes abound, and your spirit will be uplifted and strengthened each time you experience this masterpiece. Dvořak wrote it in the spirit of "faith, hope and love to Almighty God."

Evenson, *Gong with the Wind* (Soundings of the Planet). Flute, gongs and bells mix with birds, water and other animals to enhance listening experience.

September 9　　**The Ever-Flowing River**

Focus　Every moment in life is a new point of departure, an ending and a beginning, a convergence as well as a divergence. All that we are today is the result of tens of thousands of past actions, an interweaving of choices and chances, some grasped, many squandered.　　　　Yehudi Menuhin

Meditation　So many past choices influence your life today, and your decisions today shape your tomorrows.

Like a river, you will do best when you keep

flowing—moving ahead without regretting, without blaming.

You can learn from the past, working to correct your errors and ignorance, while you chart the future course of the ever-flowing river.

Musical Keynotes   Virgil Thomson, *The River*, Suite (Stokowski—Vanguard). This is a very spirited work, complete with a banjo in one movement to suggest the deep South.

Frederick Delius, *Summer Night on the River* (Beecham—Seraphim). This is another beautiful tone poem describing the waters at night.

Paul Robeson, *Ole Man River* (Robeson—Vanguard). This song describes how important it is to "just keep rolling along" and not get stuck in setbacks or disappointments.

September 10   **Focusing Attention**

Focus   You give birth to that on which you fix your mind.
                                    Antoine de Saint-Exupéry

Meditation   Today look at what you think about the most.

The power of concentration and focus has an energy that attracts its object to you.

Look again at what is most important.

Today you can fix your attention upon what is most essential.

Musical Keynotes   Boris Tchaikovsky, Symphony No. 3, *Sevastopol* (Fedoseyev—Melodiya). This symphony about this city describes the courage and rugged fortitude needed to defend a place from the hardships of war. It is a very powerful work.

Joemy Wilson, *Carolan's Cottage* (Dargason Music); Melissa Morgan, *Erin's Harp* (Melissa Morgan, Box 4024, San Diego, CA 92104). A pleasing folk-like quality emanates from these selections. They offer quickening music that brings out good spirits.

September 11	## *The Formative Influence*
Focus	The most powerful formative influence on children between 12 and 18 is *not* the school, *not* the church, *not* the home, but rock music and all that goes with it. It is not an elevating but a leveling influence. The children have as their heroes banal, drug and sex-ridden guttersnipes who foment rebellion not only against parents but against all noble sentiments. This is the emotional "nourishment" they ingest in these precious years. It is the real junk food. Allan Bloom
Meditation	Who are the most formative influences in your life? Whom do you admire the most?
	It is likely that the heroes of your life first appeared in your adolescent and early teen years.
	Remember a person you deeply admired when you were younger. See how you are still connected emotionally to this person and to patterns surrounding these feelings.
	Choose the persons you now want to model your life on.
Musical Keynotes	Ashley Heenan, *A Maori Suite* (Heenan—Kiwi). This suite from New Zealand is memorable for its appealing melodies and its settings of Maori songs. Especially lovely are *A Song of Love* and *Song of Farewell*.

Tom Barabas, *Piano Impressions* (Soundings of the Planet). This music is very expansive and stimulates feelings and imagery. It is for solo piano.

September 12   **Reverie**

Focus   In Nature the Supreme Artist has created with never-ending variety marvels of form, color, motion, sound, drama, poetry—never repeating—always creating new developments of basic motifs. The unending variety of the design of flowers... the mysterious light of the moon and the stars—pure poetry...an immense drama, spreading over centuries.   Leopold Stokowski

Meditation Sometimes you can recall the memories of the journey.

Other places, other people, other sights, sounds and fragrances suddenly return to consciousness.

Enjoy occasional times of reverie. It is enriching to allow yourself to recall past scenes and memories of the immense drama that is your continuous journey.

Musical   Salvador Bacarisse, Concertino for Guitar and Or-
Keynotes   chestra (Yepes, Acensio—DGG); Joaquin Rodrigo, *Concierto para una Fiesta* (P. Romero, Marriner—Philips). Both of these works with a Spanish flavor emanate their own atmosphere of reverie. Striking pieces that awaken deep memories, such as these, are a special benefit for meditation.

Claude Debussy, *Clair de lune; Prelude to the Afternoon of a Faun;* Robert Schumann, *Dreams* (Ormandy—Columbia). This open, spatial music

is naturally geared toward reverie. It is very good
for creative imagery. All three pieces can be found
in the same album.

September 13 *Giving What You Never Received*

Focus

Curiously, it is often the case that whatever you
did not receive, especially in childhood, will be exactly what you need to give now to someone else.

Unknown

Meditation

Sometimes you can share a part of yourself easily
because it was awakened early or you brought it
into this lifetime already prepared.

But there may be parts of yourself that have not
been awakened, loved or developed.

These areas in yourself may become increasingly
important for you to understand and share.

Today, look for parts of you that may still be asleep
or difficult for you to express. Find ways to develop
them.

*Musical
Keynotes*

Clara Schumann, Piano Concerto in A-Minor
(Ponti, Schmidt, Gertenbach—Candide). Clara
Schumann, wife of Robert Schumann, was a fine
composer in her own right. This concerto contains
some beautiful melodies and good energy.

Ray Green, *Sunday Sing Symphony* (Van
Vactor—CRI). Again, the melodic content is very
appealing here.

Daniel Kobialka/Wolfgang Amadeus Mozart,
Sonata in A, K. 300, from *Moonglow* (Li-Sem).
This is a mellifluous, easy-flowing arrangement of
Mozart's work. It is ideal for good sleep—like a
lullaby.

September 14	**Germination**

Focus   All things spring from germs. Under many diverse forms these things are ever being reproduced. Round and round, like a wheel, no part of which is more the starting point than any other. This is called heavenly equilibrium. And He who holds the scales is God.   Chuang-tsu

Meditation   Consider the marvelous spectrum of creation.

Creation is like a great wheel ever turning, active and dynamic, like a great firecracker exploding outward.

All parts are equally important to the wheel. Without any one part, it would be incomplete.

Reflect today upon the many parts of yourself. You need to use them all in order to feel "the heavenly equilibrium."

You can let the great celestial equilibrium activate and balance all parts of you.

Musical Keynotes   Maria Luigi Cherubini, Mass in A, *Coronation* (Muti—Angel). This is dynamic music bringing a wonderful feeling of pageantry and praise.

Hua Yan Jun, *Reflections of the Moon on Two Lakes* (Fang—Hong Kong). This energetic music evokes its own imagery and suggests a Chinese landscape.

September 15	**Higher Worlds**

Focus   Our music, whose eternal being is forever bound up in its temporal sounds, is not merely an art, enriching beyond measure our cultural life, but also a message from higher worlds, raising and urging us on by its reminders of our own eternal origins.   Bruno Walter

Meditation Today remember how the inner planes interpenetrate the earthly dimension.

Reminders are always coming to us from higher worlds that the visible is not all there is.

You can feel today how the temporal world is penetrated and empowered and uplifted in the eternal.

Musical Horatio Parker, *Hora Novissima* (Strickland—
Keynotes Desto). This large choral work is lyrical yet powerful in its outpouring of energy. Parker wrote:

> A composer is at times a partly unconscious instrument who records beauties thrust upon him, flowing through him from heaven to earth.

Frank Martin, *Peace on Earth, In Terra Pax* (Ansermet—London). *The Lord's Prayer* is especially conducive to serenity and opens the doors to higher worlds.

September 16 Rituals and Traditions

Focus Our [rituals], celebrations [and customs] have been diminished in strength because their original purpose has often been lost or forgotten or exploited by commercialism. The evolution of women... may also have contributed to the change in the nature of celebrations, which have been passed on in primarily matriarchal ways. People are attempting to revitalize their celebrations by understanding the origins of their traditional ceremonies and creating their own interpretations of age-old customs with rituals more befitting their lives.

Caterine Milinaire

Meditation   Today, think of the rituals in your life.

They can be small ones: having a cup of coffee in the morning before work; feeding your animals in a certain way; reflecting in the shower.

And the rituals can become celebrations: a birthday party; a yearly reunion; a summer vacation to a special place; a remembrance of a past event.

Rituals, customs and celebrations are ways to focus and enjoy specific areas of living.

Enjoy your rituals. Take time to celebrate meaningful events. Such occasions release power, and they energize you.

Musical Keynotes   Itzhak Perlman, *Tradition, A Treasury of Yiddish Folksongs* (Perlman, Seltzer—Angel). Many of the songs are deeply moving and melodic. Particularly lovely is *The Jewish Mother*, a traditional Jewish song.

Cyrille Verdeaux, *Offerings* (Soundings of the Planet). Piano, synthesizer, lyricon and natural sounds offer unusual music.

September 17   **White Peacock**

Focus   Here where the sunlight
Floods the garden,
Where the pomegranate
Rears its glory
Where the oleanders
Dream through the noontides;
...Where the heat lies
Pale blue in the hollows,

Here as the breath, as the soul of this beauty
Moves in silence and dreamlike, and slowly
White as a snowdrift in mountain valleys
When softly upon it in the gold light lingers:
Moves the white peacock...
Dim on the beautiful fan that he spreads....
Here, as the breath, as the soul of this beauty,
Moves the White Peacock.

                                    William Sharp

Meditation   Today visualize the stream of purity, like snow, like the white peacock.

Reflect upon a scene of the white peacock—watch him move, see his spreading, softly, in silence and dreamlike, rearing in glory—the white peacock.

Musical Keynotes   Charles Tomlinson Griffes, *The White Peacock*, *Clouds* (Ozawa—New World; Hanson—Mercury). These impressionistic selections suggest imagery and landscapes. They are largely quiet and removed, offering a particular enchantment.

Dawn Chorus, *Birds of Morning, Pro Musica* (Sine Qua Non). Robert J. Lurtsema, host of the morning program "Pro Musica," uses this soothing nature tape as background, and it is relaxing and pleasing. Among birds included are vireos, flickers, titmouses, thrushes.

September 18   *Essential Qualities*

Focus   Give us
A pure heart
That we may see Thee,
A humble heart
That we may hear Thee,
A heart of love

That we may serve Thee,
A heart of faith
That we may live Thee,

Thou
Whom I do not know
But Whose I am.
                        Dag Hammarskjöld

Meditation   Today reflect quietly upon these beautiful thoughts.

Focus upon the four essential qualities:
    Purity
    Humility
    Love
    Faith

They help you draw ever nearer to That which is beyond all knowing, yet intimately close.

Musical   Ulysses Kay, *Markings* (Freeman—Columbia).
Keynotes   This elegiac piece suggests the many phases of one's Path—a destiny unknown yet followed with faith and humility. Sections of great power alternate with quiet times of reflection and mystery. A sense of trust and surrender underlies the outer uncertainty.

Richard Strauss, *Festival Prelude for Organ and Orchestra* (Bernstein—Columbia). This heroic music arouses feelings of courage and power.

September 19   ***Being Authentic***

Focus   Insist on [being] yourself; never imitate. That which each can do best, none but his Maker can teach him. Do that which is assigned to you, and you cannot hope too much or dare too much.
                        Ralph Waldo Emerson

Meditation   Others may inspire you, but only you can express the true purpose for which you were created.

Part of being authentic means to do as well as you can whatever is assigned to you.

The better you do what is immediate, the larger will be your possibilities.

Musical   Ernest Bloch, *The Voice in the Wilderness*
Keynotes   (Starker, Mehta—London). This music, for cello and orchestra, suggests the feelings of an individual trying to move through mists and obstacles in order to find his way and express his own purpose. Many feelings are portrayed: restlessness, searching, some suffering, yet joy triumphs at the close.

Michael Jones, *Seascapes* (Narada); Environments, *Slow Ocean* (Syntonic Research). This combination of piano and ocean produces a strong sense of power and expansiveness.

September 20   *Opening with Music*

Focus   My friends: Music is the language of spirits. Its melody is like the frolicsome breeze that makes the strings quiver with love. When the gentle fingers of Music knock at the door of our feelings, they awaken memories that have long lain hidden in the depth of the Past.

> Heartener of warriors,
> Strengthener of souls,
> Ocean of mercy and sea of tenderness,
> O Music
> In your depths we deposit our hearts
> and souls
> Thou hast taught us to see with our
> ears
> And hear with our hearts.
>   Kahlil Gibran

Meditation   You can feel today the breeze of music.

Let beautiful melodies and powerful energies of music sweep over you and penetrate you.

Music has the power to awaken deep memories stored inside you.

Music can strengthen your soul and open your heart to the quiver of love.

Musical   Ildebrando Pizzetti, Piano Concerto (Borini,
Keynotes   Alberth—RCA). This lovely music, for piano and full orchestra, will fill you with beautiful, lyrical power. It is pictorial, and has the ability to open feelings. The composer said, "Music must be song, even when it is not sung. It must possess a lyrical impulse."

Ildebrando Pizetti, *Concerto for the Seasons* (Gardelli—London). Another beautiful pastoral piece for orchestra.

September 21   **Music and Eternity**

Focus   Music, being identical with Heaven, isn't a thing of momentary thrills, or even hourly ones: it's a condition of eternity.

Gustav Holst

Meditation   Music can open the way to the heavens.

You can hear music that will give you momentary thrills, and music can stimulate your senses.

But the greatest music echoes the heavens and resonates with the celestial imprint singing in you.

Musical   Gustav Holst, *Two Songs from The Coming of*
Keynotes   *Christ*, from *Songs of the Host of Heaven* (Aston—

University of East Anglia). This is incidental music from John Masefield's mystery play *The Coming of Christ*. The trumpet and celestial choir announce their presence with these words:

A new Life enters Earth, Who will make clear
The Beauty, within touch, of God the King;
O mortals, praise Him! O awake and sing!

Thomas de Hartmann, *Journey to Inaccessible Places* (Box 5961, Grand Central Station, New York, NY 10163). The music is mysterious and otherworldly, with a strong Oriental quality to the flow and the rhythms. It takes the listener on a timeless journey.

September 22	*Continuity*

Focus

The spiritual content of music, especially as found in the late music of Beethoven, can point directly to the evidence that LIFE IS CONTINUOUS and goes beyond this bodily shell we inhabit temporarily.   John Lill

Meditation

Behind the great succession of shapes and forms, each life continues its journey.

Today, you can feel the great continuity of life; through multiple experiences your life moves through the limitless reach of eternity.

Let the music playing through you open your shell: you move along on the great ocean of continuous life.

Musical Keynotes

Mikolajus Ciurlionis, *The Sea* (Melodiya). This is a vast and lovely piece of music, with long melodies and very suggestive imagery.

Gabriel Lee, *Heavenly Moon* (Plumeria). Especially beautiful in its flowing sense of continuity is *Heaven's River*, for solo koto.

September 23   **Struggle**

Focus   There is a law of man's nature to the effect that the more opposition a person faces the better his chances are of getting ahead.... The essence of life is struggle. Strength comes from struggle, weakness from ease.   Alfred Montapert

Meditation A productive life must offer variety and a certain friction and struggle.

An easy and predictable life is like strings on a violin that go slack.

You can decide today the appropriate proportion of struggle and ease you desire.

Strength develops from struggle.

Musical   Norman Cazden, *Three Ballads from the Catskills*
Keynotes   (Buketoff—CRI). This music has beautiful melodies, and the energies range from struggle to repose and serenity. *The Lass of Glenshee* is especially lovely.

Ernest Gold, *Exodus,* Soundtrack (RCA). The struggle and the longing of the Hebrew people for their land is described here. There is a strength and a sense of destiny.

William Dawson, *Negro Folksong Symphony* (Stokowski—Vanguard). This is another piece that describes suffering and struggle. There is a nobility in this music.

September 24   **Home Environment**

Focus   Homes should have paintings; homes should have music. The arts are the instruments for the manifestation of ideals.

Manly P. Hall

Meditation   The arts quicken your feelings for the beautiful.

When you are inspired in the presence of great music and great paintings, your ideals for this lifetime are more likely to find form.

In your home or at the office, create your own environment of sound and color.

You can enjoy continuously many varieties of music and painting.

In this way you can receive nourishment from your environment.

Your earthly residence can radiate the music and colors of rooms in eternity.

Musical   Antonin Dvořak, *My Home*, Overture (Kertesz—
Keynotes   Vox). An intimate piece of music, suggesting homeland and family.

Stephen Foster, *Songs, Americana Volume V* (Gregg Smith Singers—Turnabout). These beautiful songs suggest home and family and friendship.

September 25   **Invisible Helpers**

Focus   I owe my life work to angelic intelligences and those invisible helpers whom I try to follow as a spiritually blind man must be led through life.

Alan Hovhaness

Meditation   You are supported by many that you may not see.

There is the great underpinning, a support system, visibly human and invisible beyond.

Today, as you go about your life, you can be filled with the presence of helpers along the Path—visible and invisible.

Musical   Léon Boëllmann, *Elevation*, from *Mystical Hours*
Keynotes   (Philips). This mystical music, for solo organ, suggests the Presence and invisible helpers.

Paul Halley, *Nightwatch* (Gramavision). The beautiful organ solo *Sunset/Dusk* suggests in its own mysterious way the presences of invisible helpers, which C. W. Leadbeater described: "Help will be given through those who are [appropriate]: the grand concept of an unbroken ladder of living beings extending down from the Logos Himself to the very dust beneath our feet."

September 26   *Holiness in Action*

Focus   In our era, the road to holiness necessarily passes through the world of action. THINE—for Thy will is my destiny, DEDICATED—for my destiny is to be used and used up according to Thy will.
                                                          Dag Hammarskjöld

Meditation   The great ideals need action in order to make them become visible.

Today, consider what you can do to express your ideals in your life.

Your dedication, each day, needs the anchoring of action.

Musical Keynotes George Frideric Handel, *See the Conquering Hero Comes*, from *Judas Maccabeus; Worthy Is the Lamb* and *Final Amen* from *Messiah* (Ormandy—Columbia). This music suggests the deep dedication in action that is possible for each person.

Popul Vuh, *Hosianna Mantra* (Celestial Harmonies). Piano, harpsichord, guitar, oboe, violin, tambura and vocals provide a contemporary devotional experience.

September 27 ## *Vortices of Power*

Focus It is wiser to alter ourselves than to try to alter circumstances, for often the latter are unalterable—not so the former. Within ourselves lies the power to become what we are—vortices of joy and wisdom.   Cyril Scott

Meditation If you cannot change circumstances in your life, you can yet change yourself.

Attunement to the highest that you know produces inward power for change.

Today, you can link up again to deeper reservoirs of divine power, and to the vortices of joy and wisdom, streaming through you.

Musical Keynotes Cyril Scott, Piano Concerto No. 1 (Ogdon, Herrmann—HNH; Lyrita). Free rhythms and changing time sequences distinguish this music. It has good vitality.

The Art of the Persian Santoor (Musical Heritage). This music is related to the Zoroastrian teachings and spiritual traditions. The haunting sounds of the santoor encompass several octaves.

244   SEPTEMBER 28

September 28   ***The Way***

Focus   Knowing where the Way rests,
                a foundation is fixed.
             After a fixed foundation,
                there can be quietness.
             After quietness,
                there can be peace of mind.
             After peace of mind,
                there can be careful planning.
             After careful planning,
                there can be attainment.
                                   Confucius

Meditation You must sense your spiritual direction before you
              can attain inner growth.

              Sensing the next step ahead, you can develop your
              plan to get there.

              Having a plan and a foundation brings assurance
              and greater peace.

              In quiet action you will find attainment.

Musical   Florent Schmitt, *Psalm 47* (Martinon—Angel).
Keynotes   The music, for chorus, soloists, organ and or-
              chestra, portrays the whole race of humanity sing-
              ing glory to the Creator. This is music of power
              and "sovereign beauty." Words include the
              following:

                        O clap your hands
                        All ye people;
                        Triumphal fanfares:
                        Glory to God.

              Gabriel Lee and Riley Lee, *Oriental Sunrise*
              (Plumeria). Koto and shakuhachi play *Sunrise
              Suite*.

September 29   **Angels (Michaelmas)**

Focus   Flutes, harps and cymbals are [the angels'] favorite
                instruments, although they have no need of them.
                Their presence alone is enough to produce waves
                of harmony. There exist not only the mission of
                angels, but their jubilation....Each angel con-
                tributes his or her particular and irreplaceable
                note, comparable to that of each instrument in the
                ensemble of an orchestra.

                                                  Ania Teillard

Meditation   Today you can celebrate the great company of
                angels. You can feel again how much the angels
                bless your life: Guarding and inspiring you, beauti-
                fying nature around you, bringing healing, sending
                music and fragrance, bringing rain and affecting
                weather, releasing power, attending great shrines
                and places of worship, instructing you—their un-
                seen presence is always there.

                Today, and always, remember the angels and the
                selfless purity and joy of their presence.

Musical   Gabriel Fauré, *In Paradise*, from *Requiem*
Keynotes   (Davis—Columbia); Vangelis, *Memories of Ant-
                arctica*, from *Antarctica* (Polydor). Both of these
                pieces lift the listener into celestial realms. The
                world of angels opens through this music.

September 30   **Past Lives**

Focus   None sees the slow and upward sweep
                By which the soul from life—depths deep
                Ascends,—unless, mayhap, when free,
                With each new death we backward see

The long perspective of our race
Our multitudinous past lives trace.

William Sharp

Meditation   You are so much more now than you were in previous lifetimes.

Your challenges and opportunities this incarnation are wonderfully appropriate for what you came to learn and develop.

Today, as you reflect upon the upward climb in consciousness, you can be sure that whatever you learn this lifetime will never be lost. It will empower you into the future.

Musical   Johan Svendsen, Cello Concerto (Andersen—
Keynotes   Norwegian Cultural Fund). This is a meditative, lyrical work, filled with lovely melodies and an interior landscape.

The Bach Trumpet (Ludwig Güttler—Capriccio). The powerful openings provided by the clear trumpet sounds lead into an ascending journey of power and clarity. The listener is "cleaned out" as the strong brass music shines through.

Divine Discontent

An individual who is content where he is, is certainly not dead, but he is only half alive, for he is resisting contact with all that life has still to offer him. Instead of being part of the river, he insists on being a little stagnant pool in which pride seeks to usurp and kill the function of movement.

George Arundale

Meditation   Your life is a spiral, not a circle.

Arrivals are only temporary resting places.

Today you can realize the joy of accepting your life, knowing that life has more to offer you.

The river always flows on toward the ocean. The wonder of God's moreness awaits you.

Musical   Sergei Rachmaninov, Piano Concerto No. 3,
Keynotes   (Gavrilov-Muti—Angel; Horowitz, Ormandy—RCA). This great piece contains many high moments, where the energy erupts with power and abandon, and a sense of discontent and confinement breaks through into ecstasy, as the finale breaks forth.

Vladimir Horowitz in Moscow (Horowitz—DGG). This is a treasure of an album, portraying in music the heartfelt love of an artist for his homeland. There is a deep feeling here of the "river

that flows on" as Horowitz in his autumnal years
plays so powerfully and feelingly. His rendition of
Mozart's Piano Sonata in C, K.330, is especially
beautiful.

October 2   ## *Holding to the Truth*

Focus   Love in action is gentle, it never wounds. It must
               not be the result of anger or malice. It is never
               fussy, never impatient, never vociferous. Holding
               to the truth *(satyagraha)* is the direct opposite of
               compulsion. It was conceived as a complete
               substitute for violence.

                                            Mohandas Gandhi

Meditation   Holding to the truth relieves pressure and tensions.

               In the midst of stress, you can become more
               centered in truth.

               You can find the ways to be firm, steady and gen-
               uine without being aggressive or violent.

               Today be true but gentle.

Musical   *Gandhi*, Soundtrack (Jarre—RCA). There is
Keynotes   dramatic and powerful music here, and the music
               clearly expresses the ideals of Gandhi, and the con-
               flicts that he faced throughout his life.

               Celestial Songs of the Upanishads (Susheela,
               Parthasarathy—Oriental Records). Keeping in the
               vision of Gandhi, this music invokes peace, through
               vocal and instrumental expression of verses from
               the Isha and Kena Upanishad. The theme is the
               experience of bliss in the Absolute.

               Ravi Shankar, *Homage to Gandhi* (DGG). A mov-
               ing tribute to a great soul, by a great artist.

October 3 ## *Water*

Focus Rain, a stream, a fountain, a river, a waterfall, the sea, each makes its unique sound. In water there is cleansing, purification, refreshment and renewal.... "Water [implies] spirit that has become unconscious. The descent into the depths always seems to precede the ascent."

R. Murray Schafer and Carl Jung

Meditation The Chinese considered water to be the superior element.

Feel your contact with water today—the water you drink, the liquid surface of a pond or lake, the sounds of water flowing, like a river or a stream or a waterfall.

Let the sounds of water roll over you now, clearing and cleansing you.

And you can let deep feelings come up and be released in the spirit of healing.

Musical Keynotes Carol Rosenberger, *Water Music of the Impressionists* (Delos). The music, for solo piano, is open and transparent, giving the almost kinesthetic feeling of being in liquid. Wonderful, fragrant atmospheres rise out of the music. The playing is superb.

George Frideric Handel, *Water Music*, Complete (Van Beinum—Philips). Perhaps the most famous water music ever composed comes alive here in a compelling performance.

October 4 ## *Perseverance*

Focus Blessed are they who persevere in those things which they have begun.

Saint Francis of Assisi

Meditation   To begin is easy; to finish requires perseverance.

Today examine your life to review how you are progressing. What is there that you need to finish? Where are you procrastinating?

Today you can move ahead. Persevering in a new effort will yield progress.

Musical   Ralph Vaughan-Williams, Symphony No. 7, *Ant-*
Keynotes   *arctica* (Boult—Angel); Philip Green, *Let Me Bring Love, Mass of Saint Francis of Assisi* (Green—EMI). Both of these works in the classical vein bring a strong sense of strength and perseverance. The Green music is more popular. The first movement of the Vaughan-Williams' Symphony No. 7 is majestic and powerful. There is a sense of the trek toward higher consciousness and the effort needed.

Tim Wheater, *Awakenings* (Invincible). *Memories by the River* is especially lovely and effective.

October 5   ## The Human Family

Focus   All humankind is one vast family—
                   this world our home;
                We sleep beneath one roof—
                   the starry sky;
                We warm ourselves before one hearth—
                   the blazing sun.
                Upon one floor of soil we stand
                   and breathe one air
                   and drink one water
                   and walk the night
                beneath one luminescent moon.
                The children of one God we are
                   and brothers and sisters of one blood

and members in one worldwide
  Family of God.

Vern Grimsley

Meditation   We are all from the same divine Source.

We are all nourished by the same sun.

Today you can appreciate the richness of the diversity of humanity, yet realize that we have a common Source amid differences in appearance, background, experience, and opinions.

Whenever you feel constricted or overwhelmed, go outside in an open area and feel the unity with all others.

Musical   Cyril Rootham, Symphony No. 1 (Handley—
Keynotes   Lyrita). This is a strong symphony, with spirited rhythms and lovely tunes. Its vigor is good for energizing, but it is also quite romantic.

Teja Bell, *Breathe* (Rising Sun Records). This music effervesces into the atmosphere. It is very open.

October 6   **Sense of Wonder**

Focus   To what extent is the secret of a long and happy life never quite growing up, never becoming completely adult, settled down and no longer continually surprised and diverted by things as are the young. Keeping a youthful interest is rare as people become more staid with the years. Certainly I have never felt completely grown up. And, no doubt, that is the way I have appeared to others.

Edwin Way Teale

Meditation   Keep the sense of wonder in your life.

Always be able to marvel anew, as if seeing for the first time.

Keep your sense of wonder in marriage, in anniversaries, in friendships, the unexpected meetings where the soul suddenly shines through.

Keep the sense of wonder alive in enjoying nature; listen to the song of the bird calls, the light glistening through the leaves, the gurgle of streams, laughter of children.

The music of life always brings new wonder.

Musical Keynotes
Karol Szymanowski, *Stabat Mater* (Gadulanka, Rowicki—Schwann); *The Fountain of Arethuse, Dryades and Pan,* from *Myths* (Danczowska, Zimerman—DGG); Max Highstein, *Twelve Cosmic Healers* (Inner Directions, Box 66392, Los Angeles, CA 90066). Each of these pieces brings a sense of wonder and mystery. The Szymanowski music is for violin and piano; Highstein's music is played on piano, electric piano and synthesizers.

Valerie Dunbar, *Always Argyll* (Igus—Klub Records, 9 Watt Road, Hillington, Glasgow, Scotland G52 4RY). A marvelous sense of wonder shines through these songs of Scotland.

Aeoliah, *Majesty* (Sona Gaia).

October 7   **Stillness**

Focus
Be active in silence
Strong in peace
Keep thy strength in gentleness
Rest with the song of wings about thee
Fill the inner reaches with love
Bathe in Spirit

For It is sweetness to thy bones, flesh and health.
Keep in this holy estate and listening—obey!
                                        Anonymous

Meditation   You can use beautiful music to bathe in the Spirit.

As you live more continuously in the attitude of receptivity and listening, you will become more sensitive to the stillness.

In stillness there is divine Presence that brings both peace and strength.

Musical   Ralph Vaughan-Williams, Symphony No. 3,
Keynotes   *Pastoral* (Previn—RCA). The slow second movement emanates a sense of stillness and serenity. The music rises into majesty and then settles back in the vast whisper of the unknown. A wordless soprano intones the voice of nature in the final movement.

David and Amanda Hughes, *Flowers from the Silence* (Vedic Research Institute, 415 S. Bernardo, Sunnyvale, CA 94086). This is a beautifully meditative experience, and the music is open. The blend of Oriental and Occidental is very pleasing. A poem inspired the instrumental music:

> Winds sigh. As Autumn comes, a hawk
> Circles scarlet maples.
> Her face.
> A nocturne to touch
> Beneath the cool rain moondreams.
> A year, a lifetime, a moment
> Breathes the floating world.

October 8   **Vibrancy**

Focus   I would like to write a song that is so vibrant and intimate that the earth would adopt it as if it had sprung like a stream from the land's memory, as if no one had written it but life itself.

Vangelis Papathanassiou

Meditation   Today focus upon the quality of vibrancy.

A vibrant life scintillates with energy and power.

At the same time vibrancy radiates intimacy and warmth.

As you become more vibrant, you can feel the dynamic energy at the center of creation.

Musical   Vangelis Papathanassiou, *Memories of Antarctica*,
Keynotes   from *Antarctica* (Polydor); *Chariots of Fire*
(Polydor). In both of these pieces there is power and force. *Memories of Antarctica* has a celestial quality that is highly inspiring yet keeps you alert in the midst of peacefulness. *Chariots of Fire* releases courage and strength.

The Sufi Choir Sings Kabir (Cold Mountain Music). Kabir was a 15th century Indian poet and weaver who was initiated by the great Hindu teacher Ramananda. His poetry reflects both Hindu and Sufi traditions. Robert Bly provides the English versions. The songs are joyous and melodic:

> True love has no beginning, has no end.
> As the river gives itself to the sea,
> What's inside you moves inside me.
> Look deeply at this great love:
> It cannot be annihilated.

October 9   **Synthesis**

Focus   We have deified the intellect. Our mechanized minds need to be musicalized. We have separated intellect from the other side of human nature. We must seek a SYNTHESIS. Music as an art and science can do it. Ernst Levy

Meditation There is danger when the intellect advances ahead of feelings and the loving heart.

Music can help the hemispheres of the brain to balance and cooperate.

You can use certain pieces of music to stimulate thinking and other compositions to awaken feelings.

The more you can harmonize your thinking and feeling, the better balanced your life will be.

Musical Keynotes Camille Saint-Saens, Symphony No. 3, *Organ* (Zamkochian, Munch—RCA). This is one of the truly great pieces of romantic music. The organ, sounding out and embracing the orchestra, leads with the vision, and the orchestra, with marvelous brass, provides the underpinning and the accord.

Eino Rautavaara, *Cantus Arcticus* (Finlandia). In a quite different way this music also represents vision and a song of nature in its wildness. Actual bird calls integrate with orchestral sounds to provide the listener with a sense of a unique landscape. A sense of remoteness pervades the music, as well as feelings of strangeness. Also memorable is Rautavaara's *Requiem* (Finlandia).

October 10 **Release into the Spirit**

Focus As soon as the mind is sufficiently developed, there awakes in man the spiritual preoccupation, the discovery of a self and inmost truth of being, and the release of man's mind and life into the truth of the Spirit, its perfection by the power of the Spirit, the solidarity, unity, mutuality of all beings in the Spirit.   Sri Aurobindo

Meditation Today you can mobilize your energies and focus them into your quest for spiritual Truth.

The power of the Spirit will always strengthen and perfect your highest efforts.

You can feel your life lifting and expanding, as your interests and energies find greater release in the Spirit.

Musical Giuseppe Verdi, *Sanctus,* from *Requiem*
Keynotes (Reiner—London).

> Holy, holy, holy, Lord God of Hosts,
> Heaven and earth are full of Thy glory.
> Hosanna in the highest.
> Blessed is he that cometh in the name of the Lord.

With these traditional words, Verdi's *Sanctus* blazes with fervor and drama. This music, for chorus and full orchestra, will inspire the listener in the Spirit.

Richard Warner, *Spirit Wind* (The Source, Box 1466, Coronado, CA 92118). This haunting music, for alto and bamboo flute with wind chimes, puts the listener into an open, receptive attitude to the Spirit.

October 11   **Warmth**

Focus A person may be ultrasensitive and not warm. She can be intensely curious, plying with questions, teasing, charming questions that make a person glow at being even for a moment the object of one's attention. But I felt . . . at times as though I were

"a specimen" to be absorbed and filed away in a
store of vicarious experience.

May Sarton

Meditation   There is a difference between caring and just being
curious.

Today, reflect upon being interested in persons for
themselves, for their sake, not merely for your own
satisfaction.

If you sincerely care, you emanate a warmth that
is genuine.

Musical   C. P. E. Bach, Concerto in D for Flute and Strings
Keynotes   (Mackerras—Nonesuch). This lively music exudes
warmth and glad tidings. It is especially good for
raising the spirits.

Frank Patterson, *Peace and Joy* (Peters International). I especially like the songs *Let There Be
Peace* and *Bless This House.* A warmth fills these
pieces.

October 12   ## *Beauty of Nature*

Focus   He rises and begins to round,
He drops the silver chain of sound,
Of many links without a break,
In chirrup, whistle, slur and shake.
For singing till his heaven fills,
'Tis love of earth that he instills.
And ever winging up and up,
Our valley in his golden cup,
And he with wine which overflows
To lift us with him as he goes,
Till lost on his aerial wings
In light and then the fancy sings.

George Herbert - Text for
Vaughan-Williams' Lark Ascending

Meditation   Consider the glories of nature—how the sights, smells, sounds and shapes of Nature enriched your life.

Pick a particularly beautiful scene that comes to mind and feel it again.

You can enjoy the upliftment, like a lark ascending.

Musical   Ralph Vaughan-Williams, *In the Fen Country*
Keynotes   (Boult—Angel); *Lark Ascending* (Bean, Boult—Angel); Symphony No. 3, *Pastoral*, Second Movement (Boult—Angel). These selections exude the beauty of nature. The violin tones suggest the swoop and flight of the lark.

Donald Walters, *Rainbows and Waterfalls* (Ananda Recordings). This is a lovely, quiet journey into nature, complete with sounds of streams, birds and other voices of outside.

October 13   ## Stand Clear—Travel Light

Focus   Shake yourself clear of old habits and travel light, as you have been told. Every moment is a challenge to an act of faith, but you have joy in the companionship of the saints. . . . Frightening thoughts will tempt you down the wrong road, but blow your silver bugle and the walls will fall down before you. . . . Nothing is asked of you but the highest you can reach.   Anonymous

Meditation   "Stand clear: travel light."

Today stand clear of your destructive habits or hurtful tendencies.

Through exercising stronger will power, you can throw off heaviness and move ahead.

Visualize your strength like the bugle that "blows down the walls" of resistance and opposition.

Shaking off negative habits will help you attain the highest you can reach.

Musical   Luigi Boccherini, Cello Concerto No. 2 in D-Major
Keynotes   (Fournier, Sacher—DGG). The clear and pro-
                 pulsive tunes and rhythms in this music propel you
                 forward. It is good for "standing clear."

Victoria Looseleaf, *Harpnosis* (Goddess Records, Box 1966, Laguna Beach, CA 92652). There is a wonderful clarity in these selections, played on the harp. Some of the great classics, such as Canon in D (Pachelbel), *Clair de lune* (Debussy), and *Air on a G String* (J. S. Bach), are presented with simplicity and warmth.

October 14   ## Arabesque

Focus   An arabesque suggests a fleeting moment of
                 beauty—the mysterious encounter of an instant—
                 with a shape or melody just about to vanish.

                                                    Unknown

Meditation   Today remember magic moments and sudden en-
                 chantment you have known.

The delicately colored brush strokes in clouds at a sunset.

The dance-like movement of the human body.

Beautiful shapes or textures, a wisp of melody, a breeze caressing you, a loving touch, a fragrance passing.

When you can be in the moment, alert and recep-tive, you can feel the mystery of an arabesque.

Musical   Peter Ilyich Tchaikovsky, Symphony No. 4, Second
Keynotes   Movement (Ashkenazy—London). This is a
                 magical movement when the music wanders pleas-
                 ingly, like a will o' the wisp, taking different shapes
                 and directions.

                 Hearts of Space: Arabesque (Wilkinson—Zensong,
                 651 W. 7th Ave., Escondido, CA 92025). This is
                 a beautiful experience of contemporary mid-
                 Eastern arabesques. It is important to play the
                 pieces in the following order, because others on the
                 tape conflict with the essential flow of the mood:
                 *Light Rain, Dream Suite, Shah, Kamasutra, Al
                 Gromer Khan, Chai and Roses, Minro Javan, Per-
                 sian Songs.*

October 15   *Atmosphere*

Focus   In a world of peace and love, MUSIC would be
                 the universal language, and men (and women)
                 would greet each other in the fields in such accents
                 as a Beethoven now utters at rare intervals from
                 a distance. All things obey music as they obey vir-
                 tue. Music is the herald of virtue. It is God's voice.
                                            Henry David Thoreau

Meditation   Music can greatly enhance the atmosphere of a life,
                 a home, a relationship, and nearness to divinity.

                 Today choose the music that is most uplifting and
                 inspiring for you.

                 Wherever you go, try to lift the atmosphere by in-
                 wardly making beautiful music.

Musical   Dag Wiren, *Serenade for Orchestra* (Somary—
Keynotes   Vanguard). This is an extremely pleasant piece of
                 music, unfolding in its own natural, melodic way.
                 It creates a warm, unthreatening atmosphere.

Daniel Kobialka and Steven Halpern, *Recollections* (Halpern Sounds). I especially like the rendition of Brahms, *Lullaby* and *Greensleeves*. Halpern, who often interprets other sources and materials, shows how meaningful and transformative the great classics can be. It is interesting how many New Age composers borrow themes and inspiration from the great composers and re-clothe them into a New Age format.

October 16   # Wings of the Soul

Focus   There are moments when the soul takes wings: what it has to remember, it remembers; what it loves, it loves still more; what it longs for, to that it flies.   Fiona Macleod, *Iona*

Meditation   Certain experiences can stimulate deep memories in your soul.

A great love can expand you toward love that is eternal.

And, if you sense a great longing, your soul will not rest until it realizes its deepest desires.

Take the time today to contact and feel your soul's deep yearnings.

Your soul remembers, your soul loves deeply, and your soul flies toward what it most deeply cherishes.

Musical   Erich Korngold, *Garden Scene*, from *Much Ado*
Keynotes   *About Nothing;* E. Ponce, *Estrellita, Little Star;* Jules Massenet, *Meditation*, from *Thais* (Sakonov—London). All three pieces are intimate cameos that give wings to the soul.

Karl Goldmark, *In the Garden*, from *Rustic Wedding Symphony* (Previn—Angel). This is yet another orchestral cameo with a sense of quiet beauty.

October 17   *Choosing the Good*

Focus   Satan said, "You shall be as gods, knowing good and evil." God says, "You shall be as gods, knowing good and evil, and choosing the good."
George MacDonald

Meditation   Through knowledge and free will, you can overcome the struggle between the lower and the higher in you.

Knowledge is not enough; a choice is required.

The decision must be made: correction of ignorance and self-will can occur when you decide to choose the highest within you.

Musical   Herbert Howells, *Hymn of Paradise* (Willcocks—
Keynotes   EMI). The "white radiance of eternity" is portrayed nobly in this music. The final choral section's text is taken from the *Salisbury Diurnal:*

> Holy is the true light, and passing wonderful,
> Lending radiance to them that endured in the heat
>   of conflict.

Heraclius Djabadary, *Georgian Rhapsody* (de Froment—Qualiton). Beautiful Oriental coloring emerges from this music; there is nostalgia, and also a great joy sounds forth.

October 18   *Serendipity*

Focus   Serendipity is the faculty of making happy and unexpected discoveries by accident.
Horace Walpole

Meditation   What seem to be "happy accidents" occur through divine grace and through your own just dues.

Your constructive efforts, whether conscious or unconscious, can magnetize serendipity.

Musical Keynotes   Cesar Franck, *Psyché* (Strauss—Connoisseur Society). This is music of enchantment and strong feeling. It evokes another world, a world of dreams and interior landscapes, even of angels, that is very conducive to serendipity experiences.

Paul Sutin, *Serendipity* (Real to Reel, 1001 J. Bridgeway, Suite 440, Sausalito, CA 94965). This is strong and joyful music for keyboard, acoustic guitar, flowing water, birds and light percussion. The energy is open, kinetic and strengthening.

October 19   # Perception

Focus   The sweetness of music, the loveliness of nature, the beauties of color and form are, at times, intolerably sweet reminders, inklings of eternity, of an eternal world, lying beyond immediate perception.
J. B. Phillips

Meditation   Perception can be heightened by beautiful music, the glories of nature, and the vibrancy of colors.

Each day you are given reminders through your senses of a world beyond your present location in time, yet interpenetrating it.

Today open up to inklings of eternity. Try to sense another world already affecting you, ineffably beautiful, joyous and full of wonders.

Musical Keynotes   Antonin Dvořak, *Four Romantic Pieces* (Luca, Schoenfield—Nonesuch). These delightful pieces, for violin and piano, are filled with the joys and glistening colors of nature. The music quickens perception and feeling.

Iasos, *Jeweled Space* (Interdimensional Music, Box 594 Waldo Pt., Sausalito, CA 94965). *The Valley of Enchimed Peace* is especially vibrant and flowing.

October 20 ## Hills, Meadows and Streams

Focus
Thou Beautiful! From every dreamy hill
What eye but wanders with Thee at thy will,
Imagining thy silver course unseen,
Conveyed by two attendant streams of green.
Robert Underwood Johnson

Meditation
Visualize today a scene, in nature, a favorite of yours.

Go there in consciousness, lifting out of the thickness into the beauties of nature.

Feel the freshness, smell the fragrances, see the colors, the movements, the shapes and textures in the dance of nature.

Take time to renew acquaintance with hills, meadows and streams.

Musical Keynotes
Charles Ives, Symphony No. 2, First and Third Movements (Ormandy—RCA). These two movements of a great American symphony are filled with streams and hills; they convey a sense of pastoral delight, and they also emanate imagery and a certain nostalgic power. In this music you can let your feelings wander over landscapes that expand your imagination.

Environments, *Dawn at New Hope; Gentle Rain in a Pine Forest* (Syntonic Research, Inc.). The sounds of nature at dawn include the therapeutic gurgles of flowing streams. Along the same line is the sound of streams and rain, with occasional birds. A beautifully atmospheric experience awaits you.

October 21 **Contemplation**

Focus Man rises to the contemplation of God through the senses. He can understand absolute beauty, which is God, through the effect of precious and beautiful things on the senses. The dull mind rises into truth through that which is material.

Abbot Suger and Kenneth Clark

Meditation As your senses help you to experience greater beauty, they become more refined.

Gradually, the development of your senses leads into a deeper faculty—your intuition.

Matter is an aspect of Spirit, moving at its own rate of vibration.

Your contemplation of Spirit rises from sensory experience of dense material forms to an intuitive glimpsing of what is ever finer and clearer in the celestial worlds of Spirit.

Today focus upon appreciation of what is beautiful, wherever you find it.

Musical Keynotes Marie-Joseph Canteloube, *Songs of the Auvergne* (De Los Angeles, Jacquillat—Angel). These marvelous songs describe the beauty of nature, as well as love and feelings. Different emotions come through the various songs, enabling the listener to range throughout the spectrum of human feeling. Especially memorable is *Bailero*.

Ralph Vaughan-Williams, Symphony No. 5 (Barbirolli—Angel). A vast landscape unfolds with grandeur and nobility. Each listener can supply his or her own imagery.

October 22   *Deep Bond*

Focus   God saved me, and I believe that I must work hard and study hard.   Luciano Pavarotti

Meditation   Today consider your deepest bond.

Like an obligation or a commitment, binding yourself to a course of action leads to greater dedication.

When you have formed a bond—with God, your deeper self, others, or to a high quality of performance—your results will improve naturally.

Your bond is a heartfelt sense of feeling linked and wanting to do your best.

A deep desire and commitment to hard work bring your bond of intention to greater fulfillment.

Musical   Franz Liszt, *Les Preludes* (Muti—Angel); Franz
Keynotes   Liszt, *Sonnet No. 123 of Petrarch* (Bolet—London). The subject here is the love of divine radiance. The music was inspired by these words; "I saw on earth angelic grace."

Luciano Pavarotti, *Verismo Arias* (De Fabratiis, Chailly—London). The bond can be heard and felt clearly in this music. Especially wonderful are Faust's words:

From the fields and the meadows, now engulfed by night, from the quiet paths I return, filled with peace,
profound calm and a sense of holy mystery. . . .
I am moved only by love of man and God.

October 23   **Rebounding**

Focus   Develop the ability to bounce back: don't blame
God; draw upon God's strength. Don't blame
yourself; decide that nothing will defeat you. Bury
selfish grief; add up your joys; don't count your
sorrows. Accept help when it comes—from whatever source God uses.   Robert Schuller

Meditation   Today, you can bounce back. You can move to
overcome defeat, disappointment, discouragement
and dejection.

You can rebound by drawing on divine strength
and energy.

Already there are those on the Path who can help
you. Help may come from friends or total
strangers.

You can bounce back by meeting defeat with
courage and a larger vision and purpose.

Musical   Crystal Cathedral Choir, *We Sing the Power*
Keynotes   (Swann—Gothic). Stirring music for rebounding.

Manos Hadjidakis, *Vespers* (Hadjidakis—EMI).
The composer calls these fifteen Greek-flavored
songs "hymns to the twilight and the sanctity of
the sun." There is an echo of light, deep intentions
and "a delicate scent of love." Piano and guitar are
the leading instruments. The pieces are melodic
and reassuring. The music speaks of the goodness
of life, through all of its ups and downs.

October 24   **Unselfed Givers**

Focus   Unselfed givers leave us a legacy of friendship: they
leave to the world the unlimited treasure of their
souls, a light of friendship that never can be spent.
Barbara Cook

Meditation You are the recipient of many "unselfed givers."

Some you might have know intimately and personally.

Others have left you a legacy of kinship through their writing, the arts, service in the world, scientific advancement or a broader vision of life.

Today you can receive their friendship, and in your own special ways, you can pass on the legacy to others.

Musical Keynotes Antonin Dvořak, Trio in F-Minor for Piano, Violin and Cello (Raphael Trio—Nonesuch). This radiant and joyful work emanates friendliness and goodness. It is a paean to friendship and warmth.

Korla Pandit, *At the Mighty Pipe Organ* (Fantasy Records). "Music never dies, but ever materializes into beautiful forms." Many beautiful songs and melodies played on the pipe organ are included in this album. Among them are *As Time Goes By*, *Tara's Theme* from *Gone with the Wind*, and *Over the Rainbow*.

October 25 *Pillar of Light*

Focus Each one of us is in that pillar of light, no matter where he may go to in the space of being, nor where he may be occupied in the time of consciousness. . . . The mind finds itself now and then being irradiated as from above. It is servant now, not master.   Ernest Wood

Meditation Today reflect on the light that lights every person.

Light is the symbol for divine radiance.

Light is at the core of all created beings. In this way you *are* light.

Visualize being empowered by a pillar of light so that your life becomes radiant.

Musical   Alexander Gretchaninov, *Domestic Liturgy*
Keynotes   (Christoff, Robev—Balkanton); *Holy, Radiant Light* (Ottley—Columbia). The Liturgy, a sacred work, for soloist, chorus, and chamber orchestra, is powerful and dramatic. Surges of patriotic fervor mark the performance. The music was recorded in a cathedral and its resonance reaches toward the heavens. The anthem *Holy, Radiant Light* radiates white light into the atmosphere. The tone is devotional and the music is strong in its mystical fervor.

John Rutter, *Gloria* (Rutter—Collegium). This bright piece of sacred music pervades the atmosphere with vibrant energy.

October 26   *Spiritual Wealth*

Focus   Take time! Take time to be courteous, to be thoughtful, to remember things that mean much to others, to do simple little kindly things that most persons are "too busy to do." Spiritual wealth is to be invested in other lives. It is essentially vital, alive, alert. It deals in friendliness, in love, in service, in good judgment, in generous unselfishness. No man can possess much of it by himself alone. It has to be shared to be enjoyed. It grows and increases and multiplies as it is given away. It attaches itself by invisible arms to the sharer, and manifests surprisingly and abundantly in his life.

Ernest Wilson

Meditation   Spiritual wealth implies having inner riches to share.

Generosity is one of the key factors in being truly wealthy.

Invest yourself and what you have been given into the great fund of life itself, and you will always have abundance.

Musical   Richard Yardumian, Symphony No. 2 (Chooka-
Keynotes   sian, Kojian—Varese-Sarabande). This symphony, based upon Psalm 130, is composed in memory of the Reverend Theodore Pitcairn, a priest in the Swedenborgian Church, of which Yardumian is a member. Reverend Pitcairn supported the arts and music, and his generosity brought him and many others spiritual wealth. The music is dramatic and powerful.

Marilyn Horne, *Beautiful Dreamer: The Great American Songbook* (Davis—London). Stephen Foster songs, negro spirituals, *The Lord's Prayer*, *Simple Gifts* and other selections make up this stirring collection.

October 27   ## The Anonymous Giver

Focus   Voluntary self-sacrifice does not mean piousness, mournfulness nor eccentricity of viewpoint. It indicates happiness earned by participating in something bigger than one's self. Words of self-sacrifice may be like these: "May I do a great deal of good without ever knowing it." (Wilbur Thoburn) Miracles will happen through you, not by you, that even you will not always know about.

                                              An Initiate

Meditation	It is a wonderful privilege to be able to contribute constructively. It is often even better not to know about all the good that is accomplished.

Consider today times you have given and did not need to know whether others appreciated your gift.

You can find great joy in giving anonymously.

You will sometimes touch others' lives in ways unknowable.

Musical Keynotes
Niccolo Paganini, *The Convent of Mount Saint Bernard* (Plotino—Dynamic). This unusual work is filled with mystery and spiritual aspiration. It begins with twelve tolls of a bell and moves into a monks' call ("friars' chant"). The music then builds to dramatic intensity.

John Corigliano, *Poem in October* (Peress—RCA). This is a lyrical setting to the work of the Welsh poet Dylan Thomas:

> And freely he goes lost
> In the unknown, famous light of great
> And fabulous, dear God.
> Dark is a way and light is a place,
> Heaven that never was
> Nor will be ever is always true.

October 28

Hymn

Focus
We give thanks to Thee...for all Thy benefits known, for all unknown, for Thine open and secret favors bestowed upon us. Thanks unto Thee for the ministry of worship—thousands of Archangels and ten thousands of angels, the Cherubim and the six-winged Seraphim full of eyes, soaring aloft on their wings, SINGING THE TRIUMPHAL HYMN, crying, calling aloud, and saying:

HOLY, HOLY, HOLY,

HEAVEN AND EARTH ARE FULL OF THY GLORY.

HOSANNA.

Howard Hanson

Meditation   Let your hymn surface in your heart.

The hymn you sing is your statement of praise to the Creator.

Create the hymn and let it be heard.

Musical   Leontyne Price, *Hymns* (RCA). This is a devo-
Keynotes   tional, reverent statement of faith.

Holy, Holy, Holy and Other Hymns (Cleobury—Argo). The King's College Choir sings many outstanding hymns.

Howard Hanson, Concerto for Organ, Strings and Harp (Hanson—Mercury). This is a hymn of power and praise that also contains quiet sections of strong lyricism.

Alan Hovhaness, *Silver Pilgrimage*, Symphony No. 15 (Whitney—Louisville). The concluding *Hymn to Louisville* is especially beautiful.

October 29   # *Rapport*

Focus   Energy can be transmitted from one [person] to another, without the two being in direct physical contact....Put yourself into a constructive attitude of mind and body. Tune in to the peace and assurance of the Self. Envision the other person as peaceful and filled with the light of the higher consciousness. From the unlimited reservoir of the Life that both share, and on which they both can draw, bathe the person in vitality, poise, or strength, to meet the need. The person feels the sense of peace.

A new flow of energy has been induced from within outward, and if he picks this up and draws on it from within himself, he will continue to improve in mind, then emotions and body.

Adelaide Gardner

Meditation   You can send healing energies to others if you have a sense of rapport with them.

Rapport enables transformation and regeneration.

Today establish a collaboration in the Spirit with someone who needs your help.

Musical   Franz Schubert, Sonata in A (Richter—Angel).
Keynotes   This piano piece is lyrical, gentle, relaxed and graceful. It was composed in the memory of a close rapport Schubert felt with friends, and for the daughters of a close acquaintance.

John Green, *Raintree County*, Soundtrack (Entr'acte). This sweeping music conveys true Americana. It also contains some beautiful, intimate sections describing close rapport and love between hero and heroine.

October 30   **Remembering Meetings**

Focus   How immediately richer my life becomes when I cast my glance over all those figures who have entered into my life. . . . Often something important to us is due to the fact that one person or another came into contact with us at a certain age, and perhaps without knowing it himself, drew our attention to something important.

Rudolph Steiner

Meditation   Today think of the meetings in your life that have been especially meaningful and helpful.

Recall a time when you were at a crossroads or turning point, and someone came into your life who helped you.

All along the way, you are guided, helped and inspired—often by unexpected meetings.

See how seemingly chance meetings have helped you, and look for new meetings.

Musical Keynotes   Alban Berg, Violin Concerto, *To the Memory of an Angel* (Kremer, Davis—Philips). This is a beautiful and private work, describing the composer's memory of a beautiful young child who died prematurely.

Ben Carlile, Piano Solos (Bing Records, 204 East 2nd Ave., Suite 205, San Mateo, CA 94401). These pieces for solo piano have a power that penetrates the memory and helps to recall images from the past. Friendly melodies fill the strong currents of sound. Especially beautiful is *The Wedding Suite: Home, Joy Processional and Celebration.* This music is popular for contemporary weddings. It is more reflective than the very beautiful and stronger *There Is Love*, by Captain and Tennille, also very fine for use at weddings.

October 31   ## Hallowe'en

Focus   It is the time for the All-Hallowed Evening—a holy evening—the hour approaching midnight, when goblins, witches and all wildness are released for the new space to be filled with healing and hope.
Anonymous

Meditation   Now is the time to release all that is not beautiful in you.

Anticipating the cleansing, let go today of the glitches and goblins that clog and pester you.

Replace the howls of your nights with the new day: the sun, the clarity and light of the way you have chosen.

*Musical
Keynotes*   Modeste Mussorgsky, *Night on Bald Mountain* (Ormandy—Columbia); Franz Schubert, *Ave Maria* (Anderson—Stokowski—Disneyland). The juxtaposition of these two pieces provides a striking transition from the goblins of the night into the radiance of the dawn. The bells scatter the ominous forces of darkness, and the soprano heralds the energy of transmutation and overcoming as the sun begins to rise.

Alexander Borodin, *Polovetsian Dances*, from *Prince Igor* (Ormandy—Columbia). These dances are outstanding for release of blocked energy pockets.

November 1   # All Saints Day

Focus

This which I love when I love my God: I love a kind of light, and of melody and of fragrance, a kind of food and a manner of embracement, when I love my God; the embracement, food, fragrance, melody, and light of my inner man.

Saint Augustine

Meditation

This is a good day to remember all the saints and those whose advancements inspire us to progress along the Path.

Consider the saints and spiritual teachers that mean the most to you. Think of the power of their love and caring.

You can renew the link in consciousness with the great saints of history and those living among us now, such as Mother Teresa of Calcutta.

Musical Keynotes

Charles Gounod, *Saint Cecilia Mass* (Hendricks, Pretre—Angel); Anton Dvořak, *Saint Ludmila* (Supraphon); Franz Liszt, *Legend of Saint Elizabeth* (Supraphon); Felix Mendelssohn, *Saint Paul* (Fruhbeck de Burgos—Angel); Patrick DiVietri, *Partita Teresiana*, guitar solo (Teresiana). All of these works pertain to saints. Most of them are dramatic and quite beautiful. DiVietri's gorgeous guitar tape is wonderfully meditative and melodic. It was recorded in an actual mission. The mood is reverent and atmospheric.

November 2   *Clear Horizons*

Focus   Climb the mountains and get their good tidings. Nature's peace will flow into you as sunshine flows into trees. The winds will blow their own freshness into you, and the storms of their energy, while cares will drop off like autumn leaves. . . . The clearest way into the Universe is through a forest wilderness.   John Muir

Meditation   The great mountains and high places renew and regenerate you.

               Take the time to visit wilderness places. Even looking at pictures of them can clear you of cares.

               You can let the fresh air and the benedictions of mountain energies flow through you.

               Stretch your consciousness in the mighty horizons of great mountain wildernesses.

Musical   Larry Pruden, *Taranaki, Mt. Egmont* (EMI).
Keynotes   *Taranaki*, the Maori name for Mount Egmont on North Island, New Zealand, is portrayed here in a stirring piece of powerful nature music.

               Douglas Lilburn, Symphony No. 2; *Aotearoa Overture, Land of the Long White Cloud* (Heenan, Hopkins—Jerusalem; Kiwi Records, New Zealand). These works are genuine masterpieces. Mysteries of nature open up through the music, which is very visual and heightens the senses. The unique power and freshness of New Zealand's glorious landscapes come through the

music, especially the section portraying Milford
Sound on South Island.

November 3	***Learning***
Focus	Every day that we spend without learning something is a day lost.
	Ludwig van Beethoven
Meditation	What have you learned today?
	Make a special effort today to learn more about your job, about another person, about some subject that interests you.
	Learning is a key to growing. When you stop learning, you do not draw fully on your powers and talents. Learning removes limits.
	Keep asking the question: how am I learning each day?
Musical Keynotes	Vincenzo Bellini, *Messa Di Gloria*, *Gloria Mass* (Burger—MASSound, Box 1816, New York, NY 10185). This is a powerful and radiant choral work with energy that streams forth in melody.
	Tom Barabas, *Sedona Suite* (Tom Barabas—The Source, Box 1466, Coronado, CA 92118). These healing and relaxing piano solos are sometimes exhilarating, as for instance *Sedona Suite*, with movements entitled *Sunrise*, *Prayer*, *Joy*, and *Sunset*.
November 4	***Determination***
Focus	To believe in the wide-awake real, through all the stupefying, enervating, distorting dream: to will

to wake up, when the very being seems thirsty for
Godless sleep: these are the broken steps up to the
high fields where repose is but a form of strength,
strength but a form of joy, joy but a form of love.

George MacDonald

Meditation   Many broken steps lead finally upward—toward
the high fields of spiritual growth.

Determination finds the strength to wake up—to
move beyond the mistakes of the past, into greater
joy ahead.

Visualize a road or a path with steps leading ahead.
What are the steps you need to take today?

Through your determination your path will open
before you.

Musical   Arnold Cooke, Clarinet Concerto (King, Francis—
Keynotes   Hyperion). Cooke is a Yorkshire composer who
produces here a beautiful, lyrical concerto.
Especially lovely is the slow movement.

Spencer Brewer, *Portraits* (Narada). Oboe, English
horn, ocarina, lyricon, cello, guitar and violin play
memorable pieces such as *Carnival*, *Portraits* and
The Muse.

November 5   ***Latent Power***

Focus   In the soul is a sacred place where the spellbound
god may wake to liberty. The soul, allowing herself
to be impregnated by Nature, will give birth to the
Divine.   Rudolph Steiner

Meditation   As a person discovers the sleeping power within,
a great, creative energy begins to be released.

Today try to realize the newly awakening power
of the "spellbound god" seeking birth within you.

Look for the latent inner power and feel it moving through you.

Musical Keynotes	Johann Christian Bach, Sinfonias (Jones—Nonesuch). These delightful early pieces offer a verve and a bright energy.

Evenson, *Tropic of Paradise* (Soundings of the Planet). Bird calls, waterfalls and other water sounds combine with flute, harp, piano, violin, bells, guitar and sitar to produce power and energy.

November 6   ## Group Energy

Focus   The Seventh Ray, being the ray of ceremony and activity, means that it sets into motion those energies within humanity that stimulate group activity and relationship.   David Spangler

Meditation   Today think of the enjoyable activities you have participated in with a group.

Perhaps you have belonged to a choir, a band or orchestra, a drama group, a prayer group, a fraternity or sorority, a community project, a sports team, a discussion group or growth group.

When two or more "gather in His name," the power of such a group is squared. Can you meet with others who are on a spiritual journey?

Remember today the power of a cooperative group and its capacity to make a constructive difference.

Musical Keynotes   Ignace Jan Paderewski, Symphony in B-Minor, *Polonia* (Wodiczko—Muza). The music carries a definite feeling of the Polish people and culture, but also has a monumental quality. Beautiful melodies and tone colors make this work a pleasing experience.

Masayuki Koga, *East Meets East*, Volume 1 (Invincible Records, Box 13054, Phoenix, AZ 85002). Sahul Sariputra, sitar virtuoso, meets Masayuki Koga and his flute in a haunting blend of the sounds of the Orient. The combination of Indian and Japanese music works in a marvelous way that exemplifies the group energy.

November 7	## *Reach*
Focus	The struggle to reach. . . is itself enough to fulfill the heart of man. Albert Camus
Meditation	Consider today the ways you are reaching toward a great dream or hope.
	What goal are you reaching for? What great aspiration do you cherish?
	Whatever your area of reach, it helps you aim beyond where you are to where you might be.
	Use your capacity to stretch and to aspire. There is no limit to your reach.
Musical Keynotes	William Alwyn, *Lyrica Angelica, Angel's Songs* (Alwyn—Lyrita). This music was inspired by the English metaphysical poets of the 17th century, in particular those of Giles Fletcher. There is a mystical, rapt atmosphere in the music that will hold the listener's attention.
	Soundings of the Planet: Soundings Tapestry (The Source, Box 1466, Coronado, CA 92118). Forest sounds, streams, birds, harp, flute, plus other instruments mingle in an uplifting musical experience with a far reach.

November 8   ***Awe***

Focus   I think that in the lives of all persons there must
                be fleeting moments, investing the imagination
                from some intangible cause with a vast and awe-
                inspiring significance out of all proportion to the
                actual event. These are momentary states of
                ecstatic vision.   Sir Arnold Bax

Meditation   What inspires awe in you—great music, art, the
                majesty of nature, the life of a noble person, uplift-
                ing thoughts, the night sky?

                Today experience something that arouses awe in
                you.

                Wonder and the capacity to be divinely over-
                whelmed and inspired remain among your most
                important endowments.

                Always keep alive your capacity to feel awe and
                the thrill of ecstasy.

Musical   *Stabat Mater, Eton Choirbook* (Christophers—
Keynotes   Musical Heritage). This sacred choral music of the
                15th century awakens awe and reverence.

                Sir Arnold Bax, Symphony No. 4 (Thomson—
                Chandos). The music awakens awe, terror and
                wonder beyond understanding. It is largely an im-
                posing seascape, inspired by the west coast of
                Scotland. Bax writes these words about it: "The
                white gleam of the sea was so sharp that it seemed
                at any moment about to burst into some intenser
                expression than was possible to light alone, as if
                it must break into some trumpet tone shrilling
                above the heavy crash of the surf. . . . An enormous
                grey allurement, tender and terrible."

November 9   ***Peace in the Midst of Turmoil***

Focus   True peace does not depend alone upon harmonious environment; it is of God, and comes to us through our becoming at-one with Him. Instead of peace coming through harmonious circumstances, harmonious circumstances come as a result of inward peace.

Henry Hamblin

Meditation The greatest peace always comes from deep within you.

In the midst of any outer circumstances, there is always great quiet at the center.

Today you can feel again the divine peace sustaining you through all outer challenges.

Musical Burrill Phillips, *Paul Revere's Ride*, from *Tales*
Keynotes *from McGuffy's Readers* (Hanson—Mercury). This is an exciting piece that pictures Paul Revere riding through the towns at night giving warning that "the British are coming." There is a deep sense of mission that comes through the night and the music. The piece rises to triumph at the close.

Zamfir, *Harmony* (Philips). Zamfir and Harry van Hoof and his orchestra play several beautiful pieces from the classics and from the popular movie genres. The Pan flute blends in pleasingly with other instruments. Especially lovely is *Elvira Madigan* from Mozart's Piano Concerto 21.

November 10 **The Divine Harmony**

Focus Since music is an imitation of the divine harmony, it can, through rhythm and melody, instill a harmonious balance in a human soul that has become untuned. Music can produce in others the mood that it expresses itself, and thereby modifies the character of its listener and alleviates the ills of the mind.   Manly P. Hall

Meditation Today listen to a great piece of music. Listen to it as an expression of the Divine Harmony that sounds through the universe.

You will find readjustment in your energy field, as you hear the vibrations of great music.

The rhythms and melodies of life can have a balancing effect upon your own energies.

Musical Henri Rabaud, *The Nocturnal Procession*
Keynotes (Dervaux—EMI). The music is interior and suggestive in its landscapes. It is good for imagery, and the listener can supply visual and kinesthetic associations.

The Music of Le Comte de Saint Germain (Philosophical Research Society, 3910 Los Feliz Blvd., Los Angeles, CA 90027). This is very centering music from ancient times. It is direct, simple and beautiful, restoring a sense of peace and order.

November 11 **Concentration**

Focus One must have time to concentrate—to get into the right feeling, or else the creation of a sustained work is impossible.

Alexander Borodin

Meditation In everything in life, concentration helps to bring you focus and depth.

Find the ways to concentrate in all circumstances: alone in a quiet atmosphere or with music in the background, and in the midst of outside interferences.

Even in difficult conditions, if you deeply care about others you can center and find the necessary concentration to help them or to do your work.

Musical   Alexander Borodin, Symphony No. 2 (Svetlanov—
Keynotes   Quintessence; Ansermet—London Treasury). This
               symphony quickens the imagination. The different
               movements and the great finale take the listener
               into worlds of Oriental imagery. There is the sug-
               gestion of vast, open spaces, perhaps with gardens
               looming out of desert oases. Each listener will be
               able to supply individual imagery.

               Environments, *An English Meadow* (Syntonic
               Research, Inc., 175 Fifth Ave., New York, NY
               10010). This is a pleasing, open kind of experience,
               filling the mind with a sense of peace and sunlight.
               Bird calls blend into the landscape. This nature
               music is yin and completely different in its ap-
               proach to concentration from the more potent
               Borodin Symphony No. 2.

November 12   **Healing Space**

Focus   Healing happens between the notes. I had to allow
               the space and not be afraid, and to know that
               things happen in space. You have to let the space
               settle. If you let go, you transcend and experience
               the stillness, and that is the healing. One ingredient
               of health is rest. Activity comes from inactivity.
               The basis of sound is silence. Stillness is basic to
               health.   Paul Horn

Meditation   In the spaces of silence comes the voice of the
               divine.

               Create spaces in your life, and they will be filled
               in ways that heal and empower you.

               In the midst of busy-ness, take the time to listen
               between the notes. You can experience divine still-
               ness in the spaces of your life.

Musical *Keynotes*	Wolfgang Amadeus Mozart, Violin Concerto No. 3 (Stern, Szell—Columbia); Piano Concerto No. 21 (Casadesus, Szell—Columbia). Both pieces, in the slow movements, emanate healing space.

Paul Horn, *Inside the Great Pyramid* (Teldec—Germany). This wonderful, improvisational music for flute is performed in the King's Chamber of the Cheops Pyramid, and also in the Queen's Chamber and the Burial Chamber of the Kephren Pyramid. It contains many open spaces.

November 13   **Steadfastness**

Focus   Thank God every morning when you get up that you have something to do which might be done, whether you like it or not. Being forced to work and forced to do your best will breed in you temperance and self-control, diligence and strength of will, cheerfulness and contentedness, and a hundred virtues which the idle never know.

Charles Kingsley

Meditation In the love of a work well done, there is always steadfastness.

You can keep on going forward in the midst of delays and setbacks if you love your work and continue with strength of will.

In steadfastness there is progress.

Musical *Keynotes* Joonas Kokkonen, *Requiem* (Söderblom—Finlandia). This is beautiful, open music, with all moments directed toward the final section, *Eternal Light*. It is a genuinely heartfelt piece, composed in memory of Kokkonen's wife Maija.

Derek Bell, *Carolan's Favorite* (Shanachie,

Dalebrook Park, Ho-Ho-Kus, NJ 07423). This melodic and quickening music is both centering and stimulating to the imagination. Much of the music is played on the Irish harp and is the music of the Irish harper, Turlough O'Carolan.

November 14   *Connection*

Focus
Isn't religion that connection with something larger than oneself? All we know is that the moment of possession is the moment of inspiration. Whence it comes or how long is its duration, one can never foretell. Inspiration is the antithesis of self-consciousness.   Aaron Copland

Meditation
Today consider how the divine fills you—especially in heightened moments.

Often, crisis and inspiration are related.

The deep connection can come in times of intensity and also in repose.

You cannot control your experience of the connection, but you will feel it more when you are less self-conscious.

Musical Keynotes
Aaron Copland, *Suite from Our Town; Quiet City* (Abravanel—Vanguard). These two Copland works bring a deep connection. *Our Town Suite* contains some of Copland's most beautiful melodies, and *Quiet City* is a haunting, nocturnal landscape, suggesting the city in its sleeping hours.

Paul Horn, *China* (Kuckuck—Celestial Harmonies). The flute, cheng, chin, erhu, and ti-tze combine to bring a beautiful connection between East and West. Especially memorable is *Temple of Heaven*.

November 15	**Collaboration**

| *Focus* | True love begins when nothing is looked for in return. To love Me is, above all, to collaborate with Me.   Antoine de Saint—Exupéry |

Meditation	A willingness to love opens the door to collaborating with another.
	When you love, the willingness to give results in cooperation in a relationship.
	To love expecting nothing, yet being totally expectant, enables meaningful collaboration.

| *Musical Keynotes* | Orlando Gibbons, *Anthems and Songs of Praise* (Wulstan—Nonesuch). The music is exalted and uplifting. Its movement is spiral, lifting the listener vertically in consciousness. |
| | Tony Wells, *Collage* (Karma Productions, 701 Brush St., Las Vegas, NV 89107). Many exotic sounds mingle to produce a collaboration with a haunting effect. Flutes, Tibetan bells, singing bowls, wind chimes, gongs, sculptured percussion, African slit drums, shakers, sticks, bell clusters, Brazilian whistles, Hopi clay flutes, western bird calls, creek and wolf songs contribute to this music-making. |

November 16	**Calm**

| *Focus* | Seek always the tranquil way; cleanse your heart of all conflict, all fear. The calm, faithful spirit which rings true throughout every experience of life, in. . . adversity and disappointment as well as in success, will gain admission into the heavenly places. What you can forgive and what you can love can have no adverse or harmful effect upon you.   White Eagle |

Meditation   Calm comes when you can respond with feeling
                and interest, yet remain detached toward the
                outcome.

                It requires a delicate balance to move between suc-
                cess and failure, pleasure and disappointment.

                In the midst of every outcome, there is the still
                point; in the center there is calm.

Musical   Paul Hindemith, *Concert of Angels*, from *Mathis*
Keynotes   *de Maler Symphony* (Ormandy—Columbia). This
                music is drawn from Hindemith's opera by the
                same name. It describes moods and scenes in the
                life of Matthias Grunewald, an early German
                religious painter. The music is gentle, tender and
                serene.

                Frank Perry, *Deep Peace* (Celestial Harmonies).
                This strong and beautiful music is produced by
                many varieties of bells and gongs, but with no elec-
                tronics. The title of the music has been taken from
                an old Gaelic prayer:

> Deep peace of the running wave to you,
> deep peace of the flowing air to you,
> deep peace of the quiet earth to you,
> deep peace of the shining stars to you,
> deep peace of the son of peace to you.

November 17   ## The Rule of Love

Focus   Where love rules, there is no will to power; and
                where power predominates, there love is lacking.
                The one is the shadow of the other.

                                                    Carl Jung

Meditation   Today consider outgoing love with no need for
                power or control.

                The wish to dominate another comes from want-
                ing power, not from love.

Love occurs in the midst of mutual kindness and consideration. In genuine love there is joy participating together and mutual giving and receiving.

When you truly feel love, there is no need for power.

Musical Keynotes   Gustav Holst, *Jupiter*, from *The Planets* (Boult, EMI). This music is powerful but also good-humored, like a good belly-laugh. It is very energizing.

Erik Berglund, *Beauty* (Sona Gaia). Pieces for solo harp bring out the keynote of love.

November 18   **Purity**

Focus   Music is truly love itself, the purest, most ethereal language of the emotions, embodying all their changing colors in every variety of shading and nuance.   Carl Maria von Weber

Meditation   Sibelius once said that music is a carrier of clear streams and flowing water. The Sons of the Pioneers remind us of this when they sing the thirst-quenching tones of *Cool Water*.

Water brings purity, clarity and feelings of the un-contaminated essence that can be sensed in people's character, in the elements of nature, and in the music of relationships.

Today, in the moments of stillness, look for your own pure essence, the divine in you.

Musical Keynotes   Antonio Vivaldi, Flute Concertos (Rampal, Scimone—Columbia). These lovely concertos contain the essence of purity, freshness and colors. They sparkle with good spirits.

Evenson, Verdeaux and Kramer, *Tree O₂* (Soundings of the Planet). Here is a unique blend of fresh, flowing melodies, played on piano, flute and cello, bringing joy and clearance. A genuine purity pervades this music.

November 19	## *Soul Crystal*
Focus	The soul of man, left to its own natural level, is a potentially lucid crystal, left in darkness. It is perfect in its own nature, but it lacks something that it can receive only from outside and beyond itself. But when the light shines in it, it becomes in a manner transformed into LIGHT and seems to lose its nature in the splendor of a higher nature, the nature of the light that is in it.

Thomas Merton

Meditation	Like a beautiful crystal hanging in the open air, your soul is the transparency that awaits the light, and then shines upon your personality.
	The light, shining through, produces luminosity in the purity of your soul.
Musical Keynotes	Edvard Grieg, Piano Concerto, Slow Movement (Lupu, Previn—London); Frederic Chopin, Piano Concerto No. 1, Slow Movement (Gilels, Ormandy—Columbia). These two pieces reveal the crystal of the soul in all its radiance and pure splendor.
	Crystal Chimes, *In the Enchanted Crystal Forest* (Magical Rainbow Prod., Box 717, Ojai, CA 93023). Open spatial music offers a gentle experience, at times quite meditative.

November 20   **Harmlessness**

Focus   Non-injury is the highest religion. Master of your
                    senses and avoiding wrong, you should do no harm
                    to any living being, neither by thoughts, nor
                    words, nor acts.   Mahavira

Meditation   Revere every life's right to live. If possible, in some
                    way constructively touch each life that you meet.

                    You can hurt or help others not only physically,
                    but with your words, thoughts and feelings.

                    To make helpful contact with others, you must
                    begin to master your behavior and thoughts.

                    Today try to do no harm and to give of yourself.

Musical   Franz Joseph Haydn, Flute Quartets (Rampal—
Keynotes   Seraphim). These pieces are very cheerful and
                    filled with an energizing quality. Beautiful tunes
                    and perky rhythms help to bring the listener into
                    focus and alertness.

                    James Galway, *Song of the Seashore* (RCA). These
                    intimate Japanese songs of nature, played with
                    flute, koto and strings, emanate poignant feelings.
                    Especially beautiful are *Lullaby*, *Cherry Blossom
                    Time* and *The Evening Primrose*.

November 21   **Morning Song**

Focus   Whenever my eyes first open in the morning, let
                    my heart open likewise; from it let a flaming, fiery
                    torch of love send up Thy praise. . . . May the praise
                    sound as sweetly. . . as in this world the sweet music
                    of all lovely instruments ever sounded, in its own
                    way, to a free soul.

                                                        Henry Suso

Meditation   "Sending up Thy praise" is a perfect way to begin
                your day. You will be heard.

                Your music opens new doors.

                Free your soul by beginning the morning with your
                heart singing praise.

Musical   *The Bach Trumpet,* (Ludwig Guttler—Capriccio
Keynotes   Records). This is an empowering, joyous selection
                of Bach pieces for trumpet, orchestra and
                sometimes voice. The sound of the trumpet
                awakens you.

                Alan Hovhaness, *Gloria Patri,* from *Magnificat*
                (Whitney—Poseidon). The stirring finale to this
                sacred work builds to a heroic climax with
                adoration.

November 22   **The Great Shining**

Focus   The little earthly life hides from our glance the
                enormous lights and mysteries of which the world
                is full, and he who can draw it away from before
                his eyes, as one draws away a hand, beholds the
                great shining of the inner worlds.
                                                Rabbi Nachmann

Meditation   Behind outer appearances, there you will find the
                great shining.

                Today, tune in to the larger worlds and perspec-
                tives—see behind the surface.

                A greater understanding and acceptance of life
                come as deeper mysteries are probed.

                Larger realities unfold as the great shining of the
                inner worlds moves through you.

Musical *Keynotes*	J. S. Bach, The Harpsichord Concertos, slow movements (Kipnis, Marriner—Columbia); *English Meadow* (Environments). Combining these two selections brings out the quiet shining of the inner peace and divine order.

George Frideric Handel, Harp Concerto (Zabaleta, Kuentz—DGG); Oboe Concertos, slow movements (Lord, Marriner—Angel); Organ Concertos (Alain, Paillard—Erato). In all of these beautiful works, inner worlds shine forth.

November 23   *The Immortals*

Focus

Live for the realization of the Immortals. Spend your lives in service to their godly purposes. Seek to understand something of the Divine Plan underlying your ascent from Neanderthal man to Master of your life. Then the Divine will become more approachable, perceived and attained.

Flower A. Newhouse

Meditation

As you give yourself to the highest that you know, openings into immortality occur.

Become more sensitive to the changes and the needs around you; turn your difficulties into victories, your faults into virtues.

Walk the path of the great Immortals.

Musical
Keynotes

J. S. Bach, *Organ Chorale Preludes* (Miscellaneous Labels). These magnificent works open doors into immortal places. The chorales composed at the end of Bach's life make up some of the most profound musical utterances in the history of mankind.

Joseph Haydn, *Saint Cecilia Mass* (Kubelik—Orfeo). This is another magnificent work that

scales the heights to the Immortals. The energies
of this music are transcendent and very empowering.

November 24	*Worship*

Focus

There is material worship, spiritual worship and
divine worship: action, word and prayer, or *deed*,
understanding and *love*. The instinctive desires
deeds, the abstractive turns to ideas, and the
specialist sees the end, he/she aspires to God, whom
he inwardly perceives and contemplates.

Honoré de Balzac

Meditation

In your life there are three primary kinds of worship and attention: deeds express your focus in action; understanding arranges your perceptions;
love describes your sensitivity and compassion.

Today, you can let your needs for devotion and
worship emerge—in action, understanding and
love.

*Musical
Keynotes*

J. S. Bach, *The Brandenburg Concertos* (Casals—
Columbia). These enlivening, noble works bring
out the sense of worship and *worth*ship by uplifting the human spirit.

Peter Maxwell Davies, *Orkney Wedding and
Sunrise* (Williams—Philips). There is a wonderful
sense of celebration and warmth in this music,
which includes a bagpiper and folk melodies
played by the orchestra.

Liz Storey, *Solid Colors* (Windham Hill). An introspective, reflective quality comes through much
of this music for solo piano. Especially pleasing are
the songs, *Water Caves, Peace Piece, Wedding
Rain, Hymn,* and *Things with Wings.*

November 25   ***The Supreme Musician***

Focus   Soulful music makes us feel that we are in tune
               with the Highest, with the deepest and with the
               farthest. It also makes us feel that God Himself is
               the Supreme Musician.

                                            Sri Chinmoy

Meditation   A soulful experience can change us inside.

               In music or in relationships, moments come in
               which we are opened within ourselves and the
               divine enters.

               Remember today the Supreme Musician in your
               life, who can reestablish the central tonality of
               healing and balance within you.

Musical   Virgil Thomson, *Symphony on a Hymn Tune*
Keynotes   (Hanson—Mercury). This is an especially lyrical
               and nostalgic piece of Americana, played by the
               full orchestra.

               Gabriel Lee, *Impressions* (Narada). This is soulful
               music for solo guitar. Especially lilting and at-
               mospheric are *Earth Dances* and *Remembrances*.

November 26   ***Fruition***

Focus   Step by step we are shaped
               in Light;
               Patiently ascending higher mountains
               toward greater sight.

               Welcome every morn
               and let the point of flame
               pierce the passing clouds;
               release all tears

to let the falling rain
fill deep the hungering earth.

Anonymous

Meditation   The ways of growth are gradual; your vision grows with each new experience. Every day is gradually assimilated as the journey leads to fruition.

Today, look at your life and your progress on the path. Let your inner strength pierce the clouds of doubt and uncertainty.

Let go of past hurts and let the nurturing rain awaken new seeds of life stirring inside you.

Musical   J. S. Bach, *Six Suites for Unaccompanied Cello*
Keynotes   (Casals—Angel). These spiritual classics lead to fruition and deep contemplation.

Joaquin Rodrigo, *Music for a Garden* (Batiz—Angel). This music of fruition consists of four exquisite cradle songs—*Autumn*, *Winter*, *Spring*, and *Summer*. There is a certain elusive, haunting quality to the music. The sounds are largely transparent and lyrical.

November 27   # The Jungle

Focus   The person who has love can walk unharmed through the jungle...for there is nothing that has the message of hate to his heart. The love that radiates to the world around us draws all things in to serve and not to injure, to love and not to hate....All living things will come to the person who loves, for they are all the offspring of the Divine, and the Divine is Love.

Annie Besant

Meditation   Today imagine yourself in a tropical jungle. See
                 the lush forest, hear the birdsong, visualize wild
                 animals. The scene is open and refreshing, and the
                 sounds and sights are beautiful.

                 You are safe here, and because you feel safe, there
                 is no need for fear.

                 The animals notice you, but they feel your love for
                 them, and neither you nor they are afraid.

                 You can enjoy this visit, because your love protects
                 you.

Musical   Charles Koechlin, *The Jungle Book* (Segerstam—
Keynotes   Cybelia). *The Meditation of Purun-Baghat* is
                 especially striking. It is music of strength and
                 serenity, combining sounds of organ and orchestra.
                 Finally, the music sinks back into silence.

                 Deuter, *Cicada* (Kuckkuck Schallplatten—West
                 Germany); Yas-Kaz, *Jungle Book,* from *Jomon-Sho*
                 (Gramavision). This colorful music brings a
                 wonderful freshness. It is good for imagery and
                 enables the listener to create a personal, visual
                 landscape from the sounds. For a unique jungle ex-
                 perience, play the Deuter and the Yas-Kaz in se-
                 quence.

November 28   **Embodiment**

Focus   Music embodies the inward feeling of which all
                 other arts can but exhibit the effect. Music uses the
                 other arts somewhat as the soul uses the body.
                 Music is the soul of all seen things.
                                                          Unknown

Meditation   You can move behind your feelings today to the
                 music that plays inside your world.

There are silent melodies in all your experiences.

Listen for the soul behind all embodiment and the silent singer in your own soul.

Musical   Alexander Kastalsky, *O Gladsome Radiance*
Keynotes (Potorjinsky—Westminster); Anton Rubinstein, *Angelic Dream* from *Kammenoi Ostrov* (Ponti— Candide; Dragon—Capitol). Both of these celestial pieces emanate the presence of angels. They speak of the deeper currents infusing all life. They also carry Slavic tones of spirituality that unite heaven and earth.

Dan Gibson, *Among the Mountain Canyons and Valleys* (Solitudes, Volume 5). This is water music of nature. "The silvery flow washes through the mind: the archetypal mountain stream. Birds sing and later the rains fall, gently cleansing and renewing you."

November 29   **Circumstances**

Focus   The life which forgets itself turns to its true immortality. I will go back to the stars without any flourish of trumpets, but I won't weep as I return, or whine about circumstances.   AE

Meditation In the midst of your ever-changing circumstances, you can pour your life and love into the self-forgetfulness of eternity.

Losing yourself in something greater than yourself is the only way to find yourself.

Musical   Gaetano Donizetti, *Miserere* (Maklari—
Keynotes Hungaroton). The power of this music brings its own solutions to outer circumstances through its inner radiance.

Ralph Vaughan-Williams, *Song of Thanksgiving* (Boult—EMI). A lesser known example in music of a thankful heart.

November 30   ***Essences***

Focus   The angels use man's prayers like cosmic gold dust: white and colored energy essence, in order to surround those areas of need with healing. Prayers of love, visualization, and caring create a real essence that the Higher Ones use for good and the finer healing work. Thus God and the angels can use man's prayers to further the Kingdom of Light on earth.   Anonymous

Meditation   Sincere prayers, succinctly rendered, rise into the angels' keeping.

Your deepest thoughts, directed heavenward, make clear contact.

Let your prayers be known today, with love and clarity.

Your prayers will be used; they create a finer essence and stir the energies that can help to bring about healing and progress.

Musical Keynotes   Gabriel Fauré, *Sanctus*, from *Requiem* (Plasson—Angel); *Elegie* (Ormandy—Columbia). Both of these pieces are like prayers ascending to the heavens. The elegy, for cello and orchestra, is a bit more earthbound, although it contains a true beauty and sense of repose.

Iasos, *Angelic Music* (Interdimensional Music, Box 594, Waldo Pt., Sausalito, CA 94965). This is lovely, ethereal music that rises into the higher spheres. Distinct melodies are rare, but the feeling is of openness and space.

Resourcefulness

Focus   We are living in a world where the individual must learn to command the raw materials of expression. He must not be dependent all the time on the ready-made, the finished product. It's the transferring, the changing of the raw into what is the expression of your own self—the whole joy and satisfaction and frustration of life is built into this.
Yehudi Menuhin

Meditation   Genuine growth often means to produce something out of nothing.

You can take the raw materials of your experiences and transform them into the finished product of your character.

In the frustrations and the joys of working with life's raw materials, you will discover your true resourcefulness.

*Musical
Keynotes*   Jessye Norman, *Great Day in the Morning* (Philips); Simon Estes, *Spirituals* (Philips); *Leontyne Price Sings Spirituals* (RCA); Marian Anderson, *Spirituals* (RCA and EMI). Powerful and moving renditions of the great Negro spirituals.

Morton Gould, *Spirituals for Orchestra* (Crystal Clear Records). This music is rooted in jazz and Black folk idioms, but no spirituals as such are included.

December 2   **Union**

Focus   I have joined my heart to Thee: all that exists
                art Thou;
                Thee only have I found, for Thou art all that exists.
                O Lord, Beloved of my heart,
                Thou art the home of all;

                . . . .
                Thou hast entered every heart: all that exists
                art Thou.
                From earth below to the highest heaven,
                from heaven to deepest earth,
                I see Thee wherever I look: all that exists
                art Thou.

                                                    Ramakrishna

Meditation   In the end there is only God.

                Divinity permeates all of nature and every human
                heart.

                The more you enter the divine radiance, the more
                you find that radiance in all things.

                Focus today on union with the Beloved. Make
                divine life visible wherever you look, filling every
                space.

Musical   Sergei Rachmaninov, *Vespers* (Rostropovich—
Keynotes   Erato). This extraordinary sacred work for chorus
                brings in a deep sense of union and intimacy, in
                the midst of a divine grandeur. The music becomes
                an evolving mantram, linking the listener with
                higher spheres.

                Ravi Shankar, *Tribute to Nippon* (DGG). This
                music is a synthesis of Indian and Japanese ap-
                proaches and styles. It forms a lovely blend.

December 3   ## *Loon Lake*

Focus   The wind, silence and love; friends who have
             taught me the most.   Fiona Macleod

Meditation Imagine the sound of the wind at night. Listen to
             the silence in the open air pierced by the longing
             cries of loons. Let their mournful calls awaken
             great love in your heart.

             This is your inner journey to Loon Lake.

             In your visualization and feeling response learn
             from wind, silence and love.

Musical   *Land of the Loon: Solitudes II* (Dan Gibson Pro-
Keynotes   ductions); *Canoe Trip to Loon Lake* (Dan Gibson
             Productions); *On Golden Pond*, Soundtrack (Dave
             Grusin—MCA). All three of these recordings con-
             jure up a synesthetic delight, both visual and
             auditory. You may wish to lie in a quiet place and
             let yourself mentally wander out to a landscape as
             the sounds emerge.

December 4   ## *Readiness*

Focus   O Great Spirit,
             Whose voice I hear in the winds,
             And whose breath gives life to all the world,
             Hear me! I am small and weak, I need
             your strength and wisdom.

             Let me walk in Beauty, and make my eyes
             ever behold the red and purple sunset.

Make my Hands respect the things you
have made and my ears sharp to hear your voice.

Make me Wise so that I may understand
the things you have taught my people.

Let me learn the lessons you have hidden
in every leaf and rock.

I seek strength, not to be greater
than my brother, but to fight my greatest enemy—
myself.

Make me ready always to come to you
with clean hands and straight eyes.

So when life fades, as the fading sunset,
my spirit may come to you without shame.

                                        An Indian Prayer

Meditation   This beautiful prayer implies that every person,
every life, every experience has its place in your
life and in the great Plan.

If you walk in beauty with clean hands and straight
eyes, you are then ready to see meaning emerge
all around you.

Today you can become more receptive and willing to learn from whatever experiences come to
you.

Musical   Sir Hamilton Harty, *A John Field Suite*, Violin
Keynotes   Concerto, *With the Wild Geese* (Thomson—
Chandos). These are pleasant, enlivening pieces,
filled with the sense of nature and the out-of-doors.

Merrill Jenson, *Windwalker* (Jenson—Cerberus
Records). The music, a soundtrack for the film
Windwalker, captures the spirit of Cheyenne tribal
songs. It conveys a feeling of reverence for environment as well as a certain heroic quality. The music
is powerful, yet filled with dignity. Listen for the
haunting sounds of the Indian flute.

December 5	*Oscillation*

Focus   Life is but a daily oscillation between revolt and
             submission, between the instinct of the ego, which
             is to expand, to take delight in its own sense of in-
             violability, if not to triumph in its own sovereignty,
             and the instinct of the soul, which is to obey the
             universal order, to accept the will of God.

                                                        Amiel

Meditation Consider today the movement between the poles
              of obedience and revolt.

              There are times when an impulsive force wants to
              take over and resist, even though there is a larger
              need to accept circumstances without fighting.

              You can learn to move in harmony between the
              extremes of wanting to change things and
              acceptance—to do what is necessary without
              resisting your situation or waiting too long to
              change it.

Musical   Vitezslav Novak, *About the Eternal Longing*
Keynotes   (Sejna—Supraphon). This beautiful tone poem, for
              full orchestra, describes the sea and the soul's long-
              ing for love and the Eternal. The music moves into
              a deep, meditative power.

              Gabriel Lee, *The Seasons* (Narada). The music, for
              solo guitar, describes cycles of nature. It has dif-
              ferent rhythms which are appropriate, each in its
              own time. The music is spacious and open, with
              obvious variety.

December 6	*Imprisoned Splendor*

Focus   The supreme values which we know are Goodness,
             Truth and Beauty. . . . These three values . . . medi-

ate to us directly, not indirectly, the nature of God. They constitute together the white light which shines outwards through all the veils of Maya from the imprisoned splendor within. These beams pierce to the outermost limits of the world of nature, and when we pass them through the prism of our mind's analysis, we find in the spectrum only Love, Truth and Beauty.

Raynor Johnson

Meditation   The splendor of the light within shines through all creation.

Today try to penetrate behind appearances to the core of Love, Truth and Beauty that lies at a deeper level.

A timeless love supports and empowers you, and you move in the white light of the divine.

Musical Keynotes   Henryk Górecki, Symphony No. 3, *Symphony on Plaintive Songs* (Bour—Erato). This is a marvelous work: one continuous song, a chant for orchestra, with soprano singing vocalise. I believe this is a masterpiece. In the symphonic tradition this work is like one extended mantra.

Scott Fitzgerald, *Sojourn* (Search for Serenity). This is lovely music for piano and orchestra. The feelings of goodness permeate the listener through beautiful melodies.

December 7   **Correspondence**

Focus   One of music's effects is to awaken within the hearer corresponding states of consciousness, from coarse up to realms of beauty and truth, according to the ability of the hearer to respond to angelic ministrations. Good music therefore is a wonderful instrument for stimulating awareness in the higher nature, improving and purifying the personality, and increasing spiritual responses.

Geoffrey Hodson

Meditation   Beautiful music can change your consciousness and the rhythms of your being.

Today listen to music that moves you. In a receptive state, feel the currents of sound moving through you.

As you give yourself to the music, you begin to resonate with the rhythms and the energies of sound.

If you listen deeply, you can respond to the angelic tones and become more closely aligned with their harmonies.

You will tend to mirror the music you hear and respond in ways that correspond to it.

Musical Keynotes   Pietro Mascagni, *Intermezzo* and *Easter Hymn*, from *Cavalleria Rusticana* (Scotto, Levine—RCA). The music is deeply melodic and devotional, expanding the heart chakra and uplifting the consciousness.

Erich Tingstad, *Woodlands* (Narada). Guitar, ocarina, horn, oboe, cheng and piano play *Sequoia, Oaks* and other tree-related inspirations.

December 8   **The Governing Power**

Focus   The final form of one's work is, indeed, dependent on powers that are stronger than oneself. Later on, one can substantiate this or that, but on the whole, one is merely an instrument. This wonderful logic—LET US CALL IT GOD—that governs a work of art, is the force and power.

Jan Sibelius

Meditation   Like a great piece of music, your life moves within the larger orbit of a governing power.

At the center of your freedom there is order and a greater meaning.

Today, you can feel the wonder and the cosmic grandeur of the divine sweep throughout the universe.

You can move creatively as an instrument of a larger order.

Musical   Jan Sibelius, Symphony No. 7 (Rattle—Angel).
Keynotes   This magnificent soulscape for orchestra shows an epic economy: much is said in a short space of time. The finale expresses a great release of energy that moves into endless space. Robert Simpson, speaking as a composer about this symphony, says:

> The Seventh Symphony is like a great planet in orbit, its movements vast, inexorable, seemingly imperceptible to its inhabitants. The symphony has both the cosmic motion of the earth and the teeming activity that is upon it.

Bohuslav Martinu, *The Greek Passion* (Mackerras—Supraphon). This opera is a strong work, based upon a novel by the great Greek writer, Nikos Kazantzakis. Try to listen to parts of it. It is a very deeply felt, moving work. Martinu, the Czech composer, had these words to say about the piece:

> Those, who in their great faith, take the path to universal love, find their way blocked by those who refuse to give up their selfishness.

December 9 *Waves of Temperament*

Focus
One must adapt one's life to one's temperament. Life is not a state; it is a movement. Nowhere in nature does it present the character of a fixed and stable maximum, but rather of an undulation, successive waves of life. The really important thing in life is not the avoidance of mistakes, but the obedience of faith. By obedience, a person is led step by step to correct his errors, whereas nothing will ever happen to him if he does not get going.

Paul Tournier

Meditation
If your life is to progress, you must come to know and work with your temperament.

You respond to life's situations with successive waves of energy, some outwardly forceful, others more quiet and reserved.

You are always trying to respond to outer circumstances in ways that harmonize without disturbing your inner balance.

Observe the waves of your temperament; try to find the flow and work with the most constructive movement of energy in your feelings, thoughts and activities.

Musical Keynotes
Joaquin Turina, *The Bullfighter's Prayer* (Kostelanetz—Columbia); *Music for the Guitar, Sevillana* and *Homage to Tárrega* (Costanzo—EMI). This music, although typically Spanish, carries the energy and melody that open the consciousness. In its own ethnic tone, it transcends local definition.

Luciano Pavarotti, *Favorite Neapolitan Songs: O Sole Mio* (Guadagno—London). These melodic, expressive songs, rooted in the folk music of Italy,

bring a passionate energy. Particularly memorable
and inspiring are *O Sole Mio (O My Sun)* and *Turn
to Sorrento.*

December 10   ***Regeneration***

Focus   Christ's love falls upon regenerated humanity like
              a new light. The Divine Presence...is won
              through love. Celestial and terrestrial choirs sus-
              tain their long and serene Hosannas.

              César Franck

Meditation   Divine love is always regenerating and empower-
              ing you.

              Beatitude is the aura of blessedness that fills the
              earth from on high.

              Today let divine love bless and fill your life.

Musical   César Franck, *Panis Angelicus*, sung by Luciano
Keynotes   Pavarotti (Adler—London). In this short, beautiful
              work, for soloist, choir and orchestra, there is a
              strong angelic presence. Celestial choirs echo the
              lead of the soloist, and the text reinforces the
              angelic presence.

              César Franck, *The Beatitudes* (Allain—Schwann;
              Hampton—Sine Qua Non). This great oratorio is
              Franck's masterpiece. It contains many mystical
              sections for celestial choirs and orchestra.

December 11   ***The Whispering Wings***

Focus   The wind seems to carry the whisper of a gigantic
              spirit.   Mieczyslaw Karlowicz

Love and music are the two wings of the soul.
Music alone embodies the eternal song of the other
arts, and lifts it, in grand reverberating tones, to
the throne of the Almighty.

Hector Berlioz

Meditation   When you feel the divine Presence close to you and
in you, it is sometimes like a breeze or a whisper—a
subtle tone of celestial singing.

Today, feel again the whisper of the wings of
angels—eternal song of love and music.

Musical   Hector Berlioz, *L'Enfance du Christ* (Martinon—
Keynotes   Nonesuch). About this noble, radiant work, Berlioz
wrote the following:

> O my soul, for thee what remains now to do, but
> to bend thy pride before such a mystery! O my
> heart, fill now with a love deep and pure that
> alone can guide us to a heavenly abode.

Mieczyslaw Karwowicz, *Lithuanian Rhapsody*
(Salwarowski, Wifon—Poland). A beautiful piece
for full orchestra; the composer's words are as
follows: "The Song of Eternal Being: grandeur,
might, majesty, ruthlessness, [awesomeness],
necessity, eternity."

December 12   **Rapture**

Focus   In the tranquility of evening, when only the swells
move the surface of the sea, the eye is enraptured
by the fabulous display of colors in the endless view
over sea and land; colors fade toward midnight,
the calmness becomes even more complete, until
at last the night winds slowly begin to blow.

Kurt Atterberg

| *Meditation* | Rapture is the sudden feeling of being transported beyond oneself, into the ecstasy of a larger dimension of life. |

Often, a powerful scene in nature, a moment of deep love for another, a touch of silence, any sudden experience may hold the key to rapture.

Today try to experience something that calls forth rapture in you.

Musical Keynotes   Kurt Atterberg, Symphony No. 3, *West Coast Pictures* (Ehrling—Caprice). This compelling Swedish orchestral work describes musically the rapture of untamed nature. In one section a storm unleashes its violent power on the islands of the outer archipelago. The scene then moves to a calm body of water in a fjord. This is music of genuine rapture.

Debbie Boone, *You Light Up My Life* (Warner Brothers). In its own simple way, this song opens the listener into union with another. The music is uplifting, carrying the sense of a love that surpasses just romance.

December 13   *The Great Fountain*

Focus   In the center of our life stands the great fountain, the drink for healing. Every step that is not toward the fountain is toward the desert....Every power has its work to do, every capacity its gift to fill it, every motive its wheels to turn..., achieving finally the soul's great work.

Phillips Brooks

Meditation   As the soul discovers its true calling this lifetime, it begins to expand like a fountain.

You can feel the fountain of your heart, opening, spreading, lifting, as your capacities unfold.

See your life now moving forward into its own larger purpose, rising, like a great fountain.

Musical Keynotes Antonio Vivaldi, *Concertos for Guitar and Mandolin* (Yepes, Ochi, Kuentz—DGG). These melodic works, composed in clear baroque fashion, emanate joy and fountains of gladness.

Ottorino Respighi, *The Fountains of Rome* (Muti—Angel; Ormandy—Columbia). The gushing waters of Rome's beautiful fountains are described in the music of this memorable composition. Quiet moods alternate with effervescence and strong energy.

December 14   *The Shining Point*

Focus Nothing could stifle my inner certainty that a shining point exists where all [moving] lines intersect.
Czeslaw Milosz

Meditation Your thoughts, feelings, and body are in constant motion.

At the center, beyond the movement and changes, is YOU.

You are centered in the shining point that weaves all lives together.

Musical Keynotes Joseph Jongen, *Symphonie Concertante for Organ and Orchestra* (Fox, Pretre—Angel; Murray, DeWaart—Telarc). This is one of the great pieces of mysticism—very powerful and cleansing.

Antonin Dvořak, Symphony No. 8 in G, First Movement (Marriner—Philips). This music for full orchestra is sunny and radiates good spirits into the atmosphere. The energy is pleasing and kinetic.

Hiroshi Yoshimura, *Green* (Narada). Amid the sounds of a gurgling creek and bird songs, the synthesizer creates continuous movement of energy, busy and somewhat "minimalist" in its subtle changes. The music dances around a central rhythm and pattern.

William Ellwood, *Renaissance* (Narada). This clear music, for solo guitar, offers its own focus of energy, especially *Magic Road* and *Gabriella*.

December 15 *The Healing Touch*

Focus In the higher sense, touch gives us all kinship. There is something Godlike about the power every one of us possesses in our hands and fingers to bring pleasure and give meaning to another human being. We can all be creators of "social enzymes" that add up to well-being. Like Walt Whitman, writing in "Song of Myself," we can say, "I make holy whatever I touch or am touched from."

Helen Colton

Meditation Let your touch bring healing. Feel the energy of love and goodness radiate from your fingers. Your hands can be carriers of kindness.

Even more, let your love touch others, in the look of a moment—the magic instant of true kinship.

Musical Keynotes Franz Joseph Haydn, *Choruses from The Creation* (Willcocks—EMI; Marriner—Philips). These powerful, proclamatory choruses, for singers and orchestra, deliver strength and glory.

Sir Arthur Sullivan, *The Lost Chord* (McCormack—RCA; Burrows—London). This music touches the listener to the core. The energy rises into a great crescendo, and there is total release.

December 16   ## *Higher Worlds*

Focus   Music is the one incorporeal entrance into the higher worlds. O Divine One, thou lookest into my inmost soul, thou knowest it, thou knowest that love of mankind and desire to do good live there-in.... O God, give me strength to conquer myself, nothing must chain me to life. All men are brothers.   Ludwig van Beethoven

Meditation   Just as music builds a bridge to the higher worlds, your desire to live with greater love and under-standing and giving opens you to the Highest and leads you beyond a narrow life.

Today try to realize your connection with the great brotherhood: visible and invisible.

Musical Keynotes   Ludwig van Beethoven, *Hallelujah Chorus*, from *Mount of Olives* (Mormon Tabernacle Choir—Columbia). This is a strong, uplifting piece of music. The energy is catalytic and martial at the close.

Johannes Brahms, *How Lovely Is Thy Dwelling Place*, from *A German Requiem* (Walter—Odyssey). A radiant work! The words of wisdom are as follows:

How lovely is Thy dwelling place, O Lord of Hosts! For my soul, it longs, yea faints for the courts of the Lord.

Georgi Sviridov, *Prayer* and *Holy Love* from *Tsar Fedor Ivanovich* (Ukhov—Melodiya). These pieces are hauntingly played, and *Holy Love* includes a mystically beautiful soprano solo.

December 17   ***Dharma***

Focus   Each person has his own dharma—a purpose to
                 fulfill in action. It is the way of wisdom to learn
                 and accept it. Accept the conditions of your life
                 with a cheerful attitude. Right reaction to condi-
                 tions can minister as much to your spiritual
                 development as any others which you might much
                 prefer. Know your dharma and accept it coura-
                 geously....To achieve peace amid stormy sur-
                 roundings is greater....To find the Presence of
                 God in the Beyond is good, but to find it on Earth
                 is a greater achievement.

                                                    Raynor Johnson

Meditation   As you begin to sense your dharma, your true pur-
                 pose, you will be able to face conditions more
                 cheerfully.

                 You will feel an increasing sense of fulfillment as
                 you do what you are here to do.

                 When you feel in the flow, living out of your
                 strengths, it is easier to work on your weaknesses
                 and blind spots.

                 Today consider again your life purpose, your
                 dharma.

Musical   *Little Marches by Great Masters* (Netherlands
Keynotes   Wind Ensemble—Philips). Marches by Beethoven,
                 C. P. E. Bach, Vranicky and Haydn bring power
                 and energy to this recording. There is a determina-
                 tion in the music which is very motivating.

                 Franz Liszt, *Hungarian Coronation Mass*
                 (Lehel—Hungaroton). The music has a festive
                 sparkle and also moments of intimate, celestial joy.
                 The *Hosanna* and *Benedictus* are especially
                 moving.

December 18   ## *Origin*

Focus   In the deep mystery of things as they really are in themselves, we are released from our fixations and attachments to them. When the Ten Thousand Things are seen in their Oneness, we return to the Origin where we have always been.

Sengtsan

Meditation   Today is a good time to look at life again, to see with new eyes and behold without judgments.

Looking at the great variety of life all around you, try to sense their Origin, the Oneness that lies behind them.

At the center, all is One.

Musical Keynotes   Edward MacDowell, *To a Wild Rose* (Ormandy—Columbia); Suite No. 2, *Indian* (Hanson—Mercury). These compositions show MacDowell at his most poetic. There is a strong sense of origin and the land in the various episodes of the *Indian Suite*.

Camille Saint-Saëns, *Softly Awakes My Heart*, from *Samson and Delilah* (Horne—RCA). This is a strong and fervent love song, which hits the center of all origins.

December 19   ## *The Great Crescendo*

Focus   The weightless beating of the heavenly hosts' wings accompanies the song of the angels. The gates of heaven are opened in a blinding crescendo: heaven and earth are full of the majesty of Thy glory.

Otto Olsson

Meditation   Feel the great crescendo in a blaze of sunset, the
                deep love of a moment shared; an instant of
                discovery, the inbreaking of invisible worlds
                around you.

                Center today on the ecstasy you can feel as music
                plays.

                Think of the Great Crescendo that sounds from the
                gates of heaven.

Musical   Otto Olsson, *Te Deum* (Bis); *Requiem* (Caprice).
Keynotes   These grand romantic works from Sweden contain
                many great crescendos. The energy of the music
                is impressive, and the melodies are outstanding.

                Ludwig van Beethoven, Symphony No. 5 (Klei-
                ber—DGG). Powerful moments occur throughout
                this music. The dynamics are strong and allow for
                release of tensions in triumph.

December 20   *Nuances*

Focus   You must have music first of all,
                and for that a rhythm uneven is best,
                vague as the air and soluble,
                with nothing heavy and nothing at rest. . . .

                Never the Color, always the Shade,
                always the nuance is supreme!

                Let there be music, again and forever!
                                              Paul Verlaine

Meditation   Nuance suggests subtlety.

                In the subtleties of music, you can feel the endless
                array of nuances. So in your life, there is the domi-
                nant rhythm, and also the subtle variations—what
                is stated and what is suggested, what you know and
                what you may be sensing.

Listen for the nuances of life today.

Hillel, *The Ancient Shepherd Pipes* (Folkways).
This is an extremely evocative recording; the ancient days of Israel mix with the present, especially
in the pieces *Night Galilee* and *The Legend of the
Sea of Galilee.*

Tom Barabas, *Magic in December* (Invincible
Records). The music for piano is both joyful and
introspective, filled with lovely melodies and a
warm spirit.

December 21   *Adoration*

Focus   The angels help man as far as he can be helped.
They intensify all his highest aspirations, stir up
his adoration and his love, and to give effect to the
ancient and beautiful words of their traditional
Hymn: "Glory be to God in the highest, on earth
peace to men of goodwill."

Dora van Gelder

Meditation Feel the angels today, stirring your sense of joy and
adoration.

Let your heart open now; feel the surge of the
Spirit, the current of life coursing through you.

The glory of God shines through you.

*Musical
Keynotes*   Jakub Jan Ryba, *Czech Christmas Mass* (Matl—
Supraphon). This very ancient setting of the Mass,
for soloists, chorus and orchestra, brings a devotional quality and contains many beautiful melodies of adoration.

Zdenek Fibich, Symphony No. 3 (Belohlavek—
Supraphon). Love and nature are the themes of this
wonderful music. In the adagio (slow movement)

a sense of bliss and deep devotion emerge to bathe the listener in sound.

Soundings of the Planet: Joy to the World (Box 43512, Tucson, AZ 85733). This contemporary statement of Christmas contains a joyful spirit of adoration.

December 22   ## *One Fine Day*

Focus   One fine day we'll see
a wisp of smoke arising
from the far horizon of the sea,
and then the ship will appear.
Then the white ship
will sail into the harbor,—
it roars out its salute!
You see? He's come!
                    Giacomo Puccini

Meditation   Today look for your ship appearing on the horizon.

What is "the white ship" for you? Let the image emerge: hear the salute—the roar, and the glad tidings.

Accept this fine day, for whatever your ship brings into port.

Musical Keynotes   Giacomo Puccini, *Un bel di (One Fine Day)* from *Madame Butterfly; Oh! mio babbino caro (My Dear Father)* from *Gianni Schicchi* (Mitchell, Adler—London). These gorgeous arias from two of Puccini's operas are spacious and very strongly evocative in feeling. Let this romantic music fill you: breathe into it and welcome the new day.

Franz Schmidt, Intermezzo, from *Notre Dame* (Karajan—DGG). This music has the blaze of the inner worlds. It rises in glory, as if transporting

the listener to higher spaces. After swirling heavenward, the music eventually levels and recedes.

Kim Robertson, *Celtic Christmas* (Invincible
Music); Sylvia Woods, *Three Harps for Christmas*
(Tonmeister Records). This music conveys a
joyfulness and a festive folk quality.

December 23   ## The Great Profusion

Focus   Is it not by His high superfluousness we know
Our God? For to be equal a need
Is natural, animal, mineral: but to fling
Rainbows over the rain
And beauty above the moon, and secret rainbows
On the domes of deep sea-shells,
And make the necessary embrace of breeding
Beautiful also as fire,
Not even the weeds to multiply without blossom
Nor the birds without music:
There is the great humaneness at the heart of
    things,
The extravagant kindness, the fountain
Humanity can understand, and would flow
    likewise
If power and desire were perch-mates.

Robinson Jeffers

Meditation   Today, you can feel the great profusion of God's
creation.

At the center of nature and of humanity, there is
abundance of beauty and variety.

This reflects the moreness of God, the fling of
divine blessings, the emerging blossoms behind
every weed.

See and feel the great humaneness in the ex-
travagance at the center of creation.

Musical   Pablo Casals, *El Pesebre, The Manger* (Casals—
Keynotes   Columbia). This is one of the truly outstanding
                   Christmas pieces. There is a quiet yet joyful
                   reverence and devotion in the presentation of the
                   shepherds, and the singing of the soprano, Iglesias,
                   is especially lovely.

                   Alfredo Ortiz, *Navidad* (Ortiz, Box 911, Corona,
                   CA 91720). A beautiful Christmas festival, played
                   on the Paraguayan harp. It radiates joy.

December 24   **Sing Imperial Heavens**

Focus   Sing heavens imperial, most of height!
                   Regions of air make harmony!

                   All Gloria in excelsis cry!
                   Heaven, earth, sea, man, bird and beast,
                   He that is crowned above the sky
                       Pro nobis Puer natus est.
                                              William Dunbar

Meditation   Listen to the heavens singing today. The glory of
                   God sounds forth in praise.

                   You can hear the coronation ringing forth, high
                   in the imperial heavens. Join the throng!

Musical   Sir Hubert Parry, *Ode on the Nativity* (Will-
Keynotes   cocks—Lyrita). This is a sublime work, filled with
                   innocence and a sense of wonder. A mystical
                   simplicity and exaltation fill the atmosphere.

                   Georges Schmitt, *Eternal Noels* (Carrere). Flute
                   of Pan, organ and percussions sensitively render
                   well-known carols and other folk compositions.
                   Again, the sounds are open and pleasing.

                        At Christmas the bells ring out,
                        always in their own way.

From the mountain tops they resound
into the valleys.
At Christmas the bells ring out,
awaking the entire world.

December 25   *Christmas*

Focus   In silence and joy I await the midnight hour that
brings You. All the world awaits the Light and love
You give again. The Angels and shepherds join in
song to herald Your approach. A mighty burst of
music swells; the Light glows into splendor. The
bells ring out, and You are here within my sanc-
tuary, within the shrine of my own heart. Lord,
I love You; I would give You more than love. . . . I
give myself wholly to Your cause. . . . Accept me
for Your work. . . . may I radiate to everyone I meet
the love and good will that He exemplifies.

Flower A. Newhouse

Meditation Today in the aura of the Christmas spirit, let the
purified tone of this moment inspire you for the
coming new year.

What has been difficult can now be met and
overcome.

Let the Christ Spirit, larger than any religion or
creed, shine through into all lives.

Feel the Christ's loving Presence now, go forth
today in greater light, feeling the divine love of
God.

Musical   George Frideric Handel, *Choruses from Messiah*
Keynotes   (Willcocks—Arabesque; Marriner—Argo). These
stirring musical statements radiate the Christ Spirit
as it fills the earth. This music remains a pinnacle
of inspiration.

Christmas in Westminster Abbey (Preston—DGG); *The Glorious Sound of Christmas* (Ormandy—Columbia); Luciano Pavarotti, *O Holy Night* (London); *On Christmas Night* (Willcocks—Argo); Jessye Norman, *Christmastide* (Philips); New Troubadours, *Festival of Light* (Lorian); Kathleen Battle, *Christmas* (Battle, Slatkin—Angel).

December 26   ## *Taking Command*

Focus   A person of genuine achievement has the quality of NEGATIVE CAPABILITY; he is capable, being in uncertainties, mysteries, doubts, etc., without any irritable reaching after fact or reason.
                                                      John Keats

Meditation   There are times when we must move ahead in the midst of outer doubts and uncertainties.

                  Often, you may be required to take a step without being able to see completely what lies ahead.

                  Using good judgment, you can do what is required.

                  Consider today how you can become more capable of taking charge.

Musical   Ottorino Respighi, *Saint Gregory the Great,* from
Keynotes   *Church Windows* (Simon—Musical Heritage Society). This music, for full orchestra, bells and organ, intones power and grandeur. The score carries this inscription: "Bless the Lord. . . Sing the Hymn to God. Alleluia." The whole piece is a fantasia on the *Gloria* from *The Mass of the Angels.*

                  Victor Hely-Hutchinson, *A Carol Symphony*

(Rose—EMI) Memories of the Christmastide come through here in music that is gentle and lyrical, but also powerful and dramatic.

December 27	## *The Love for Mankind*
Focus	I shall go forth, against all sorts of things, towards bright, strong and righteous aims, towards a genuine art that loves mankind, lives with his joys, his grief and his sufferings.

Modest Mussorgsky

Meditation	Let your heart open to humankind, not just your chosen friends, but everyone that comes across your path.

Like a good Samaritan, you can recognize the bond and kinship with all lives.

Let the needs of others touch you. There is always some new way that you can give—of your energies, substance and talents.

In the great love of mankind, you will find yourself in God.

Musical Keynotes	J. S. Bach, *The Great Bach Choruses* (Ormandy—Columbia). These stirring, uplifting choruses proclaim the glory of God.

Modest Mussorgsky, *The Great Gate of Kiev*, from *Pictures at an Exhibition* (Liebowitz—Quintessence; Reiner—RCA). This epic-like music gathers in all the weight of the ages and transforms it into a great triumphal surge that wipes away resistance and heaviness. Bells and gongs sound forth, signifying the deeper glory underlying all the travail of humanity.

December 28   **A Fruitful Life**

Focus

[Love, hope and joy—]
These three flowers of fruitful life
Scatter their precious perfume with wings
    of angels.
Their unseen power transforms the world's
    ugliness to beatific vision,
Storms of anger to gentle peace,
And brute passion to divine affection.

                            Paramananda

Meditation

Consider your life today and how fruitful you feel it is.

Remember again the three fragrant flowers, love hope and joy, can bloom in your heart and cause the tree of your life to flourish.

Musical
Keynotes

Michael Haydn, *Vespers for Holy Innocents' Day* (Szabo—Harmonia Mundi). The composer, who deeply loved children, wrote this gladsome music, for soloists, chorus and orchestra, in hopes that life would be fruitful for children everywhere.

Randall Thompson, Symphony No. 2 (Bernstein—Columbia). This work is a unified statement of a life well-lived. Especially beautiful is the slow movement (Largo), with its baroque-like songfulness and peaceful, flowing melody.

December 29   **The Tree of Life**

Focus

We are one of the leaves of the tree. The tree is all of humanity. We cannot live without the other leaves of the tree. We need intelligence, and when there is intelligence, there is love.

                            Pablo Casals

Meditation   Today consider the parts and the totality.

Think of the importance of the leaves to the tree. Without its leaves, the tree could not live.

Each leaf contributes to the life of the tree.

Without the individual contribution, the greater totality remains incomplete.

Musical   Pablo Casals, *Song of the Birds* (Munroe,
Keynotes   Kostelanetz—Columbia); *Sardana for 8 Cellos* (Orion); *Casals Conducts J. S. Bach's Brandenburg Concertos* (Columbia). These compositions and recordings must be counted among the greatest of musical experiences. The music is alive, vital, and passionately felt. *Song of the Birds,* a Catalan folksong, portrays the longing and sorrows of Casals' country, Spain.

José-Luís Lopátegui, *Catalan Guitar,* (Harmonia Mundi). These beautiful works, for solo guitar, echo the homeland of a great artist like Pablo Casals.

December 30   *How Can I Help?*

Focus   How supportive it is merely to be in the presence of a mind that is open, quiet, playful, receptive or reflective....And there is INTUITIVE AWARENESS—that links us most intimately to the universe and, in allegiance to the heart, binds us together in generosity and compassion. Often it leaps to vision and knowledge instantaneously.

How can I help?

In the clarity of a quiet mind, there is room for all that is actually happening and whatever else might also be possible.... The quiet appreciation of the total situation and its inherent possibilities steadily moves things toward resolution; we find ways to step back. In a spirit of compassion and reverence for life, these various skills flourish and combine appropriately.

Ram Dass and Paul Gorman

Meditation In your life ahead, you will ask more and more, "How can I help? What are the ways I can best serve?"

A listening mind does not react or rush in, although there may be instant caring and sensing of perspective.

Quiet appreciation of the larger situation leads to appropriate action or non-action.

You *can* help. By caring and listening and acting in the rhythm of the need, you can come to the leap of understanding and insight that contains the way of service.

Musical Keynotes Felix Mendelssohn, *Hear My Prayer* (Norrington—Argo); *Psalms* (Corboz—Musical Heritage). Mendelssohn's choral music is serene and flowing, lulling the listener into a receptive condition. It fits the qualities of the listening mind.

André Messager, *The Two Pigeons* (Lanchbery—EMI). The music of this ballet supports the story of a young man and woman whose love undergoes ups and downs. Their final reconciliation is mirrored by two pigeons also coming back together.

December 31 The Eve of a New Tomorrow

Focus The perfection of the soul consists not in speaking, nor in thinking much on God, but in loving Him sufficiently.

Miguel de Molinos

Be active in silence
Strong in peace
Keep thy strength in gentleness
Rest with the song of wings about thee
Fill the inner reaches with love
Bathe in Spirit
For it is sweetness to thy bones, flesh and health.
Keep in this holy estate and listening—obey!

Anonymous

Meditation   Tonight is the finale of another year—lived through and learned through.

Tune in to themes of the New Year that you also worked with in the old:

Be joyful in your vision and your goals.
Feel the closeness and intimacies of life.
Share the beauty and the tasks.
Keep on moving ahead.
Find ways to make a contribution.
Return to the quiet place where God is shining.
Make constructive decisions and carry them out.
Turn forgiveness and compassion into brother-
    hood.

Enjoy the New Year!

Musical   *New Year's Eve in Vienna: Strauss Waltzes and*
Keynotes   *Other Music* (Maazel—DGG; Boskovsky—
               London). It's a wonderful time to release the old,
               and celebrate the New Year. You can feel the dance
               of life tonight.

Giuseppe Verdi, *The Four Seasons* from *I Vespri
Siciliani* (Maazel—London). Beautiful music,
beginning with *Winter*, provides the listener with
flavors of the New Year.

Ernest Moeran, *Symphony* (Dilkes—EMI
Greensleeves). This is a wild, impassioned and
powerful nature symphony, filled with imagery
and beautiful melodies.

Composers' Birth Dates

January

4 –Josef Suk (1874)
6 –Max Bruch (1838)
  Alexander Scriabin (1872)
7 –Francis Poulenc (1899)
8 –Jaromir Weinberger
    (1896)
9 –John Knowles Paine
    (1839)
11 –Christian Sinding (1856)
13 –Richard Addinsell (1904)
14 –Albert Schweitzer (1875)

20 –Guillaume Lekeu (1870)
21 --Ernest Chausson (1855)
22 –Charles Tournemire
    (1870)
23 –Rutland Boughton
    (1878)
27 –Wolfgang Amadeus
    Mozart (1756)
29 –Frederick Delius (1862)
30 –Charles Loeffler (1861)
31 –Franz Schubert (1797)

February

1 –Victor Herbert (1859)
2 –Giovanni Pierluigi Da
    Palestrina (1525)
  Fritz Kreisler (1875)
3 –Felix Mendelssohn
    (1809)
9 –Alban Berg (1895)
12 –Roy Harris (1898)
15 –Michael Praetorius
    (1571)
17 –Arcangelo Corelli (1653)

19 –Luigi Boccherini (1743)
21 –Leo Delibes (1836)
22 –Frederic Chopin (1810)
23 –George Frideric Handel
    (1865)
27 –Sir Hubert Parry (1848)
28 –Elias Parish-Alvars
    (1808)
29 –Gioacchino Rossini
    (1792)

331

March

2 –Bedrich Smetana (1824)
4 –Antonio Vivaldi (1678)
5 –Heitor Villa-Lobos
  (1887)
7 –Tomaso Vitali (1663)
8 –Alan Hovhaness (1911)
9 –Samuel Barber (1910)
10 –Pablo de Sarasate (1844)
12 –Thomas Arne (1710)
14 –Georg Philipp Telemann
  (1681)

18 –Nikolai Rimsky-Korsakov
  (1844)
21 –Johann Sebastian Bach
  (1685)
23 –Dane Rudhyar (1895)
  Franz Schreker (1878)
27 –Vincent d'Indy (1851)
29 –Sir William Walton
  (1902)
31 –Franz Joseph Haydn
  (1732)

April

1 –Sergei Rachmaninoff
  (1873)
5 –Albert Roussel (1869)
8 –Giuseppe Tartini (1692)
11 –William Byrd (1543)
  Jean Mouret (1682)
18 –Leopold Stokowski
  (1882)
19 –David Fanshawe (1942)

20 –Nikolai Miaskovsky
  (1881)
21 –Randall Thompson
  (1899)
22 –Guiseppe Torelli (1658)
28 –Hermann Suter (1870)
29 –Wallingford Riegger
  (1885)
  Rod McKuen (1933)

May

1 –Hugo Alfven (1872)
2 –Alessandro Scarlatti
  (1660)
4 –Marisa Robles (1937)
7 –Johannes Brahms (1833)
  Peter Ilich Tchaikovsky
  (1840)
8 –Oscar Hammerstein
  (1847)

9 –Dietrich Buxtehude
  (1637)
11 –Irvin Berlin (1888)
12 –Gabriel Fauré (1845)
13 –Sir Arthur Sullivan
  (1842)
14 –Claudio Monteverdi
  (1567)
15 –John Lanchbery (1923)

18 –Karl Goldmark (1830)

19 –Albert Hay Malotte
(1895)

22 –Richard Wagner (1813)

24 –Martin Kalmanoff
(1920)

25 –Ralph Waldo Emerson
(1803)

27 –Joachim Raff (1822)

28 –Sir George Dyson (1883)

29 –Isaac Albeniz (1860)

30 –Ignaz Moscheles (1794)

31 –Walt Whitman (1819)

June

1 –Mikhail Glinka (1804)

2 –Sir Edward Elgar (1857)

5 –Adolf Wiklund (1879)

8 –Robert Schumann (1810)

11 –Richard Strauss (1864)

12 –Werner Josten (1885)

15 –Edvard Grieg (1843)
Guy Ropartz (1864)

17 –Charles Gounod (1818)

18 –Eduard Tubin (1905)

23 –Carl Reinecke (1824)

28 –George Lloyd (1913)

29 –Bernard Herrmann
(1911)

30 –Georg Benda (1722)
Laszlo Lajtha (1892)

July

2 –Christoph von Gluck
(1714)

3 –Leos Janáček (1854)

5 –Paul Ben-Haim (1897)

6 –Alberto Nepomuceno
(1864)

7 –Gustav Mahler (1860)

8 –Percy Grainger (1882)

9 –Ottorino Respighi (1879)

10 –Henryk Wieniawski
(1835)
Carl Orff (1895)

14 –Gerald Finzi (1901)

18 –R. Murray Schafer
(1933)

21 –Isaac Stern (1920)

24 –Ernest Bloch (1880)

26 –John Field (1782)

August

1 –Benedetto Marcello
(1686)

2 –Sir Arthur Bliss (1891)

3 –Richard Adler (1921)

4 –William Schuman (1910)
5 –Ambroise Thomas (1811)
7 –Sir Granville Bantock
   (1868)
8 –Cecile Chaminade
   (1857)
9 –Albert Ketèlby (1875)
10 –Alexander Glazunov
   (1865)
11 –Anton Arensky (1861)
13 –John Ireland (1879)
14 –Samuel Sebastian Wesley
   (1810)

15 –Samuel Coleridge-Taylor
   (1875)
   Lukas Foss (1922)
16 –Gabriel Pierné (1863)
18- Herman Berlinski (1910)
22 –Claude Debussy (1862)
23 –Moritz Moszkowski
   (1854)
24 –Theodore Dubois (1837)
27 –Sri Chinmoy (1931)
31 –Amilcare Ponchielli
   (1834)

September

1 –Johann Pachelbel (1653)
2 Saverio Mercadante
   (1795)
3 –Pietro Locatelli (1695)
4 Anton Bruckner (1824)
5 –Amy Beach (1867)
6 –Wayne Barlow (1912)
8 –Antonin Dvořak (1841)
10 –Boris Tchaikovsky (1925)
11 –Ashley Heenan (1925)
12 –Salvador Bacarisse
   (1898)
13 –Clara Schumann (1819)
   Ray Green (1909)
14 –Maria Luigi Cherubini
   (1760)
15 –Horatio Parker (1863)

   Frank Martin (1890)
17 –Charles Tomlinson
   Griffes (1884)
20 –Ildebrando Pizzetti
   (1880)
21 –Gustav Holst (1874)
   Thomas de Hartmann
   (1885)
22 –Mikolajus Ciurlionis
   (1875)
23 –William Dawson (1899)
   Norman Cazden (1914)
25 –Leon Boëllmann (1862)
27 –Cyril Scott (1879)
28 –Florent Schmitt (1870)
30 –Johan Svendsen (1840)

October

1 –Vladimir Horowitz
   (1904)

2 –Gandhi (1869)
5 –Cyril Rootham (1875)

6 –Karol Szymanowski
   (1882)
9 –Camille Saint-Saens
   (1835)
   Eino Rautavaara (1928)
10 –Giuseppe Verdi (1813)
12 –Ralph Vaughan-
    Williams (1872)
15 –Day Wiren (1905)
17 –Héraclius Djabadary
    (1891)

Herbert Howells (1892)
20 –Charles Ives (1874)
21 –Marie-Joseph Canteloube
    (1879)
22 –Franz Liszt (1811)
25 –Alexander Gretchaninov
    (1864)
26 –Domenico Scarlatti
    (1685)
27 –Niccolo Paganini (1782)
28 –Howard Hanson (1896)

November

3 –Vicenzo Bellini (1801)
4 –Arnold Cooke (1906)
5 –Johann Christian Bach
   (1735)
6 –Ignace Jan Paderewski
   (1860)
7 –William Alwyn (1905)
8 –Sir Arnold Bax (1883)
9 –Burrill Phillips (1907)
10 –Henri Rabaud (1873)
11 –Alexander Borodin
    (1833)

13 –Joonas Kokkonen (1921)
14 –Aaron Copland (1900)
16 –Paul Hindemith (1895)
18 –Carl Maria von Weber
    (1786)
25 –Virgil Thomson (1896)
27 –Charles Koechlin (1867)
28 –Alexander Kastalsky
    (1856)
29 –Gaetano Donizetti
    (1797)

December

4 –Sir Hamilton Harty
   (1879)
5 –Vitezslav Novak (1870)
6 –Henryk Górecki (1933)
7 –Pietro Mascagni (1863)
8 –Jean Sibelius (1865)
   Bohuslav Martinu (1890)
9 –Joaquin Turina (1882)

10 –César Franck (1822)
11 –Hector Berlioz (1903)
    Mieczyslaw Karlowicz
    (1876)
12 –Kurt Atterberg (1887)
13 –Phillips Brooks (1835)
14 –Joseph Jongen (1873)
16 –Ludwig von Beethoven
    (1770)

18 –Edward MacDowell (1861)
19 –Otto Olsson (1879)
21 –Zdenek Fibich (1850)
22 –Giacomo Puccini (1858)
Franz Schmidt (1874)

26 –Victor Hely-Hutchinson (1901)
29 –Pablo Casals (1876)
30 –Andre Messager (1853)
31 –Ernest Moeran (1894)

Suggested Reading

Arundale, George. *You*. Wheaton, IL: Theosophical Publishing House, 1976.

Aurobindo. *The Life Divine*. New York: India Library Society, 1965.

Beethoven, Ludwig van. *Think of Me Kindly*. Boulder, CO: Blue Mountain Press, 1978.

Carpenter, Edward. *Towards Democracy*. New York: Mitchell Kennerly, 1922.

Chinmoy, Sri. *Song of the Transcendental Soul*. Blauvelt, NY: Rudolph Steiner Press, 1973.

Clark, Kenneth. *Civilization*. New York: Harper & Row, 1969.

Codd, Clara. *Trust Yourself to Life*. Wheaton, IL: Theosophical Publishing House, 1975.

Colton, Helen. *The Gift of Touch*. Putnam, NY: Seaview Press, 1983.

Daniels, Robin. *Conversations with Menuhin*. New York: St. Martin's Press, 1979.

Gandhi, Mohandas, *Autobiography*. Washington, DC: Public Affairs Press, 1948.

———. *Letters to a Disciple*. New York: Harper & Row, 1950.

Gardner, Adelaide. *Meditation*. Wheaton, IL: Theosophical Publishing House, 1973.

Gibran, Kahlil. *Treasured Writings*. Seacaucus, NJ: Book Sales, Inc., 1982.

Goswami, Satsvarupa. *Prabhupada*. Los Angeles: Bhaktivedanta Book Trust, 1983.

Guillaumont, A., ed. *Gospel According to Thomas*. New York: Harper & Row, 1959.

Hall, Manly P. *The Blessed Angels*. Los Angeles: Philosophical Research, 1980.

Hammarskjöld, Dag. *Markings*. New York: Alfred Knopf, 1965.

Hein, Rolland. *The Harmony Within*. Washington, DC: Christian University Press, 1982.

Herman, E. *Creative Prayer*. New York: Harper & Brothers, 1940.

Hodson, Geoffrey. *The Brotherhood of Angels and Men*. Wheaton, IL: Theosophical Publishing House, 1982.

———. *The Kingdom of the Gods*. Madras, India: Theosophical Publishing House, 1952.

———. *Clairvoyant Investigations*. Wheaton, IL: Theosophical Publishing House, 1984.

Howell, Alice. *Jungian Symbolism in Astrology*. Wheaton, IL: Theosophical Publishing House, 1987.

Hubbard, Barbara Marx. *The Evolutionary Journey*. San Francisco: Evolutionary Press, 1982.

Jeffers, Robinson. *Selected Poetry*. New York: Random House, 1959.

Johnson, Raynor. *The Imprisoned Splendor*. Wheaton, IL: Theosophical Publishing House, 1971.

Kyber, Manfred. *Three Candles of Little Veronica*. London: Waldorf Press, 1967.

Krishnamurti, Jiddu. *Education and the Significance of Life*. New York: Harper & Row, 1953.

———. *The Mind of J. Krishnamurti*. Luis Vas, ed. Bombay, India: Jaico Publishers, 1971.

Leadbeater, C. W. *Invisible Helpers*. Madras, India: Theosophical Publishing House, 1976.

Mikkelson, Patricia. *Sing for Service* (Newsletter). 1106 2nd Street, Suite 107, Encinitas, CA 92024.

Milinaire, Catherine. *Celebrations*. New York: Harmony Books, 1981.

Myers, Isabel. *Gifts Differing*. Palo Alto, CA: Consulting Psychologists Press, 1984.

Newhouse, Flower A. *Insights into Reality*. Isaac, Stephen and Phyllis, ed. Escondido, CA: Christward Ministry, 1975.

———. *The Sacred Heart of Christmas*. Escondido, CA: Christward Ministry, 1978.

Paramananda. *Daily Thoughts and Prayers.* Cohasset, MA: Vedanta Center, 1926.

Picard, Max. *The World of Silence.* South Bend, IN: Gateway, 1952.

Ram, N. Sri. *Thoughts for Aspirants.* Wheaton, IL: Theosophical Publishing House, 1972.

Rudhyar, Dane. *The Magic of Tone and the Art of Music.* Boulder, CO: Shambhala, 1982.

Safranek, Milos. *Martinu.* London: Allan Wingate, 1962.

Saint-Exupéry, Antoine. *The Wisdom of the Sands.* Chicago: University of Chicago Press, 1979.

Sarton, May. *Journal of a Solitude.* New York: W. W. Norton & Co., 1973.

Schweitzer, Albert. *Reverence for Life.* New York: Harper & Row, 1969.

Scott, Cyril. *The Greater Awareness.* York Beach, ME: Samuel Weiser, 1981.

Spangler, David. *Festivals in the New Age.* Forres, Scotland: Findhorn, 1975.

Steiner, Rudolf. *Christianity As a Mystical Fact.* New York: Anthroposophic Press, 1947.

Swedenborg, Emanuel. *Conjugal Love.* London: Swedenborg Society, 1978.

Tame, David. *The Secret Power of Music.* New York: Destiny Books, 1984.

Thomas, Dylan. *Collected Poems.* New York: New Directions, 1957.

Tournier, Paul. *The Seasons of Life.* Richmond, VA: John Knox Press, 1972.

Valle-Inclan, Ramon. *The Lamp of Marvels.* West Stockbridge, MA: Lindisfarne Press, 1986.

Way, Robert. *The Wisdom of the English Mystics.* New York: New Directions, 1978.

Wilson, Ernest. *Adventures in Prosperity.* Unity Village, MO: Unity Books, 1931.

Wood, Ernest. *The Seven Rays.* Wheaton, IL: Theosophical Publishing House, 1985.

Yeadon, David. *When the Earth Was Young.* Garden City, NY: Doubleday & Co., 1978.

Quest publishes books on Healing, Health and Diet, Occultism and Mysticism, Philosophy, Transpersonal Psychology, Reincarnation, Religion, The Theosophical Philosophy, Yoga and Meditation. **Other books on music and meditation include:**

Concentration: An Approach to Meditation *by Ernest Wood*
Meditation approach uses 36 physical and mental exercises.

Creative Meditation and Multi-Dimensional Consciousness *by Lama Anagarika Govinda.*

Finding the Quiet Mind *by Robert Ellwood*
How to attain serenity through mental stillness.

Gifts of the Lotus, *comp. by Virginia Hanson*
366 quotations from spiritually oriented philosophers.

The Healing Energies of Music *by Hal A. Lingerman*
Reference for musical compositions as therapy.

Meditation: A Practical Study *by Adelaide Gardner*
Purpose and benefits of yoga and meditation.

Music Forms *by Geoffrey Hodson*
Occult value of music as seen by clairvoyant. Illustrated.

The Royal Road *by Stephan Hoeller*
The tarot and Kabbalah are adapted for meditation.

Self-Transformation through Music *by Joanne Crandall*
How music can help us become aware of our inner nature.

Available from:
The Theosophical Publishing House
306 West Geneva Road, Wheaton, Illinois 60187